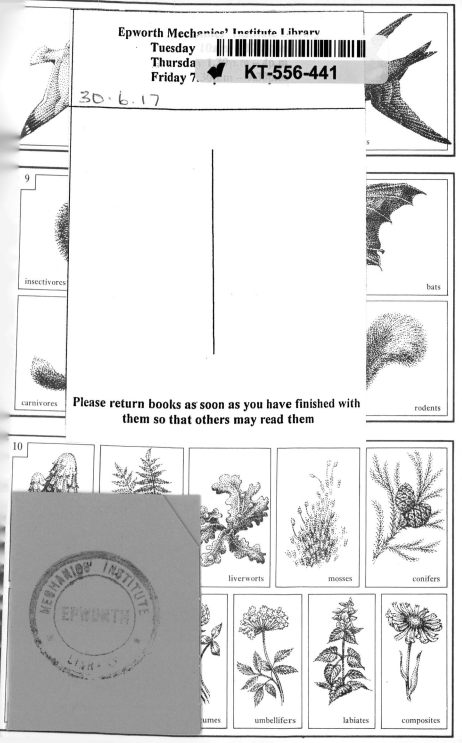

THE NATURAL HISTORY OF BRITAIN
AND NORTHERN EUROPE

TOWNS AND GARDENS
DENIS OWEN

Editors JAMES FERGUSON-LEES & BRUCE CAMPBELL

Contributors Franklyn and Margaret Perring (Plants);
Paul Whalley, Frederick Wanless, Roger Lincoln (Invertebrates);
James Ferguson-Lees (Birds); Gordon Corbet (Mammals)

Hodder & Stoughton
LONDON·SYDNEY·AUCKLAND·TORONTO

This book was designed and produced by
George Rainbird Limited,
36 Park Street, London W1Y 4DE
for Hodder & Stoughton Limited,
Mill Road, Dunton Green,
Sevenoaks, Kent

House Editor: Karen Goldie-Morrison
Designer: Patrick Yapp
Indexer: Diana Blamire
Picture Researcher: Barbara Fraser
Cartographer: Tom Stalker Miller
Cover Illustrator: Hilary Burn
Endpapers Designer: Marianne Appleton
Production: Sheila McKenzie

Printed and bound by
W. S. Cowell Limited,
28 Percy Street, London W1P 9FF

ISBN 0 340 22614 5

CONTENTS

FOREWORD

With increased travel and an expanding interest in Europe as a whole, many books and field guides on its natural history have been published in the last two decades, but most either treat a wide field in general terms or cover a single class or group of animals or plants. At the same time, inspired by the need for conservation, the pendulum is swinging back from the specialization of the post-war years to a wish for a fuller appreciation of all aspects of natural history. As yet, the traveller-naturalist has to be armed with a variety of volumes and, even then, has no means of understanding the interrelations of plants and animals. We believe that this new series will help to fill that gap.

The five books cover the whole of the northern half of Europe west of Russia and the Baltic States, and include Iceland: the limits are shown by the map on pages 84–85, which also marks various subregions and the abbreviations used for them and the individual countries. Four of the volumes deal with (a) coniferous forests, heaths, moors, mountains and tundra; (b) deciduous woods, hedgerows, farmland, lowland grassland and downs; (c) lakes, rivers and freshwater marshes; and (d) coasts, dunes, sea cliffs, saltmarshes, estuaries and the sea itself. Thus, in broad groupings of related habitats, they cover the whole rural scene. This book is about urban and suburban habitats.

Each book is divided into two. The first half is an ecological essay about the habitats, with examples of plant and animal communities as illustrations of interrelationships. The second is a field guide of selected species, each illustrated and described, with its habitat, the part it plays in food webs, and its distribution. Obviously there are limitations: about 600 species are illustrated in each book, or around 3000 in the series, but the north European total is probably at least 50,000. Whereas good proportions of the characteristic vertebrates (148 mammals, 364 birds, 18 reptiles, 22 amphibians and more than 300 fishes) are included, some single *families* of insects have more species than the total of these; there are over 4000 different beetles in Britain alone, and probably 8–9000 in the whole of our area, while some 3500 plants are also native or naturalized in north Europe. On the other hand, the identification of many insects and some groups of plants is a matter for the specialist and we believe that many readers will be satisfied if they can identify these at the family level. So our list of invertebrates and plants is selective, but we hope that it will form a useful groundwork from which interest in particular groups can be developed.

All plants and animals are grouped into classes (*eg* Angiospermae, Insecta, Aves), orders (*eg* Campanulatae, Lepidoptera, Passeriformes), families (*eg*

Compositae, Nymphalidae, Turdidae) and genera (*eg Aster, Inachis, Turdus*), groups of increasingly close affinity. Each plant or animal has two scientific names, the first of which is the genus and the second the species. These are often considered to be outside the scope of a work of this kind, but many invertebrates and some plants have no vernaculars and, at the same time, such names are invaluable in showing relationships. Consequently, each species is given its scientific name at the first mention in the body of the text and again in the field guide, where the family name is also inserted in capitals.

The specially commissioned colour paintings which illustrate the field guide are a delight in themselves. It has become customary to illustrate plants and animals in field guides as individual specimens, but here they are arranged in attractive compositions. Scale has had to suffer, but the sizes are always given in the facing descriptions, as are the correct food plants.

The first volume in the series, on towns and gardens, is inevitably rather different from the others. It is being published first because, in a way, it is an introduction to the rest: many readers will want to begin by widening their knowledge of the plants and animals of their immediate surroundings and, as a result, this is a book to be used at home; the others will have to be taken out in the field. At the same time, towns and gardens form a completely artificial habitat which in various ways overlaps with, and yet differs markedly from, the open countryside. Many lowland plants and animals occur in urban gardens and parks; many towns are by rivers or the sea; and microcosms of fields, woods, lakes and cliffs are provided by lawns, tree-lined avenues, ponds and tall buildings. Yet, whereas heather moors or forests of pine or oak show considerable uniformity, and agricultural land is simplified by man's monocultures, gardens are complicated by a contrived diversity of plants, which results in more varied food webs. The plants selected for illustration are a mixture of ornamental and native species, many of the latter often being thought of as 'weeds' by gardeners. The gardening cult is most developed in Britain, but a special section is included on Iceland because, as the field guide repeatedly shows, that country differs markedly from all the rest in its comparative paucity of species.

Indeed, one of the main messages of Denis Owen's ecological essay in this book is the effect of this contrived diversity of plants. Dr Owen is a zoologist, whose interest in the potential of gardens was aroused in Africa and then developed by intensive studies in England. We believe that no one has looked more closely at the natural history of individual gardens, and we hope that his wide knowledge and obvious enthusiasm will fire many people.

JAMES FERGUSON–LEES
BRUCE CAMPBELL

TOWNS AND GARDENS

A view from the air

The north European countryside is virtually everywhere man-made or man-modified. Few truly natural areas remain; instead, the landscape is designed for food production, industry, transport, housing and recreation. The need for continued industrial expansion is accepted and there is seemingly no end to our efforts at changing the countryside to suit ever-increasing demands. Even the apparently wild areas in the far north are affected. Much of the natural vegetation of Iceland has disappeared or been altered by sheep grazing; the Fenno-Scandian spruce forests are now harvested for wood for the paper industry with such regularity that the average height of the regenerating trees is decreasing year by year; and the English countryside, with its patchwork quilt of many-coloured fields surrounded by hedges, is entirely man-made and totally different from the oak forest that once covered the land. An even more extreme example is shown by the polders which have replaced the former Zuider Zee, now known as the IJsselmeer, in the Netherlands.

Nowhere is the influence more profound than in towns and cities. Seen from the air a modern town, with its tall buildings in the centre and smaller houses towards the outskirts, is rather like the top of a mountain. It appears barren of wildlife, but here and there are patches of greenery: the parks and open spaces set aside for the enjoyment of the inhabitants, and the more or less green corridors that are verges of railways and main roads coming right into the town centre. A closer inspection reveals trees in even the most heavily industrialized towns, trees planted in rows along roadways and from every point of view growing in unnatural surroundings. Away from the centre, looking down on the suburbs, there is more greenery, the gardens and yards of householders, and then an abrupt transition as the town ends and the countryside begins.

There is of course much variation in our view from the air, between both towns and countries. Some towns are greener, and many would say more beautiful, than others; there are national differences in attitudes to gardens and gardening; and varied social and economic approaches to the need for parks, golf courses and tree-lined roads, and to the housing of people. These and other considerations, including the past history of each town, account for the differences in the extent of greenery.

An aerial view of Middelburg, Netherlands. Where the town ends, there is an abrupt transition to countryside.

A recent survey revealed about a million trees within the 14,000 hectares comprising the City of Edinburgh. About 84 per cent are in gardens and the remainder in parks, cemeteries and similar open spaces, and along roadways. The urban part of Edinburgh supports about 56 trees to the hectare, compared with 43 to the hectare in the surrounding rural area. Edinburgh probably has more trees than some towns and fewer than others, but all urban areas support trees, and there is an increasing awareness of their aesthetic, recreational, and even commercial value.

Without green plants, there is no significant animal life, or at least no life that can be sustained for more than a short time. Plants acquire energy by photosynthesis, a remarkable process in which radiant energy from the sun is converted into the stored chemical energy of plant tissues. Some of the energy from photosynthesis is used for the growth and maintenance of the plant; what is left over is available as food, and all is eventually used by other organisms, mostly animals, themselves incapable of obtaining energy other than by eating.

Many species of animals, most of them insects, feed directly on living plants. Others are predators or parasites, which, in turn, are attacked by other predators and parasites. There are also decomposers, so called because they utilize dead plants and animals. All species of plants provide food for at least some species of animals, but some plants support a greater variety of animals than others. Why is this? The answer, it seems, is that some plants are more palatable and are therefore used by more plant-feeders. Most plant-feeders are severely restricted in the range of plant species they can eat.

It follows, then, that the variety of animal life found in an area depends on the plants available and, more importantly, on the diversity of species. If, for example, there is only one species of plant, there may be plenty of individual animals but relatively few species, whereas if there is a great variety of plant life a corresponding variety of animal life may be expected.

With few exceptions, the plant life of towns is extremely varied, especially in gardens; other things being equal, this should lead us to expect a varied fauna. But whether this is so depends on how well animals have become accustomed to feeding on the many non-native species of plants found in towns. About three-quarters of the species of animals found in northern Europe are insects. Many of them are plant-feeders and, if these have become adjusted to feeding on town plants, there is no reason why a wide array of predators and parasites should not be feeding on them in turn.

Webs of life

Let us look more closely. The view from the air is interesting and promising, but to find out more we must be on the ground poking about in vegetation and trying to detect and understand the food webs that exist.

People interested in natural history tend to notice birds. They are conspicuous and relatively easy to identify and many town-dwellers derive considerable pleasure from watching birds that live in gardens and parks. Most birds are predators, especially of insects, and few feed directly on plants, apart from the seed- and fruit-eaters; even they also take some insects and other invertebrates, particularly when feeding their young. Each species of bird is something of a specialist. The insect-feeders exploit different kinds of insects in different places. Hence the variety of bird life in a town depends partly on the variety of insects, which in turn depends on the variety of vegetation. Indeed, it could be said with some justification that birds are attractive but relatively unimportant links in the web of life dependent on town vegetation, while the insects are vitally important and deserve special attention. Without insects there would be few birds and without plants no insects.

The suburbs are greener and therefore probably richer in plant life than the town centre, so why not start in suburban gardens? At first sight all seems confusing. There is a huge variety of plants, some exotic-looking trees, plenty of birds, and in summer a wealth of insects. Sorting out the interrelations of plants and animals in a suburban garden looks as if it might require a life-time of study and observation. Certainly, a great deal of specialized knowledge is needed: most insects, for example, are difficult to identify. Nevertheless, a start can be made and the best approach is first to forget about the garden as a whole and focus instead on single species of plants to try to find out what they support and how they are exploited by animals. It should then be possible to move to assemblages of plants and extrapolate to the entire town and garden environment.

The holly *Ilex aquifolium* is a native of northern Europe and may be found in some places growing wild in woods and hedges. It has been extensively planted in gardens because it retains its attractive foliage throughout the year and, traditionally, branches bearing berries are used as Christmas decorations. Each individual tree is either male or female and it is the females that produce the bright red berries in late autumn and winter. Female trees are more common than males because people tend to remove those that fail to produce berries. The flowers appear in late spring, and pollen is transmitted from tree to tree by small insects attracted by the nectar.

Ripe holly berries are devoured by blackbirds *Turdus merula* and the flowers are visited by insects; but the tough, prickly leaves seem at first sight relatively immune from any attack. Yet there are insects that feed on the leaves, among them the larvae of the holly leaf-miner fly *Phytomyza ilicis*. Examination of holly leaves, particularly in February–April, should reveal large pale blotches on the upperside. These are caused by the fly larvae which live inside and feed internally on leaf tissue. The small and inconspicuous adult flies appear in June and the females lay their eggs at the bases of the midribs of the holly leaves. The tiny larvae hatch soon afterwards and mine their way forward to the centres of the leaves. They grow slowly and their presence is not easy to detect until the blotches begin to appear.

Often more than half the leaves on a holly tree are attacked by the larvae of this leaf-miner fly. Mined leaves tend to drop off prematurely and one effect of the larvae is to spread out the season of leaf-fall. Trees not attacked drop their leaves in June and July at about the time new leaves are formed, but trees severely affected lose some all the year round. This means that decomposition of dead holly leaves goes through different seasonal cycles beneath affected and unaffected trees.

In March, when the fly larvae are fully-grown, blue tits *Parus caeruleus* seek them out as food. These birds peck at the spots where the larvae are positioned and clearly have difficulty in getting a grip on the slippery outer coverings of the leaves; when one does, it makes a V-shaped tear on the leaf surface and removes the larva from beneath.

Blue tits eat insects that disfigure holly leaves; clean holly leaves are pleasing to look at and desirable as Christmas decorations, so an immediate reaction is that blue tits are 'useful'. But it is more complicated than this. The fly larvae are parasitized by about nine species of tiny wasps which always kill their hosts. As a result, a high but variable proportion of fly larvae never produce adult flies. Blue tits take both parasitized and unparasitized larvae and may therefore reduce the numbers of the insect enemies of the fly, which, in turn, may favour the fly population. A further complication in this food web is that cultivated varieties of holly trees (often called 'cultivars') differ in their susceptibility to attack by the flies. Those with very prickly leaves tend to be most affected by the larvae, and are also less often attacked by blue tits. It therefore looks as if the prickliness of holly leaves affords some degree of protection for the larvae against the attacks of blue tits. No one can say for certain if the birds control the numbers of the fly; they probably do not because, despite fairly heavy predation during a short period of the year, the larvae are relatively unimportant in the total diet of blue tits.

As we have seen, the holly leaf-miner fly is the most obvious consumer of holly leaf tissue and its presence leads to the development of a food web involving birds and parasitic wasps. There are other animals associated with holly, among them soil organisms as varied as bacteria and earthworms that decompose vegetation slowly, but there is no long-term accumulation of leaves and all eventually disappear. The dead leaves lying beneath a tree provide shelter and a place to seek insect food for such predators as hedgehogs *Erinaceus europaeus* and many spiders. The green leaves on the tree also provide winter shelter for small invertebrates and a safe roosting place for birds.

The presence of a holly tree in a suburban garden contributes a small but significant part to the total food web in that garden. All the species of animals associated with holly are connected in one way or another to the wide range of plants and animals living nearby. Thus, blue tits and blackbirds exploit food from many other sources; the adult leaf-miner flies and their parasites are eaten by other predators; and hedgehogs seek food among fallen leaves of many other garden shrubs.

Predator and prey. The blotches on the holly leaves are caused by the larvae of the holly leaf-miner fly which are eaten by blue tits in late winter.

Since the holly is a native tree, its food webs have been able to develop over many thousands of years. What about non-native, introduced species, particularly those that have no close counterparts among the indigenous flora? Have they developed similar food webs?

The butterfly-bush *Buddleja davidii* is a good example. It was introduced from China into Britain and France as an ornamental bush in about 1896 and has subsequently become a conspicuous weed of building sites and wasteland in towns. But, whether cultivated in a garden or growing wild on wasteland, it is very much a town plant and has never become properly established in the countryside. Its flowers are extremely attractive to butterflies, hoverflies (Syrphidae), bumblebees *Bombus* and other nectar-seeking insects, and it has no close rival among the native flora.

Almost all species of butterflies visit *Buddleja* flowers and, wherever a bush grows, even in the centre of a town, it is certain to attract at least some. Exactly which species depends on the locality and on the proximity of the surrounding countryside, but nearly everywhere it attracts large whites *Pieris brassicae*, small whites *P. rapae*, peacocks *Inachis io*, red admirals *Vanessa atalanta*, small tortoiseshells *Aglais urticae* and, in years when there is a substantial immigration from the south, painted ladies *Cynthia cardui*. Twenty or more species of butterflies may be expected at a flowering *Buddleja* bush in a well-established English suburban garden, a figure just short of a third of the species known from the whole of Britain.

The sugary nectar of *Buddleja* flowers is no different in chemical composition from that of other flowers, and so butterflies and other insects have no difficulty in switching to it. The same may not be true of the leaves and flowers. All species of plants produce chemical compounds which play no part in the normal processes of growth and development, but which act as deterrents to potential consumers, mostly insects. These compounds may be toxic, but more often they are distasteful to many plant-feeders, although attractive to others. One result of this arrangement is that most plant-feeders are restricted to a narrow range of plants for their food; another is that long-established, native plants tend to support a richer fauna than introduced, non-native species simply because there has been more time for the consumers to become adjusted to the chemical compounds. *Buddleja* is not native and it might therefore be expected that its leaves and flowers would be left alone by plant-feeders. But there are insects that feed on *Buddleja*, among them the aphid *Macrosiphum euphorbiae* which, like other aphids, extracts liquid food from plant tissues with its specially structured mouthparts. Most species of aphids are restricted to a narrow choice of plant species, even to a single species, but *M. euphorbiae* is one of the several able to make use of a wide range and to switch between species, an ability that probably explains how it manages to exploit *Buddleja*.

The presence of aphids on *Buddleja* in late spring and early summer leads to the development of an intricate food web. Ladybirds (Coccinellidae) lay small clusters of bright yellow eggs on aphid-infested leaves and stems, and the resulting larvae prey on the aphids, sometimes so effectively that all are eaten up. About eight species of ladybirds can be expected in an average garden in the southern part of our area. Those most frequently encountered on *Buddleja* are the small, red and black-spotted two-spot *Adalia bipunctata*, the large, red and black-spotted seven-spot *Coccinella 7-punctata* and the small, chequered yellow and black 14-spot *Propylea 14-punctata*. Many, but by no means all, species of hoverflies also lay eggs near aphids and their slug-like larvae are voracious predators. The commonest are the wasp-like *Syrphus corollae* and *S. balteatus* whose larvae are easy to find among clusters of aphids and whose adults seek nectar from *Buddleja* flowers. In turn, hoverfly larvae are frequently parasitized by tiny wasps of the family Ichneumonidae. The female wasps lay eggs on young hoverfly larvae and the resulting wasp larvae feed internally on the tissues of the hosts, which eventually die.

The ladybirds, hoverflies and parasitic wasps associated with aphids on *Buddleja* are themselves eaten by predators, including spiders and birds. Winged adult ladybirds are not especially palatable to birds: their bright coloration serves as a warning of their unpleasant taste; nevertheless, they are occasionally eaten, particularly by swifts *Apus apus*, which catch them in the air above gardens.

There are also insects that chew the leaves and flowers of *Buddleja*. Among them are caterpillars of small moths of the family Geometridae, which feed on flowers and green seed-pods, and those of another moth family, the Noctuidae, which feed on leaves. Most of these species are known to range widely in their choice of food-plants and presumably they had no difficulty in switching to yet another species. The caterpillars are eaten by birds and are hosts for parasitic Ichneumonidae and parasitic flies of the family Tachinidae.

It seems then that *Buddleja* is not only attractive as a nectar-source for adult butterflies, bumblebees and hoverflies, but also serves as a food-plant for a variety of insects. This, in turn, means that it supports a food web of its own, developed quite recently and consolidated as the bush became more popular and then escaped to become a weed of wasteland.

Buddleja usually grows as an isolated bush in a garden, as a dense thicket on wasteland, or as an opportunist colonizer of cracks in old walls. Holly generally grows as a medium-sized tree in suburban gardens and parks. But both these species are likely to be surrounded by totally different and unrelated trees and plants, all with an array of dependent insects and their associated predators and parasites. Each species of plant supports a characteristic food web and each food web overlaps widely with those on other kinds of vegetation. Predators and parasites move freely between different species of plants, seeking suitable prey and hosts; on the other hand, although there are many exceptions, most plant-feeders are restricted in the range of plant species they exploit.

Whether or not a plant supports an insect depends on a number of factors, not the least of which is the chance of colonization from other plants; this, in turn, depends on how far away the nearest neighbour is and on the mobility of the insect in question. Plants of the same species grown together in a flowerbed or vegetable patch, or as a line of trees along a roadway, are more likely to be colonized and therefore to support larger populations than plants that are well isolated from others of their species. Indeed, growing a lot of plants of the same species together provides one of the requirements for the establishment of insect populations at such high densities that they become pests. The problem of pests arises largely because of man's preoccupation with uniformity, a preoccupation best exemplified in gardens where roses, cabbages and many other ornamental and crop plants are grown in pure stands with everything else excluded.

Lime trees *Tilia* are common along roadways in the southern part of our area. In a single street, there may be a large number of them, all equally spaced from one another. The tree usually seen is a hybrid between the large-leaved lime *T. platyphyllos* and the small-leaved lime *T. cordata*, known as *T. × europaea*. Limes support a variety of insects, some of which are so abundant as to be a nuisance in places where there are many trees together. Lime aphids *Eucallipterus tiliae* occur in vast numbers and, at the height of summer, there may be up to a million on a 15-metre tree. Aphids tap the phloem (food-conducting system) of leaves and shoots and extract large quantities of sugar which is in solution together with the amino acids (nitrogenous com-

A row of lime trees along a suburban roadway. At the height of summer, each tree may support about a million aphids, which deposit large amounts of sugary honeydew on the road below.

pounds) aphids require to form protein for growth and development. But the phloem is rather poor in amino acids, so in order to obtain sufficient amounts, the aphids have to take up a lot of sugar which is promptly ejected through the anus. This ejected sugar is the familiar honeydew which in fine summers makes a sticky mess beneath lime trees, as motorists who have parked their cars there will know. The sugar released by aphids is an excellent energy source for other organisms, including a sooty mould which can give the impression that the trees have been affected by some form of industrial pollution. Many insects feed on the honeydew, including ants (Formicidae) and, especially when nectar is scarce, hoverflies and moths. The aphids themselves attract predators, including the larvae and adults of ladybirds and the larvae of hoverflies and their predators and parasites.

Our analysis of the food webs on holly, *Buddleja* and lime could be extended to all of the many species of plants found in towns and gardens. From what we know, we can predict that certain plants support more complicated webs than those described, while others may support very little.

A patchy and varied environment

Parks, cemeteries, golf courses and roadways all support vegetation and therefore food webs, but it seems that suburbia, with its patchwork of houses and gardens, is the most varied of the town environments and should, as a consequence, offer the most promise for wildlife. There are, however, regional and national differences in the essential characteristics of suburbia, which can be best understood in terms of differences in attitudes to gardens and gardening.

About 80 per cent of British households own or have regular access to a private garden and, because of the modern tendency to live on the outskirts of towns, most gardens could be described as suburban. These gardens are lovingly cultivated, much money is spent on maintaining them, and the advice of experts is often sought; indeed, gardening is second only to watching television as a national pastime. It is flowers that really matter to the British, flowers of every conceivable type that can be grown in beds and herbaceous borders, imported from all over the world. British gardens have a far greater array of flowers, trees and shrubs than those in other European countries, the only possible runners-up being the Dutch. Vegetables and fruit are also grown, because most gardeners like to feel they are contributing something to the family budget. The lawn is important: even the tiniest garden has one, and a good deal of effort is devoted to keeping it in trim. A well-established British suburban garden may contain between two and three hundred species of flowering plants, including trees and weeds, about half of them native. This figure is far in excess of what the land could support if left to its own devices.

In contrast, only 42 per cent of Swedish households own or have access to a garden and, except in the south where they are more like the British, Swedish gardens are much wilder. Most of the plants, especially the trees, occur in the area naturally and little attention is paid to the detail of herbaceous borders and the maintenance of lawns. Less time is spent on gardening and a typical Swedish suburban garden is less varied and more reminiscent of the surrounding countryside.

German gardens are in some ways intermediate between the British and Swedish patterns. They are rather formal and, as in the Netherlands, are more often used for outdoor activities and entertaining than in Britain. Flowers are favoured, especially in well-arranged beds, but crops are not popular. The French are more practical and nearly everywhere the growing of fruit is seen as a priority; they do not like lawns. The rather bare gardens in Iceland result from the climate and there, as in Scandinavia, people are more disposed towards indoor plants than in Britain or France. Thus, there is plenty of variation between the various countries of northern Europe, which affects the abundance and diversity of wildlife and the complexity of food webs.

In all European countries, the appearance of a garden is used rightly or wrongly as a way of judging the prosperity of the householder. In Britain the front, which can be seen from the road, is invariably better cared for than the back and is rarely used for growing vegetables. The Scandinavians probably care least about this aspect of gardening, but almost everywhere there is a feeling that a tidy garden indicates an orderly household. The sociology of gardening is a fascinating subject in itself, beyond the scope of this book, and all we need conclude is that, even allowing for national differences, gardens constitute the most varied and patchy environment for wildlife in northern Europe today.

But we must be a little cautious before we become too enthusiastic. Many of the more conspicuous garden plants are not native and, as a consequence, may be unsuitable for animals that feed directly on plants, although as we have seen this does not apply to *Buddleja*. Even the native species occur in unnatural assemblages, mixed with non-natives or grown in beds and rows. Naturalists are understandably suspicious of introductions and some feel that, so far as wildlife is concerned, gardens are biological deserts because of the multitude of exotic plant species grown. But even casual observations quickly suggest otherwise. There are, after all, plenty of birds feeding on lawns and lurking in the shrubbery: they would not be there unless there were food and shelter. Most of their food must be insects whose existence is ultimately dependent on the abundance and diversity of vegetation. The swifts that circle over towns in summer would not do so unless there were plenty of aerial insect life, which must originate from the land below.

If the centre of a town may be compared to the top of a mountain, or a cliff, then suburbia can be envisaged as the vastly extended woodland edge below. Naturalists know that the meeting of two habitats often produces a rich flora and fauna. For example, where woodland meets farmland there is a narrow strip supporting a rich variety of flowering plants, an abundance of insects, and more kinds of birds than in either of the adjacent habitats. The strip is narrow, often no more than a few metres wide, but its richness is apparent. Suburbia is much the same, but the strip is spread out over thousands of square metres. It consists of a complex mosaic of contrived plant diversity, blatantly man-made, to which nature has added a variety of species of plants and animals adjusted to suburban life. Perfectionists claim it is not natural; maybe not, but it is certainly not a biological desert.

Some colonizers

We have seen that plants support a variety of animal life and that each species of plant is likely to offer something different. Another approach is to select certain plants and animals to see how they have adjusted to town life.

Willowherbs *Epilobium* have exploited towns with remarkable success. Three or four species may be expected as garden weeds and they are among the first plants to colonize building sites and recently created open spaces. But exactly what is meant by a weed, a word which I have already used several times? The simple answer is a plant whose presence is unwelcome because it gets in the way or is unpleasing to look at. People have varying opinions about what constitutes a weed: a cabbage is not a weed in a cabbage patch, but it would be promptly removed from the middle of a well-trimmed lawn.

The most successful of the town willowherbs, the rosebay *E. angustifolium*, is treated by most people as a weed even though it looks attractive in a herbaceous border. Indeed, if seeds of rosebay were made available for sale in nicely designed packets, the plant might be prized by gardeners. It is a pity that plants which come up by themselves are less favoured than those that have to be planted and looked after.

A hundred years ago, rosebay was considered uncommon in Britain. In the 1940s, during and after the war, it became one of the first plants to colonize the open areas of bombed sites in London and other European cities; it came up almost everywhere and its wind-borne seeds no doubt aided dispersal. It is now one of the commonest town plants, not only in Britain but far north of the Arctic Circle.

The population explosion of rosebay resulted in an increase in numbers of the elephant hawk-moth *Deilephila elpenor*, whose large and conspicuous caterpillars feed on its leaves. In the 1940s and 1950s, there were elephant hawk caterpillars all over London; they sometimes caused alarm among people unfamiliar with insects of this size in the middle of a city, and no doubt many were destroyed by those who knew no better.

Some of the town plants we now call weeds were deliberately introduced many years ago. The Oxford ragwort *Senecio squalidus* occurs naturally on volcanic ash in Sicily and was introduced into the Botanic Garden at Oxford towards the end of the 18th century as an interesting and unusual plant. With the development of the railways in the 19th century, a suitable British environment for the species was created, not volcanic ash but clinkers along the tracks. The plant spread rapidly from Oxford, mainly along railway tracks, reaching London in 1867 and Scotland in 1940, and has now spread to almost all building sites and similar disturbed places rich in lime. Its appearance in Cork in 1839 was evidently a separate introduction by sea. It can be a common weed in the garden of a new house where there is little topsoil and plenty of rubble left over from building operations, but it does not survive in older gardens rich in humus and is rarely seen in the countryside except along roadways. Oxford ragwort is an attractive plant, originally introduced as something of a novelty, and even in winter will produce a few flowers; but, like other ragworts, it is not tolerated by gardeners. The plant has also been introduced into Denmark and France.

Rosebay and Oxford ragwort both support several species of insects. They are certainly food-plants of the spittlebug or froghopper *Philaenus spumarius*,

LEFT *One of the first plants to colonize building rubble and wasteland in towns, rosebay willow-herb growing among the ruins of St Andrews Church, London.* RIGHT *It can establish itself virtually anywhere.*

our next example of a successful town colonizer. Gardeners have probably noticed the little patches of frothy foam that appear on plants in late spring. Farmers and countrymen also know 'cuckoo spit', so called because its appearance coincides with the arrival of the migratory cuckoo *Cuculus canorus*: it is one of the signs of spring and occurs everywhere on a huge variety of both weeds and cultivated plants. The foam is produced by the immature stages, or nymphs, of several species of bugs of the family Cercopidae, the commonest being *P. spumarius*, an incredibly abundant insect throughout Eurasia and North America, and sometimes a pest of clover *Trifolium* and lucerne *Medicago sativa*. In one English garden it has been found on 62 species of plants of 31 families.

The nymphs of the spittlebug pierce plant tissue with their beak-like mouthparts and extract water from the xylem (water-conducting vessels). The water in the xylem contains nutrients in the form of amino acids and it is these that the spittlebug is after. In its mode of feeding, *P. spumarius* is similar to an aphid which, however, taps the phloem, not the xylem. A plant deprived of amino acids fails to form enough protein for proper growth and, as a result, can end up rather undersized. To obtain the amino acids it needs, a spittlebug nymph must extract a lot of water which is promptly discharged through the anus. Air bubbles are introduced into the discharge and make the foam that surrounds the nymph. It is unusual to see a nymph without its coating of foam; indeed, without the foam, it becomes desiccated and soon dies. The foam also protects the delicate nymph from predators.

Spittlebug nymphs tend to remain more or less stationary on the same part of a plant; but they sometimes crawl short distances and, once they have done so, quickly hide themselves in new foam. Adult spittlebugs, as their alternative name of froghopper suggests, are more active: they jump, fly and do not produce foam. Although tending to be static, they are capable of long-distance movements if disturbed, as when a crop is harvested or a garden cleared of weeds. Should the succulent vegetation upon which they depend become too hard to pierce, they then fly off and it may be that town populations are constantly replenished by repeated immigration from field crops in the countryside.

P. spumarius has been recorded on more than 400 species of plants, mostly non-woody, herbaceous kinds and is thus one of the most successful exploiters of garden plants and weeds. It is not often found on grasses and trees, where its place is taken by related species, but occurs on most garden plants, including aromatics, such as mint *Mentha*, sage *Salvia* and lavender *Lavandula*, and a few woody shrubs, such as privet *Ligustrum* and young birch *Betula*. It does not seem to occur often on members of the Cruciferae (cabbages and many of the common rock-garden plants), but, unlike most plant-feeding insects, exploits a wide range of species and is apparently not deterred by the strong smell of some of the herbs.

Is the spittlebug a pest? The answer must be a cautious yes: although the damage it does is not obvious and there is no visible destruction of plants, it attacks the water and nutrient flow, especially near growing points; this means that plants lose water, which could be serious in dry weather, and are depleted of nutrients. But a large, healthy plant can easily withstand a few spittlebugs.

Aerial plankton

The abundance of insect life in the air above towns is astonishing. This is particularly the case on warm, still days in July when many of the smaller species leave the ground eventually to settle far away from their place of origin in gardens and trees in parkland. These dispersal flights explain how a crop can suddenly and unexpectedly become infested with aphids. Most 'aerial plankton' consists of small invertebrates carried on air currents, but later in the year insect predators also follow the plankton and feed on it.

Both fall prey to house martins *Delichon urbica* and swifts. Swifts arrive in northern Europe from tropical Africa in late April and May, later than most other trans-Saharan migrant birds. The sudden appearance of flocks of screaming swifts is one of the signs of summer. They nest in colonies in holes under roofs of buildings (and in holes in trees or cliffs on the Continent) and are thoroughly adapted to town life. They feed entirely on insects and tiny spiders caught in the air. In wet and windy weather, when airborne insects are scarce, they feed low over the ground or water. Everything they eat is taken out of the air and their survival and the well-being of their young depends entirely on the availability of aerial plankton.

The female swift usually lays two or three eggs and the young are in the nest in July, the best month of the year for aerial plankton. If the weather is fine and sunny and there is not much wind, the young swifts receive adequate food from their parents, but in spells of rough weather their growth is retarded and some may die of starvation.

Swifts arrive, breed, exploit the seasonal peak of aerial plankton, and then disappear to more productive places in Africa. Why do they come here at all? The answer is that in July there are more insects in the air in northern Europe than in even the most favourable African environments. Swifts hunt by sight, missing very small items, and avoiding those too large. They have weak bills, but large gapes and throats in which they accumulate insects to feed their young. They seek out and exploit places where insects are common and usually hunt at between two and ten metres up in the air, flying back and forth over the same area until they have enough food to return to the nest and feed one of the nestlings.

A parent swift brings a compact ball of between 300 and 1000 insects and spiders each time it arrives to feed its young. The whole ball is passed to one nestling and there may be a struggle, a smaller nestling receiving food less often than a larger one. A brood of swifts is fed about 40 times a day and may receive about 20,000 insects and spiders in that time, a phenomenal total as each food item must be individually seen and caught by one of the parents. Young swifts are fed in the nest by their parents for about 43 days, and, allowing for the food that the adults must take for themselves, a pair of swifts and its brood probably consume nearly a million insects and spiders during July. The total removed by a pair of swifts during three and a half months in Europe might be double this figure. Swifts are common birds and the most recent estimate puts the British and Irish population at a conservative 100,000. Thus it seems certain that every season they remove many thousands of millions of invertebrates from the air above the towns of northern Europe.

An astonishing variety of insects has been found in swift food-balls collected and examined at Oxford, including at least 65 species of aphids, many of them well-known pests of garden crops. Small flies are also common, and among the many identified in swift food-balls are about 20 different hoverflies, all of them common garden species. Beetles are less abundant, although 80 species have been found and these have included several ladybird species, which are usually considered unpalatable. There are also plenty of spiders and 25 species have been found in the Oxford samples, most of them immature individuals that must have been using air currents as a means of dispersal.

Insects and flowers

A herbaceous border to a butterfly or bee is like a filling station to a motorist: it is gaudy and conspicuous, and advertizes a source of liquid fuel. But what is it about flowers that is so attractive to butterflies, bees and other insects? Most flower-visiting insects are adults. They have ceased growing and merely require refuelling and restocking with energy from time to time to enable them to move around in search of mates and escape enemies.

To us, the most attractive attributes of flowers are their colours, patterns and scents. People differ in their preferences, however, and exactly the same is true of insects that visit flowers for food: indeed, even a single species of bee includes individuals with marked preferences. Most garden plants are insect-pollinated, very few fertilize themselves; thus, the wide variations in flower structure, colour and scent can be explained by the need to attract nectar-feeding insects which transfer pollen from flower to flower. Each species of insect is selective in the flowers it visits: this means that pollen tends to be transmitted between flowers of the same species, an essential preliminary to fertilization and seed formation.

The structure of a typical flower is adapted to attract and receive insect visitors. Flower petals are distinctively coloured and provide a strong visual stimulus. The petals of, for example, pansies *Viola* have clear markings which act as a guide to the source of nectar. Other flowers, which appear to be uniformly coloured, have guide marks that become clear to us only when photographed through interference filters. As insects are much better at differentiating colours at the blue end of the spectrum, they can see marks and patterns on petals that are invisible to us.

The colour of petals is produced either by pigments or the reflection and refraction of light, and often a combination of the two. Flower scents are notoriously varied, but most people would describe them as either sweet or aromatic; a few are really unpleasant. The smell of the flowers is quite different from that of the foliage of most species, but in a few cases, such as lavender, the leaves and flowers have the same strong smell, which, although pleasant to us, is probably a repellent to immature insects that might otherwise attack the leaves and yet attractive to adults which are potential pollinators. Scent is produced from volatile oils in the tissues of the petals, sometimes from special secretory areas and sometimes more diffusely. The chemistry of flower scents is a subject in itself, but many different compounds are involved to give each species a characteristic fragrance. Some scents originate at the nectar source and in many plants there are cycles of scent and nectar production adjusted to the activity patterns of the insects that regularly visit them. Honeysuckle *Lonicera*, for example, which is visited in the evening by moths, produces a more powerful scent at dusk than at other times.

Flowers use both scent and colour to attract insects, which are, however,

LEFT *An evening primrose flower as it appears to us.* RIGHT *Photographed with an ultra-violet light source, the flower shows a dark central pattern. Moths and other insects can see such patterns, which are guides to the nectar source.*

interested in these attributes only as a means of finding and exploiting nectar. This is a solution of several different kinds of sugars and is therefore a valuable energy source. It is nearly always formed in small quantities in special structures called nectaries at the bases of the flowers. It is never produced in abundance, but just a little at a time, which encourages insects to keep moving in search of new sources, transferring pollen from flower to flower as they do so. Most flowers are bisexual and have filamentous stamens bearing anthers that produce pollen, and carpels that make up the ovary and receive pollen via the stigma. Cross-fertilization is brought about as insects move between flowers.

Pollen is used as food by some insects. Bumblebees carry it back to their nests and feed it to their larvae, and several groups of beetles and some hoverflies also eat pollen as well as nectar. It seems likely that, millions of years ago, insects once visited flowers primarily for pollen and that nectar production is a more recent adaptation evolved as a means of dispersing pollen. Transport by insects is more reliable than transport by wind, especially as each insect tends to visit the same plant species over and over again.

Butterflies about town
There is no really typical town butterfly; that is, there is no equivalent to the swift or the Oxford ragwort. Yet there are plenty of butterflies to be seen in towns. The main attraction is the abundance of flowers in gardens and parks.

Small tortoiseshell butterflies feeding from the flowers of Buddleja.

Most insects are difficult to identify, but butterflies are an exception: apart from birds, they attract more attention than any other group of animals. Most adult butterflies feed on nectar, but some also visit rotten fruit, especially in autumn. Few breed in towns. Patches of common nettles *Urtica dioica* sometimes support caterpillars of small tortoiseshells, peacocks and red admirals, but in the main these species breed in the countryside and come into towns to feed from flowers. The orange-tip *Anthocharis cardamines*, usually considered a rural butterfly, has recently become common in some English towns and the caterpillars are found feeding on the green pods of garden rockcress *Arabis caucasica* introduced as a rock-garden plant from south-east Europe. Two species of butterflies, the large white and the small white, are common garden pests: their caterpillars can be extremely destructive to cabbages and other cultivated brassicas. Caterpillars of the rather similar green-veined white *Pieris napi* feed on many other Cruciferae grown as decorative rock-garden and herbaceous border flowers, but very rarely on cabbages. In some towns, the holly blue *Celastrina argiolus* is common and may be seen flying high over thick shrubbery; its caterpillars feed on the flowers of holly in spring and ivy *Hedera helix* in autumn, but may take to flowers of other species as well.

A town garden well supplied with flowers always attracts a few butterflies and occasionally, in fine summers, a great many, especially if there is a suitably placed *Buddleja* bush. But is the individual red admiral seen in the morning the same as the one in the afternoon? Are the small whites busily inspecting the cabbages the same ones day after day or is there a constant stream of fresh arrivals? One way of finding out is to catch the butterflies with an ordinary insect net and carefully mark each individual on the wing with a tiny spot of coloured ink from a felt-tipped pen. In this way new arrivals can be recognized and, if marking and releasing are continued throughout a season or, better still, repeated for several seasons, some estimate of abundance and diversity can be obtained.

The results from one garden in Leicester, central England, are astonishing: during five years, nearly 11,000 individuals of 21 species were marked and released, including several species previously unknown in the area. Three butterflies (small white, large white and small tortoiseshell) were really common, each being recorded more than a thousand times; and three more (green-veined white, peacock and red admiral) were each recorded more than a hundred times. Nine species (small skipper *Thymelicus sylvestris*, large skipper *Ochlodes venata*, brimstone *Gonepteryx rhamni*, orange-tip, small copper *Lycaena phlaeas*, painted lady, comma *Polygonia c-album*, wall brown *Lasiommata megera* and meadow brown *Maniola jurtina*) were relatively infrequent; and six others (common blue *Polyommatus icarus*, white-letter hairstreak *Strymonidia w-album*, silver-washed fritillary *Argynnis paphia*, small heath *Coenonympha pamphilus*, marbled white *Melanargia galathea* and gatekeeper *Pyronia tithonus*) were found once only. Both the marbled white and the silver-washed fritillary are considered great rarities in this part of England.

The results from this garden suggest that towns support a highly mobile community of butterflies and that individuals remain in one place for only a short time: very few of the 11,000 were recaptured. It seems that, if a small area is watched closely over a period of years, rare and unexpected species will be found, but only a few butterflies are common in towns and a special watch must be kept for the remainder.

A plentiful supply of moths

There are many more species of moths than butterflies. Except in Iceland and the far north of Fenno-Scandia, three or four hundred may be expected in an average garden, but most of them are not often seen because they fly at night.

Most species occur just as abundantly in the countryside, but many are town-dwellers and several are intimately associated with the urban environment. Indoors are several species that will attack anything from books and clothes to wine-bottle corks; the one causing the most damage is the brown house moth *Hoffmannophila pseudospretella*. An outdoor urban moth is the vapourer *Orgyia antiqua*, the males of which fly by day through city streets and in gardens, while the fat, wingless females sit around on the cocoons from which they have emerged and await the attentions of passing males. In 1974, Londoners were astonished to find enormous numbers of brightly coloured vapourer caterpillars in Berkeley Square, right in the city

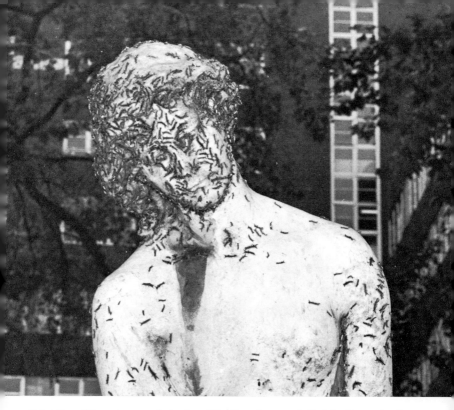

Caterpillars of the vapourer moth that have fallen from plane trees in Berkeley Square, London, grouped on the Greek statue there.

centre. The caterpillars fell from trees and were so abundant as to be a nuisance to passers-by and to people sitting around on benches eating their lunchtime sandwiches. The caterpillars were feeding on the leaves of London planes *Platanus × hybrida*, trees not normally used by moths. It seems that a population was suddenly established in Berkeley Square where, in the absence of competing species, numbers built up to plague proportions. These events, however, were not new: there are several reports of the vapourer becoming excessively abundant in towns and then disappearing just as suddenly. The caterpillars feed on the leaves of most species of broadleaved trees and shrubs. They are hairy and presumably unpalatable to birds and other predators; if handled, too, they cause an irritating rash on the skin. Exactly what the vapourer likes about towns is a mystery, but its position as an urban moth is well established even though it still occurs in the countryside.

On any warm night, hundreds of moths of dozens of species visit the flowers in herbaceous borders. Most are after nectar: those with short tongues go to flowers where the nectar is easily accessible and those with long tongues probe deep into tubular flowers, while others even crawl inside and disappear for a time. The demand for nectar is seemingly never satisfied, individuals sometimes driving each other away from choice flowers. The nectar obtained provides energy for the moths to seek more nectar, and the intense activity may at first sight appear rather pointless, but moths also fly about in search of mates and the correct food-plants on which to lay eggs, while some species migrate long distances.

In most years, the silver-Y *Autographa gamma* is one of the commonest town moths. It feeds from flowers by day as well as by night and is thus more often seen than the many similar species that feed only at night. It is migratory and cannot survive the north European winter in any of its stages. Individuals arrive from southern Europe in late spring and early summer; they lay eggs and the caterpillars feed on low-growing plants, including many species cultivated in herbaceous borders, and produce a large number of adult moths late in the summer. The volume of immigration from the south varies from year to year: sometimes silver-Ys are everywhere, but at other times there are very few. At least some of the offspring of the early summer immigrants make the return flight to southern Europe and large swarms have been reported at coasts and over the sea in October and November.

Other species have colonized northern Europe in relatively recent times, some of them especially associated with towns and gardens because their caterpillars feed on introduced plants and rarely on native ones. Among them is the golden plusia *Polychrisia moneta*, first recorded in Britain in 1890, now common and widespread, and nearly always found in gardens where its caterpillars feed on *Delphinium* and related plants. The varied coronet *Hadena compta*, whose caterpillars feed on cultivated *Dianthus*, has a similar history. Quite a few of our common garden plants originate in southern Europe and, now that they are grown north of their natural ranges, it looks as if they are being followed by certain moths and other insects. Finding their native food-plant may well enable chance migrants – brought sometimes from as far south as north Africa by strong southerly updrafts – to establish themselves.

Indeed, the herbaceous border, with its rich diversity of flowers, is an ideal breeding place for moth caterpillars. Almost all plants, including shrubs and trees are used. Caterpillars may be found by searching leaves and stems, but many are well concealed and easily overlooked. The large caterpillars of hawk-moths (Sphingidae) are often encountered, the eyed hawk *Smerinthus ocellata* on willow *Salix* and apple *Malus*; the poplar hawk *Laothoe populi* on poplar *Populus* and willow; the lime hawk *Mimas tiliae* on lime and elm *Ulmus*; and the privet hawk *Sphinx ligustri* on privet. Although large, the adult moths of these species are rarely seen except when an occasional individual is attracted to a street lamp or found resting by day on a tree trunk or fence. Other caterpillars, including those of the garden tiger *Arctia caja*, are boldly marked and hairy, and very easy to find; while some, such as those of the magpie moth *Abraxas grossulariata*, may become pests of fruit bushes. There are moths and caterpillars everywhere, but they have to be searched

LEFT *Full-grown fifth instar caterpillars of the elephant hawk-moth. When crowded, the caterpillars often turn black in the fourth instar, instead of remaining green; fifth instar caterpillars are usually black, but solitary individuals are sometimes green.* RIGHT *A drone-fly, one of the hoverflies, in flight.*

for. In terms of the number of species, moths are among the most successful exploiters of towns and gardens.

How towns favour elephant hawk-moths

The elephant hawk is one of the most beautiful insects in Europe; indeed, it looks like a denizen of a tropical forest and not a common inhabitant of our towns and gardens. The adult moths fly at dusk in early summer and may sometimes be seen hovering in front of flowers, from which they extract nectar with their long tongues. Females lay eggs in ones and twos on the undersides of willowherb leaves and the tiny green caterpillars hatch after a few days. They feed at night on the willowherb leaves; when fully grown they rest during the day near the base of the plant, but often climb to the top in late afternoon. They grow quickly, moult their skins five times, and eventually attain a length of about 8 cm.

As described earlier, elephant hawk caterpillars became exceedingly abundant in the 1940s and 1950s on bombed sites overgrown with rosebay willowherb. At first, the caterpillars were relatively free from the attacks of parasitic flies and wasps, which in rural areas are responsible for the deaths of a high proportion. Later, the parasites arrived in numbers, and they and the gradual redevelopment of the wasteland probably accounted for the decline of the elephant hawk, though it is still fairly common in towns.

Each stage between the moults of a caterpillar is called an instar. Elephant hawk caterpillars are normally green during the first four instars and black in the fifth; just occasionally they remain green throughout. During the 1940s and 1950s, however, when elephant hawks were abundant, many fourth instar caterpillars were also black: no one knew why, except that these occurred whenever the caterpillars appeared to be crowded. Later, experiments were designed to find out whether crowded conditions really were responsible for the production of black fourth instar individuals: young first instar caterpillars were reared either singly or in groups of ten in containers of a standard size; they were given plenty of food and a record was kept of dates of successive moults and of the colours of the caterpillars after each moult. The results confirmed that crowding is the stimulus for the production of black fourth instar caterpillars; those reared singly nearly always remained green until the fifth and last instar. But it was also found that crowded caterpillars grew more rapidly and pupated earlier than single ones, which suggested that they interacted with one another and fed more frequently; this behaviour would be advantageous in a natural situation where food might be in limited supply. We can imagine that, stimulated by the presence of potential competitors, a caterpillar responds by eating more food in less time, resulting in earlier pupation. Why they turn black prematurely is a mystery, but since there is no question of genetic control, the darkening is possibly no more than a secondary reaction to internal metabolic changes which occur in response to crowding. Similar changes have been noted in the caterpillars of other moths, including the silver-Y.

The populations of most town moths remain relatively stable, although there may be sudden ups and downs as in the case of the vapourer. A sudden abundance of a suitable food-plant, as on newly created wasteland, can lead to temporary upsets in density. It appears that some moths, and other insects, possess the ability to change their behaviour in ways useful for exploiting food in circumstances where competition with other individuals is likely to intensify.

An abundance of hoverflies

Seemingly motionless, they hover over flowers in bright sunshine and then disappear, only to reappear a few seconds later in the same place. There are big ones and little ones; some mimic bees, many bear a superficial resemblance to small wasps, and a few are so wasp-like that we are at first deceived. They are among the most obvious insects in towns, found wherever there are flowers, and a wide variety of species occurs in even the smallest city garden.

The hoverflies make up a distinctive family of the Diptera (or true flies), within which there is much variation in superficial appearance and, especially, in life history. The features of these Syrphidae include a thickening along the middle of the wing, looking like an extra vein, and veins running parallel to the wing margin, not easy characteristics to see in a rapidly moving fly. But they have only one pair of wings, like all true flies, and are unrelated to wasps and bees, which have two pairs. They are harmless and do not sting or bite.

Adult hoverflies are nectar- and pollen-feeders; they also take the juices of fallen fruit and, especially in dry weather, the sugary honeydew produced by aphids. The females of some species must have a meal of pollen for their ovaries to develop properly. A few species are notorious migrants: they fly south in autumn along sea coasts and swarms are often reported on beaches, where holidaymakers are apt to mistake them for wasps.

As a group, hoverflies illustrate well the complexity of relationships between insects and their food resources. Thus, although there is much similarity in the ways in which the adults acquire food, the larvae show a remarkable diversity of feeding habits. Those of the various species of *Eristalis* (known as drone-flies) and *Helophilus* feed on decomposing vegetation and dung, frequently in damp places and sometimes in stagnant water; the larvae of the large narcissus-bulb fly *Merodon equestris* and the small, black species of *Eumerus* feed on living bulbs; *Xylota segnis* takes sap exuding from trees; and *Volucella* larvae scavenge on bits and pieces lying around in bee and wasp nests. The majority of garden hoverflies, however, and we are speaking of about 50 species in some localities, are predators of aphids and thus compete with ladybirds in seeking out and exploiting clusters of these bugs on plants. Indeed, the feeding requirements and many aspects of behaviour of the seven-spot ladybird and one species of hoverfly, *Syrphus corollae*, are virtually identical. Their larvae are aphid-feeders and both exploit nectar, fruit and honeydew as adults. Numbers vary markedly from year to year, but both migrate and swarm and they may be found together on beaches where they end up as a result of attempted long-distance dispersal.

The slug-like larvae of *S. corollae*, *S. balteatus* and *S. ribesii* are particularly voracious consumers of aphids, but are often mistaken by gardeners for destructive caterpillars; this is a pity, for if any insects are to be judged useful, these particular hoverflies are strong candidates. In some years, especially when the early part of the summer is dry and warm, which also favours a build-up of aphid numbers, these hoverflies are extremely abundant on farmland. They may even exhaust their food supplies, in which case the adults start flying around in search of new sources of food and places to lay eggs. If the weather is exceptionally fine, flights of *Syrphus* can lead to large-scale movements involving millions of individuals; then there is often a massive invasion of gardens, with hoverflies at every suitable flower.

The large narcissus-bulb fly is a splendid mimic of bumblebees. It has many colour patterns and nearly all make this hoverfly look like one or another species of its model. Thus, there are red-tailed, brown and yellow-banded forms of *M. equestris*, just as there are species of bumblebees. The resemblance is enhanced by the bee-like buzz produced by the narcissus-bulb fly when

A wingless adult aphid giving birth to a live young.

touched or alarmed. It flies in May and June, at the same time as peak numbers of worker bumblebees, which it resembles in size. The advantage of mimicry is that the unarmed hoverflies tend to be avoided by predators because they are mistaken for bumblebees, which of course can inflict a nasty sting.

M. equestris was accidentally introduced into Britain about a hundred years ago, probably arriving as eggs or larvae in a consignment of bulbs from the Continent. The expansion of the bulb industry similarly extended its range northwards in Europe and promoted its dispersal to many other parts of the world, including North America, Japan and Australia. It is everywhere a mimic, but, since the extension of its range is only recent and the assemblage of species of bumblebees varies from place to place, we must assume that the colour varieties of the narcissus-bulb fly have not always had time to become well-adjusted to those of the local bumblebees in either frequency or form. The presence of a common species of bumblebee should lead to the establishment of the appropriate colour form of *M. equestris*. Mimics are almost invariably less frequent than the stinging or noxious animals they resemble; if they were not, birds and other predators would soon learn by repeated experience that many insects looking like bees were not bees at all, but both harmless and palatable. It is not easy to distinguish a mimetic hoverfly from the bee it resembles, but with experience it is possible to see slight differences in behaviour and even the bee-like buzz of the hoverfly has a slightly different tone.

Adult hoverflies like flat, open flowers and are unable to exploit the 'double' varieties commonly cultivated. They are especially attracted to the Compositae (notably golden rod *Solidago* and Michaelmas daisy *Aster*), the Umbelliferae (leave a carrot or celery to flower), *Sedum spectabile*, *Buddleja* and mint.

The gardening industry makes available an extraordinary variety of insecticides designed to destroy aphids. Advertisements state that these concoctions do not kill 'useful' insects. This may be true, but if a hoverfly larva, or a ladybird, is deprived of food it will die and, of course, a garden without aphids is less attractive to hoverflies seeking places to lay eggs than one in which at least some aphids are tolerated.

Social wasps

Most people think of wasps as black and yellow insects with the annoying habits of disrupting picnics or entering houses and stealing items of food from plates. Everyone knows they are capable of inflicting nasty stings and they are destroyed without mercy. Although there are many other kinds of wasps, even in towns and gardens, they are less obvious and rarely cause concern. The well-known black and yellow species are called 'social wasps', but what exactly does the term mean? The easiest way to explain is to outline their life history.

The fertilized females of social wasps, known as queens, make nests and during the year produce three sorts of individuals: males, queens and infertile females. The infertile females are called workers and their role is to collect food for the larvae produced from eggs laid by the queen. They far outnumber queens and males; indeed, most of the wasps we see in summer are workers, and it is only in autumn that males and queens are produced. Queens are larger than workers; they mate in autumn, the males then die, and the queens hibernate before starting a nest in spring. Thus, there is a degree of division of labour, also found among ants and bees, in which the sole function of the majority is to provide food for the larvae in the nest.

Most of the north European social wasps belong to the genus *Vespula*. Of several similar-looking species, the common wasp *V. vulgaris* and the German wasp *V. germanica* are the two most often encountered in towns, although occasional individuals of other species, notably the red wasp *V. rufa* and the tree wasp *Dolichovespula sylvestris*, may also be present. They are by no means easy to differentiate and people are apt to assume that all black and yellow wasps are the same.

The female workers are not always completely sterile; some may lay eggs at the end of the season, especially if the queen dies, but these are not fertilized and produce males only. In early spring, the fertilized queens that have survived the winter almost immediately seek out places suitable for nests. Common and German wasps use holes in the ground and make paper nests from wood fibres, which the common wasp chews from rotten trees and palings and the German from sound wood. The nest is constructed of hexagonal paper cells; the queen lays an egg in each and the resulting larva remains in its cell. At first, there are only about 20 cells, representing the number of larvae she can successfully feed; the larvae live in an upside down position and, when fully fed, they spin silken cocoons which form caps over the bottoms of the cells. Later on, as workers begin to hatch from the first pupae, the nest is enlarged to form a comb; gradually more combs are added, each hanging from the earlier sections by a paper stalk. As the nest grows, the workers enlarge the hole containing it by removing pellets of soil, often first bringing in water to soften the earth. A wasp nest at the height of summer contains all stages of development: eggs in the most recently formed cells, young larvae, fully grown larvae, pupae, and cells from which wasps have emerged.

The food brought to the nest consists of pieces of insect and other animal remains, which the workers chew up before offering them to the larvae. On the other hand, adult wasps feed on nectar and the juices of fruit, and are unusual in having a diet so different from that which they give to their larvae.

It takes about 30 days for an egg to develop into an adult. Workers are produced throughout the summer and a nest may eventually contain 10,000 or more cells, arranged in about eight combs and attended by two or three thousand workers. The existence of so many infertile workers means that a queen is able eventually to produce a large number of males and potential queens in autumn, in marked contrast to the solitary wasps which do not have workers and whose larvae have to be fed by the parents alone. Killing a few social wasps because they are annoying is really a waste of time: there are plenty more and, unless a whole nest is destroyed, which can be a hazardous operation, the best policy is to leave them in peace.

Social wasps are more common in some years than others. Exactly why is uncertain, but it seems that the weather in spring is important. A cold, wet spring is unfavourable for establishing nests, as is one that starts warm and then turns cold: this brings queens out of hibernation but leaves them with little opportunity to feed the first larvae produced. On the other hand, the severity of the previous winter does not seem to affect numbers. In general, a spring that starts well and is followed by a fine summer produces plenty of wasps.

Queens and workers will sting when disturbed or when an attempt is made to examine or destroy a nest, but the sting is essentially defensive and is not used to catch prey. Wasps are much 'fiercer' near their nests: there is, in effect, a collective defence of the colony, and the larger the nest the greater the danger to an intruder. Like most other insects, wasps are more active when the weather is hot; they then require more liquid fuel, and it is in these conditions that they cause alarm by descending on food and fruit. It would be difficult to estimate the importance of wasps to the economy of the garden, but there is little doubt that they consume many insects and, by making holes, they are responsible for the first stages of decomposition of ripe fruit.

Bumblebees

Bumblebees occur almost everywhere there are flowers. The queens are among the first of the larger insects to emerge from hibernation in spring. They are big, conspicuous and clumsy-looking; there is a story of a physicist who, after making extensive calculations and measurements, concluded that bumblebees were too heavy to fly.

About eight species may be expected in an average garden in the southern part of our area. Among the commoner ones are *Bombus pascuorum, B. lapidarius, B. terrestris, B. lucorum, B. pratorum* and *B. hortorum,* but the occurrence and frequency of these and others vary from place to place and to some extent from season to season. Only one species, *B. jonellus,* may be expected in Icelandic gardens. Despite their coloration they are by no means easy to identify as species: there is much geographical variation and, even in a single locality, individuals may differ in colour and pattern.

Bumblebees are social and many aspects of their life history are similar to those of the *Vespula* wasps. Unlike most winged insects, they are capable of flight in quite cold weather, even in near-freezing temperatures; this explains why they are among the first to appear in the spring, and why they are often flying when the weather is overcast, cool or wet. A bumblebee being cold-blooded, its temperature should be the same as its immediate surroundings, but then flight would be impossible in cold weather. In fact, bumblebees warm up before flight by shivering the muscles of the thorax, an activity that requires energy but at the same time conserves it by avoiding the need to warm up the entire body. The temperature of bumblebees has been recorded by inserting tiny thermistors into the thorax, where it has been found that something between 30° and 37°C can be generated; this is astonishingly high, especially if the surrounding temperature is near freezing. Warming up requires a prodigious rate of energy expenditure for insects weighing only about 0·1 gram, but their furry coats help to conserve heat once it has been generated. Bumblebees keep up high thoracic temperatures even when not flying, presumably because to start and stop repeatedly would be inefficient in terms of energy expenditure. They keep themselves ready for take-off throughout the day and cool down only at night. This requires an ample intake of energy in the form of sugary nectar from flowers, and so bumblebees feed continuously from dawn to dusk. The various species prefer different flowers and it has also been found, by marking bumblebees with a spot of coloured paint and following their movements, that even individuals have distinct preferences. They are among the most efficient pollinators, and they also collect pollen as food for their larvae. Indeed, bumblebees seem to visit certain flowers for nectar to acquire the fuel for longer flights, and other species of flowers with plenty of pollen suitable for taking back to the nest.

The nest is in a hole in the ground, a bank or a wall. The fertilized queen hibernates and starts it early in the spring; until the first workers appear, she provides all the food for the larvae, which are enclosed in wax cells of an irregular shape. Once there are plenty of workers, the queen stops feeding the larvae and devotes her time to egg-laying. The workers are very numerous. Towards the end of the summer – exactly when varies with the species – males are produced; these fertilize the new queens and then die before the winter sets in, as do all of the workers.

Bumblebees are especially attracted to blue flowers and the best way to observe them feeding is to allow a clump of sage to develop. In June and July, workers are very partial to sage flowers and, by careful observation, it should be possible to distinguish at least some of the species. Queens and the smaller workers have a special modification of the hind leg, known as a pollen basket, as do honey bees *Apis mellifera*, and it is usually possible to see a compact lump of pollen mixed with nectar attached to this. Individuals without pollen baskets may be males, which do not carry food to the nest, or they may be cuckoo bees *Psithyrus*, so-named because they take over the nests of bumblebees and become social parasites.

The life history of cuckoo bees is generally similar to that of bumblebees, but there are differences associated with their parasitic habits. Males and females are produced in autumn and, after fertilization, the females hibernate to reappear in spring slightly later than the queen bumblebees. They then search for and try to enter new bumblebee nests, but sometimes fail and may even be killed by bumblebee workers. It is thought that a female cuckoo bee that has gained entry to a nest often kills the bumblebee queen, but this is certainly not always the case. Whatever happens, the cuckoo bee lays eggs and the queen bumblebee either stops laying or her eggs are destroyed by the cuckoo bee. The bumblebee workers then feed the cuckoo bee larvae. No worker cuckoo bees are produced and we thus have a clear case of exploitation of one species by another. Two or three species of cuckoo bees may be expected in a garden in the southerly part of our area, but they are by no means common, and not easy to recognize among the large numbers of bumblebees usually present.

Are insects useful or harmful?

The gardening books tell us that insects are harmful if they feed on the plants we grow and useful if they are predators, parasites or pollinators, or if they feed on weeds. The damage caused by the allegedly harmful species is not just what they eat or extract from plants, but also what they transmit in the form of viral, fungal and bacterial diseases. In particular, aphids transmit

Seven-spot ladybirds feeding on blackfly on broad beans. Gardeners regard ladybirds as useful.

viruses from plant to plant and are indirectly responsible for a lot of the diseases of crops and flowers.

In approaching the question whether insects are useful or harmful, we must remember that, although the energy they require ultimately comes from plants, and although the most abundant and conspicuous species are plant-feeders, most are predators and parasites of other insects. An average garden probably supports two or three times as many species of predators and parasites as plant-feeders. Thus, in one way, most kinds of insects could be judged as useful and a few as harmful, but this is patently an over-simplification.

Each individual and species has an ecological role, or niche, and the spectrum of insects in a garden, park or patch of wasteland is a reflection of what that area can support and what it has to offer in terms of amount and variety of vegetation, availability of cover, and climate. There are always consumers of vegetation and their predators and parasites, and decomposers of dead vegetation and dead animals: exactly how many in each category depends largely on the variety and number of plants present.

Spittlebugs and aphids tap the water and nutrient flow in plants, bumblebees and hoverflies take nectar and pollen, caterpillars chew leaves, butterflies and moths search constantly for nectar and other liquid food, wasps kill other insects, and a host of small species from a variety of groups feeds on dead plants and animals. All have close relationships with plants, and all are preyed upon and parasitized by other insects. If there were no insects, flowers would not be pollinated and the much slower decomposition of dead plants would lead to an accumulation. Insects are therefore vital in maintaining 'orderliness'. These considerations should cause us to hesitate about killing a troublesome wasp or about pouring boiling water on an ant nest which appears in the garden path.

Our somewhat uneasy attitude towards ants illustrates well the problem of deciding whether insects are useful or harmful. No one is bothered about a few ants running around on the ground, but it is a different story when they swarm. The social organization of ant colonies is similar to that of bumblebees and *Vespula* wasps. Ant nests are partly or wholly underground and food is brought to the larvae by the workers. Males and potential queens are winged and on still, warm days in summer leave the nest in swarms to ascend into the air on 'marriage flights'. The males die soon after fertilizing the queens, which then remove their own wings and often start new colonies. Swarming flights of garden black ants *Lasius niger* may cause alarm and even disrupt traffic, while the workers frequently invade houses in search of food morsels. It is the sudden and unexpected increase in numbers in unusual places that leads to action being taken against ants. Most of the time they are inconspicuous, although *L. niger* sometimes nests so close to buildings that it constitutes a minor threat to masonry. Most town ants are scavengers and all make use of the sugary honeydew produced by aphids. Two species, Pharaoh's ant *Monomorium pharaonis* and the Argentine ant *Iridomyrmex humilis*, both introduced into northern Europe, survive only in heated greenhouses and houses: they are regarded as pests because they live in intimate association with man.

Each insect's niche must be understood in terms of food acquisition, escaping enemies and competitors, and realizing full breeding potential. The question, 'Are insects useful or harmful?', therefore has only a limited meaning. Each has its role and removing those considered undesirable inevitably leads to disruption of what might otherwise be a stable community. This is not to say that obvious pests should never be killed: gardeners are understandably proud of what they produce and, if they see their efforts thwarted by particular insects, there is every reason to take action. What is less understandable is the feeling that, with a few exceptions, insects are there to be destroyed at all costs.

Our question can be approached in another way. Thousands of species of small parasitic wasps belong to the Ichneumonidae, Braconidae and Chalcidoidea; several hundred species may occur in an average garden. The larvae of the wasps are parasites of other insects, particularly, but not exclusively, attacking species that eat living vegetation. The wasp larvae eventually kill their hosts and must therefore be responsible for the deaths of vast numbers of plant-feeders, not only those that attack cultivated plants but also those that eat weeds. Are these parasites useful? It is impossible to say: we would need to know exactly which hosts, and how often, each of the many species of parasites attacks. Even if we had this information, there would be uncertainties over passing judgement: does the caterpillar feeding on the leaves of the dahlias produce a moth that pollinates apple blossom? We can but conclude that insects should not always be viewed as candidates for destruction; many of them are also beautiful and have fascinating life histories. Is it not better to observe them and try to understand what they are doing?

Bird residents and visitors

Birds are the best-known of all town animals. Most of us put out food for them in winter, and there are some, even if only house sparrows *Passer domesticus* and feral pigeons *Columba livia*, in the centres of the most heavily industrialized cities. These two species are believed to have been associated with man since the Stone Age, probably following him into northern Europe in neolithic times and becoming dependent on the crops he cultivated. In modern cities, they are able to subsist largely on food accidentally provided by man. Both pigeons, descended from cliff-dwelling stock, and sparrows find niches for all their activities in the cliff-like urban centre. Both have attracted their own predators, kestrels *Falco tinnunculus* and, in suburbia, tawny owls *Strix aluco* taking sparrows, and occasional peregrines *F. peregrinus* striking down pigeons.

Apart from the attraction of towns because people feed them, birds make good use of insects and other invertebrates in gardens, parks and wasteland, and of seeds, berries and fruits of wild and cultivated plants and trees. A few species nest in or on buildings; many others do so among vegetation in gardens and parks.

The thrush that sings in the city of Reykjavik in Iceland is the redwing *Turdus iliacus*; in London, it is the blackbird *T. merula* or the song thrush *T. philomelos*; in Stockholm, it may be the fieldfare *T. pilaris*. Many birds are only occasional visitors to some towns, but common residents in others: it all depends on the locality. A moderate-sized, English suburban garden with plenty of shrubbery attracts blackbirds, song thrushes, blue tits, great tits *Parus major*, robins *Erithacus rubecula*, wrens *Troglodytes troglodytes*, chaffinches *Fringilla coelebs* and greenfinches *Carduelis chloris*. In summer, swifts and house martins are likely to be feeding on the aerial plankton and nesting in or on buildings. In winter, gulls *Larus* often fly overhead and flocks of starlings *Sturnus vulgaris* perch in the trees and feed on the lawn. Tawny owls are often heard at night and sometimes seen as silhouettes on chimney pots. But many more species are there to be found by a patient observer; we tend to notice the noisy resident birds, but miss the silent migrants because they

Waterfowl on Reykjavik's city lake. The lake supports colonies of eiders and other birds which do not breed in towns in other parts of Europe.

skulk in vegetation and stay for only a short time. One way to see them is to get up early and watch carefully.

Particularly revealing are the results of ringing birds in town gardens. For many years, ornithologists have been catching birds in traps and nets, and placing numbered, metal rings on their legs before releasing them. The rings give the address of a central office so that if a marked bird is found again, dead or alive, its whereabouts may be reported. Millions of birds have now been ringed in northern Europe, and all over the world, and the information obtained provides a firm basis for what is known about migrations, local movements, and the ages at which birds die. Equally interesting, ringers have discovered that, when the same area is worked for an extended period, all manner of unexpected species may be found.

One ringer in an English suburban garden discovered an astonishing variety of birds, some of which he never saw other than in his traps. The species included several unlikely town birds, such as marsh warbler *Acrocephalus palustris*, sedge warbler *A. schoenobaenus*, grasshopper warbler *Locustella naevia*, nightingale *Luscinia megarhynchos* and brambling *Fringilla montifringilla*; in all, he ringed 55 species, about 25 of which would not normally be expected in a suburban garden. The success of this particular ringer can be attributed partly to the variety of traps and baits used to catch the birds. Good use was made of seasonally available fruits (blackberries *Rubus fruticosus*, raspberries *R. idaeus* and honeysuckle berries), grain, fat, nuts, stems infested with aphids, mealworms, bread, and even sardines to attract gulls. But the best results came from dripping water: many small birds, particularly migrating warblers, cannot resist this and readily enter a trap for a drink or bathe.

The obvious and familiar species in gardens and parks are either breeding birds or winter visitors. Breeding males defend territories against other males of the same species. Defended territories may occupy a whole garden, several gardens or parts of several gardens, and just as the territories of the human inhabitants of suburbia are divided up, so are those of its breeding birds. Even the fences, hedges, walls and similar barricades built by human beings to keep out their fellows are used by birds as vantage points and song posts in defence of territories. The songs of such species as the robin and the blackbird may sound sweet and pleasant to us, but their true function is to warn intruders away. It is a way of staking out a space, in which to breed and forage for food, and from which others of the same species are excluded.

Male blackbirds defend territories and breed within them. In gardens, the nests are generally low in evergreen shrubs, but occasionally on buildings. Three to five eggs are usually laid and there may be three or even more broods in a season. Many clutches and broods disappear mysteriously, probably falling to marauding cats and crows. Late in the spring, newly fledged blackbirds appear on lawns; they look helpless and kind-hearted people sometimes mistakenly assume that they are injured or abandoned, pick them up and try to take care of them. But these and other young birds are usually still being fed by their parents and should be left alone.

Winter visitors to towns include other birds of the same species as the residents, but what pertains to the north of our area, where for example the robin is a summer visitor, may not be true in the south. Rural blue tits come into gardens from woodland during the winter in search of food, but there is a rapid turnover in any one area. Ringers have found of the order of four or five hundred blue tits passing through a single garden each winter; thus, the blue tits seen one day may well be different from those present the previous week. Winter visitors also come from other countries: for example, a general westward displacement of starlings occurs every autumn to such an extent that those seen in winter in a French, English or Irish town may have originated in five or six different countries of northern and eastern Europe. They mingle with the residents and compete fiercely for the limited food resources available in winter. Evidently, the town environment provides a better and more reliable year-round supply of food than the countryside, partly because of the rich variety of invertebrate food, and partly because people put out scraps in winter.

But town bird-watching in northern Europe is not only a matter of studying the ways in which a few species have adapted themselves; considerable variety is involved. Over a hundred species have been recorded in Hamburg, on the face of it both highly urban and industrialized. Reykjavik supports not only breeding redwings, redpolls *Carduelis flammea* and white wagtails *Motacilla alba* but, on its lake, the only urban colonies of arctic terns *Sterna paradisaea* and eiders *Somateria mollissima* in the world. The eiders feed with scaup *Aythya marila*, one of Iceland's commonest ducks, and the more usual mallard *Anas platyrhynchos* and tufted duck *Aythya fuligula* on scraps thrown to them by children. The little redpolls stick out the winter, joined by snow buntings *Plectrophenax nivalis*. Greylag geese *Anser anser* and black-necked grebes *Podiceps nigricollis* nest on the outskirts of Copenhagen, and mallard-haunted Amsterdam boasted urban grey herons *Ardea cinerea* long before Regent's Park, London, attracted a small colony; Stockholm has a heronry too.

Short-toed treecreepers *Certhia brachydactyla*, virtually unknown in Britain, are resident in French, Dutch, German and Polish parks, whose summer visitors include golden orioles *Oriolus oriolus*, icterine warblers *Hippolais icterina*, whitethroats *Sylvia communis* and lesser whitethroats *S. curruca*, pied flycatchers *Ficedula hypoleuca* and red-backed shrikes *Lanius collurio*. Urban species spreading north and west include the serin *Serinus serinus* and, most notably, the collared dove *Streptopelia decaocto*. Other birds are tending to spread more into towns: thus, the tree sparrow *Passer montanus*, unusual in urban areas in the west, is very much commoner in towns in eastern Europe, even outnumbering the house sparrow in some cases. The black redstart *Phoenicurus ochruros* is usually regarded as the replacement in Continental towns of Britain's national bird, the robin, but many robins sing in Paris's Bois de Boulogne in autumn and may also be seen in the city centre there.

Birds as opportunists

If you watch a wren moving about the herbaceous border searching for food, you will be impressed by its inquisitiveness. It searches everywhere, among dead leaves, bricks, stones, flower-heads and stems, and seems to peck at and examine anything that might remotely yield a morsel of food. All through the winter, when there are few obvious changes in the vegetation and insect life, wrens and other small birds search the same patch over again and again. Clearly they find food – if not, they would have to go elsewhere or die – but it is not easy to see what they are after.

Most of the common garden birds feed at least partly on insects and other invertebrates. The places they search vary with the time of year and the weather, and there is every reason to suppose that, as they hunt for food, resident individuals rely upon familiarity with the local environment. Learning acquired by trial and error plays an important part in the feeding routines of birds and, more than most animals, they can accurately be called opportunists – a quality that has led them to exploit some really unusual food sources.

One of the best examples of opportunism is the habit of some species of opening milk bottles and taking the top of the cream. It is not certain when and where this started, but by 1949 there were over 400 records in Britain alone, and it has since been reported from Denmark, among other European countries. The earliest known record in England was in Southampton in 1921. Most reports refer to blue and great tits, but several other birds have followed suit, including great spotted woodpeckers *Dendrocopos major*.

If a milk bottle top is of foil, it is necessary for the bird to hammer it to make a suitable puncture; this hammering and puncturing is comparable with the way in which a nut is opened, an operation great tits in particular perform with speed and efficiency. Cardboard tops are opened with a tearing action and the behaviour is similar to that used in stripping bark from a twig when searching for small insects; it is also reminiscent of the way in which, as we have seen, a blue tit opens up the mine of the holly leaf-miner fly in a holly leaf. Thus, the same techniques are used to open milk bottle tops as to deal with more natural foods; new skills do not have to be acquired and, once a bird has successfully sampled the contents of a milk bottle, it tries again and again, improving at each attempt. But how were milk bottles recognized as a source of food in the first place? It is most likely that many species of birds have an inborn tendency to inspect unusual objects and constantly to test them as potential foods. Great and blue tits, like wrens and many other small birds, always seem remarkably 'busy', and there is little doubt that they learn by imitation as well as from their own experience. In this way, the habit could spread rapidly among tits and other species that tend to occur together in winter flocks.

Imitation is not, however, the whole explanation. For example, the great spotted woodpeckers already mentioned do not associate in flocks, except sometimes on migration. The exploitation of new food sources also arises spontaneously in widely separated areas, with different individuals independently making the same discovery. A magpie in Surrey, England, in May 1975 was seen to break into a papier-mâché carton and remove a hen's egg, even though the box was closed and its contents were invisible. Publication of this observation resulted in further reports from a town in another county, South Yorkshire, where the habit is so regular that the delivery men are asked to cover the cartons with inverted bowls, though the magpies sometimes overturn these and take eggs. As we shall see later, magpies are becoming commoner in urban areas in parts of Scandinavia, Britain and Ireland, and it may well be that this habit will develop in the same way as the opening of milk bottles.

We have already seen how swifts are thoroughly adapted to urban life and how they exploit the aerial plankton above towns at the height of summer. House martins, also summer visitors from Africa, feed in much the same way. On still warm days, aerial plankton occurs in great concentrations, and other birds normally restricted to terrestrial habitats take to the air and catch winged insects, including the flying ants which are apt to swarm on their marriage flights in hot weather. Among the birds involved are house sparrows, starlings, carrion crows *Corvus corone* and several species of gulls. None is especially good at catching aerial insects – indeed, they are often re-

An opportunist young blue tit hammers the top of a milk bottle to get at the cream.

markably inefficient – but exceptionally abundant aerial plankton is exploited by even the most inept of flying predators, another example of opportunism.

Some birds, such as swifts, house martins, house sparrows and feral pigeons are now more closely associated with towns and villages than any other habitat throughout much of northern Europe. From Ireland to Poland, the blackbird is as at least common in gardens and parks as in the countryside. The black redstart, originally and still commonly a mountain and sea-cliff species, now breeds widely in urban areas from France to Poland and, more locally, in England. Evidently, then, towns have a lot to offer, and it is interesting to speculate about additional species that may sooner or later colonize the urban environment of northern Europe.

We certainly cannot assume that the present variety of town birds in our area represents all the species that may be expected in the future. For one thing, a number of birds are extending northwards in Europe and several of these are associated with towns. Two hundred years ago, the serin was confined in Europe to the south. By the second half of the 19th century, it was in the southern part of our area, including Germany, Czechoslovakia and Poland; it had reached the southern shores of the Baltic by 1925 and since then has started to nest, sometimes in suburban areas, in Finland, Sweden,

Denmark and England, where breeding was first proved in Dorset in 1967.

Even more spectacular has been the spread of the collared dove. Its original home is believed to have been northern India, but by the 16th century it had reached the Balkans. Then, about 1930, began an explosive extension north-west. Collared doves reached Czechoslovakia in 1936, Poland in 1940, Germany in 1943, the Netherlands in 1947, Denmark in 1948, Sweden in 1949, France in 1950, Belgium and Norway in 1952, Britain in 1955 and Ireland in 1959. Early in the 1970s, they even nested in the Faeroe Islands and Iceland. The general pattern has been for the first arrivals to be rapidly followed by a build-up in numbers at a rate unprecedented in any other species.

In Britain and Ireland, as earlier in the Netherlands, the numbers doubled annually for the first decade until by 1964 there were probably about 3000 breeding pairs and an autumn population of at least 19,000 birds, many of them in suburban gardens and parks, and along tree-lined roadways. By 1970, the breeding population was thought to be between 15,000 and 25,000 pairs, but, again as in the Netherlands, the annual rate of increase had evidently slowed down to less than half. Nowadays, collared doves can be seen in many north European towns, perching on television aerials and chimney pots and breeding in trees along busy roads. They feed chiefly on grain and seeds, and seem to exploit places where people are apt to be untidy. Mills, docks and chicken runs are especially favoured because of the grain lying around.

It appears that there was what might loosely be termed a vacant niche for a small dove closely associated with man. The feral pigeon is more a scavenger in city streets, while the larger woodpigeon *Columba palumbus* prefers open parks, and is not especially associated with gardens. The collared dove is clearly an opportunist and, because it was able to adjust to modern suburbia, has become familiar in much of northern Europe within the short space of 40 years, a remarkable achievement. Can we expect other species to behave in this way? One possible candidate is the Syrian woodpecker *Dendrocopos syriacus*, a species very similar to the great spotted woodpecker except that it is much more a bird of man-made habitats. Originally confined to the southern Balkans and south-west Asia, it began to extend its range in the wake of increased cultivation, reaching Bulgaria in 1890, Hungary in 1949 and Austria in 1951. The spread appears, however, to have slowed right down: although the species has colonized Czechoslovakia in the last 25 years and now breeds quite widely in lowland areas in the south-east and centre of that country, it has still not reached Poland, despite having been reported close to the Polish border as long ago as 1954. If it does continue to spread, it may one day be found in parks and gardens in Poland, Germany and Denmark, but perhaps it is already having difficulty in competing with the well-established great spotted woodpecker, which is more of a suburban and farm-land species in northern Europe than it is where the two overlap in range farther south.

So much for range extensions by suburban species; but at the same time several other birds have quite recently become more associated with gardens than in the past. One is the bullfinch *Pyrrhula pyrrhula*, essentially a seed-eater, restricted throughout most of its vast range in Europe and Asia to coniferous forest. In Britain and elsewhere in north-west Europe, at the extreme west of its range, and also in Japan, at the extreme east, the bullfinch occurs in deciduous woodland, and it is only in these two areas that it has become associated with gardens and, especially, orchards. Indeed, it has become a pest, as it eats the buds of cultivated fruit trees. In Britain, it was not until the 1950s that bullfinches began to become common in gardens. Their natural summer food consists of the seeds of trees and of the plants forming ground cover in woodland; in winter, they eat the buds of wild trees.

Bullfinches probably turn to buds when seeds are not available and, since the seed crop on wild trees is notoriously variable from year to year, the extent to which they eat buds also varies. Buds lack the concentration of nutritive protein found in seeds and so, when forced by circumstances to eat them, bullfinches tend to take large quantities as if to make up for a dietary deficiency. Just one in a pear tree can eat as many as 25 buds a minute, and several together can remove thousands of buds a day, thereby seriously reducing flower production the following spring. Buds of cultivated fruit trees are of higher nutritive value than those of many wild trees. Indeed, the recent infiltration of bullfinches into gardens and orchards can be explained by their discovering that cultivated fruit trees are the better substitute for the failing seed crop. And, of course, once the first step is taken, the birds discover additional food sources in gardens, quickly becoming less shy and more used to people.

The magpie provides another example of opportunism. Magpies are still persecuted by gamekeepers and farmers in the belief that they take eggs and young of gamebirds. They are also disliked because they eat the eggs of small birds and have gained for themselves the reputation of being crafty and cruel. But they are basically insect-eaters, obtaining much of their food on the ground near bushes and hedges. In Britain and Ireland, magpies occur in woodland and well-grown hedgerows; recently, they have shown an increasing tendency to come into towns – a notable example is Dublin – and feed on scraps, but they rarely breed in urban areas: they are too shy for that. In Sweden and Norway, magpies really are town birds: they perch on roof-tops and breed in gardens, and are now more common there than in the countryside. It seems that Scandinavian magpies have done well for themselves; they have found a refuge from persecution, for few people try to shoot birds in a densely populated area. But in one place, the city of Lund, policemen are authorized to kill magpies and it is believed that each year about 90 per cent of the breeding pairs are destroyed. This policy arises from public demand, chiefly from bird-lovers who claim that magpies steal the eggs of small birds. Nevertheless, the magpies persist and those shot are soon replaced by new arrivals from the countryside.

Another new urban opportunist, at least in England, is the siskin *Carduelis spinus*. Until the severe winter of 1962/63, this was essentially a forest species which fed in winter on the seeds of streamside birches and alders *Alnus*; it was almost unknown at bird-tables. Then some individuals started feeding in gardens in Surrey, taking chiefly shelled peanuts and meat fat, and by 1971 this behaviour had been noted in over 90 gardens in nearly 20 counties, mainly in south-eastern England, so it seemed likely that the spread was due to learning. Most of the records are in the second half of the winter, and the peak each year is in March, when natural food sources may be depleted. Many siskins wintering in south-east England have been shown by ringing to be of north European origin. This species is extending its range to some extent and it is most interesting that, at the same time, it should be developing a change in winter feeding behaviour.

A characteristic species of many European towns is the blackbird. It occurs widely, provided there are shrubs in which it can nest. The year 1949 was the first recorded date that a pair bred on a bombed site near St Paul's Cathedral in central London to become one of the first birds to colonize successfully the new environment created by human destructiveness. The blackbird is really a woodland species and only in the last 150 years has it become a common town resident. Most of its food is taken on or near the ground: earthworms are all-important, which is one reason why the blackbird is associated with lawns; it also eats insects, especially caterpillars, and berries.

Many blackbirds migrate from Fenno–Scandia and eastern Europe, and spend the winter in Britain, Ireland and France. The winter population in the west is thus considerably larger than the breeding one. We know from recoveries of ringed blackbirds that relatively few of these immigrants come into gardens: they tend to remain in the open countryside, where they join flocks of other species of thrushes. Many of the blackbirds born and bred in towns stay where they are all the year round; it is the rural blackbirds that are restless, which suggests that the countryside is more hazardous or has less to offer in the way of food. Similarly, breeding densities in towns, notably in gardens, may be six times as high as on farmland and nearly three times as high as in woodland, the original home of the species.

If we take into account losses of eggs and young, it can be calculated that each pair of town blackbirds produces, on average, 3·5 fledged young a year. The majority die before the next breeding season: as with all birds, the death rate of individuals less than a year old is extremely high, presumably because of inexperience in finding food and escaping enemies. Just over 40 per cent of the adult blackbirds (those at least a year old) also die each year and their territories are occupied by surviving one-year-olds or by adults that have previously failed to gain territories.

All things considered, it seems that this species' move from woodland to towns has resulted not only in more blackbirds but also in a less migratory population. The extent to which this has been made possible by people providing food in winter is a matter for speculation: blackbirds certainly take food scraps, but it is equally likely that, for them, towns are altogether better year-round feeding places than woods and fields.

Blackbirds construct their own nests and all they need to have are safe sites not occupied by other pairs. Several other species of town birds, among them blue and great tits, carry moss, grass, wool, hair and feathers into holes. Natural holes are often in short supply, particularly where there are few mature trees; if artificial holes in the form of specially designed nest-boxes are provided, they usually attract blue and great tits. Indeed, the provision of nest-boxes can considerably increase the breeding populations of these birds in places that are otherwise unsuitable.

The blue tit is one of the most frequent winter visitors to feeding tables and readily takes to breeding in nest-boxes in gardens. Its natural habitat is broad-leaved woodland, especially oak *Quercus*, where it is among the most abundant and successful of birds. Females usually lay seven to sixteen eggs and in woodland they are often successful in raising the entire brood unless it is destroyed by predators, such as weasels *Mustela nivalis* or squirrels *Sciurus*. Blue tits feed their young on moth caterpillars, particularly those of the winter moth *Operophtera brumata* and the green oak tortrix *Tortrix viridana*, two of the species capable of defoliating oaks in spring. In summer, when young blue tits have left their nests, less food is available in the woods – there are few caterpillars then – and so many of the birds move and eventually settle in gardens.

But gardens are not especially good breeding places for blue tits. Though they readily make use of nest-boxes, the trouble is that suburban trees never seem to produce the great flush of caterpillars characteristic of the woodlands. The same moths are present, but are not especially abundant, partly because town oaks and similar trees are usually well isolated from others of their species and so do not ever build up vast populations of caterpillars. Studies of blue tits nesting in boxes reveal that nestling mortality from food shortage may be eight times as great in gardens as in woods; indeed, blue tits breed in gardens chiefly because suitable sites are provided for them, and so whether this is a good policy is open to question. It is probably better to acknowledge woodland as the proper home for breeding blue tits and to think of towns and gardens as places where they can find food in winter.

Flocks of feral pigeons are a familiar sight in town squares and parks in most parts of our area, and they are also common scavengers in dockyards and around warehouses, but they rarely enter gardens. They are the same species as the rock dove, which breeds on cliffs in remote places.

There is a love-hate relationship between man and feral pigeons. People feed them in city squares and in some places it is possible to buy packets of grain specifically for pigeons. At the same time, they are regarded as a nuisance, because they foul buildings with their droppings, and city authorities take steps to destroy them.

Feral pigeons in Amsterdam's Dam Square.

The birds we now call feral pigeons were first domesticated in Iraq over 6000 years ago. Various cultures in the Middle East regarded them as sacred, the Romans bred exotic-looking varieties and, much later, they were reared in dovecotes throughout Europe as a source of food. During this long period, many must have escaped or been released, to become the ancestors of the feral pigeons of modern towns. It is also clear that wild rock doves interbreed with feral pigeons, thus impairing the purity of their own stock and yet increasing the chance of 'rock dove types' in urban populations. Feral pigeons are remarkably variable in colour and markings, due partly to past domestication and partly to adaptation to the town environment.

The feral pigeon is probably more dependent on man than any other bird. It nests on buildings and we provide virtually all of its food, either intentionally or by allowing it to steal from grain stores. In some areas it eats the seeds of weeds, but this is less usual. Unlike most birds, feral pigeons nest throughout the year, even in the depth of winter, but in all months there are substantial numbers of non-breeding individuals. Eggs and young are preyed upon by cats and rats, resulting in heavy losses in the nest.

The mess feral pigeons make with their droppings is not only unattractive, but is said to be a health hazard and certainly can cause corrosion to buildings. On the other hand, the grain and other seeds they steal reflect inefficiency in transport and storage more than anything else. Attempts to control pigeons by shooting, trapping and poisoning have met with little success: even when thousands have been killed, they have been rapidly replaced by others coming in from elsewhere; each pair also raises several broods a year. Although the general public likes to feed them, pigeons are not especially popular among naturalists. Perhaps they are a little too domesticated and dependent on man to make us feel they are genuinely wild birds. But their behaviour and social organization are worth observing: they must be among the easiest birds to approach and watch in what for them is now a natural environment.

Wild mammals

Human beings, dogs and cats are town-dwelling mammals, but, except to note that cats are predators of birds, we shall ignore them and concentrate on wild species that have taken to town life. Wild mammals are less obvious than birds and, with one or two exceptions, attract less attention.

Hedgehogs are now more easily seen in towns, especially in the suburbs, than in the countryside. Many are killed by traffic on roads, but even so they seem to flourish and breed in quite small gardens where there is sufficient cover. They are chiefly insect-eaters and are frequently discovered at night among dead leaves or scuffling about under bushes. They will also take food put out for them and are especially partial to saucers of milk. Exactly what hedgehogs like about towns is a mystery.

The grey squirrel *Sciurus carolinensis* is the most obvious wild mammal in British towns. It is common in parks, where it readily accepts food offered by people, and often enters gardens. Yet is is not a native species and was first successfully introduced from North America at the turn of the century into Woburn Park, Bedfordshire, where, reputedly, the local gentry had run out of things to shoot. There followed a series of about 30 additional introductions, and what at the time seemed a harmless experiment carried out in the interests of shooting generated one of the most remarkable population explosions recorded for an animal of this size. The grey squirrel has now spread all over Britain and, wherever it has become established, the indigenous red squirrel *S. vulgaris* has declined and usually disappeared. This suggests that the two species compete, and that the red squirrel is a consistent loser, but exactly what they compete over is by no means certain, except that at some seasons the grey is the better at exploiting scarce food sources. The grey squirrel is condemned by forestry officials because it attacks the bark and inhibits the growth of trees; it also damages twigs and branches and removes tree seeds planted in nurseries. None of these activities can be considered to be destructive in urban areas and, on the whole, grey squirrels are tolerated and even admired by town people. They are now part of the town scene in Britain and Ireland and, even if we wanted to, it would be difficult to displace them. City parks on the continent of Europe are still strongholds of the red squirrel, which sometimes occurs in a black mutant form.

Red foxes *Vulpes vulpes* are now relatively common in many north European towns. Their strongholds are railway embankments: green corridors projecting in and out of urban areas. There they can burrow and raise their cubs undisturbed, having at the same time good access into towns where they will scavenge food from dustbins, although rats and chickens are their chief prey.

Foxes are more versatile than another of the larger mammals reported in towns, the badger *Meles meles*, which needs quiet surroundings to establish itself. The undisturbed railway embankment next to a playing field is ideal, since it can emerge at night and grub around for worms. Rabbits *Oryctolagus cuniculus* and various species of deer are also seen in towns. Again, urban areas provide them with refuges from persecution by country people, who are more likely to take up guns to shoot large mammals; town people, it might be added, are more prone to attack one another.

The smaller mammals have become used to the food resources and shelter in towns, and perhaps also to the warmth. The house mouse *Mus musculus*, the common rat *Rattus norvegicus* and the ship rat *R. rattus* are all common city residents destructive to stored food and generally disliked and destroyed whenever possible. It is difficult to imagine how these three species could survive without man-made structures. Ship or black rats are associated with sea ports and warehouses, and in Britain they have been largely ousted by the common or brown rats. House mice and common rats are as much rural as urban, but abound in untidy surroundings.

Additional small mammals may occur and become established, particularly in gardens – where the mouse one sees is as likely to be a wood mouse

A fox cub among the railway lines. Railway embankments now provide a regular urban habitat for these mammals.

An alien opportunist. A grey squirrel exploits nuts put out for birds.

Apodemus sylvaticus as a house mouse. Nearly everywhere there is a mouse, a shrew or a vole of one species or another, but they are rarely seen because they come out at night; indeed, their presence is most often detected by the chance discovery of a corpse, perhaps the victim of a pet cat.

Bats are even more of a mystery. They are often seen over towns in the twilight, but it is not easy to identify the species. Long-eared bats *Plecotus auritus* and pipistrelles *Pipistrellus pipistrellus* are widespread and have exploited the roosting potential in towns. All bats feed on night-flying insects, especially moths, and spend the winter in hibernation in hollow trees or in secluded places in buildings and outhouses. Three species, two of them new to science, have been added to the British list since 1956, which shows how little is known about bats as a group.

Indoor opportunists

Many small organisms now live mainly or entirely inside human dwellings and buildings. Leaving aside the internal parasites of our bodies, there are two broad categories of species intimately associated with man: parasites living on human skin and among hair, which include mites and ticks, fleas (Pulicidae), lice, bugs, bacteria, viruses and yeasts; and scavengers, such as rats, house mice, cockroaches (Blattidae), crickets (Gryllidae), silverfish *Lepisma saccharina*, clothes moths (Tineidae) and the beetles that feed on stored products and wood. Some of those in the second category are eaten by predators, the most conspicuous of which are spiders. We could perhaps add a third category: the pests of indoor plants, such as the greenhouse whitefly *Trialeurodes vaporariorum* and red spider mites *Tetranychus*, but these are perhaps associated more with heated greenhouses than with dwellings.

How did such a varied assortment of organisms come to be associated with man? The ectoparasites present no special problem: they have evolved with us and so have always been a part of our lives, though some survive better now that we live in houses. Thus, the bedbug *Cimex lectularius*, which periodically feeds on human blood during the night, spends most of its time in crevices in walls and furniture or among bedclothes, where it lays its eggs. It is a south European species, well-known to the Greeks and Romans, which was probably brought to the north in the 16th century and quickly established itself indoors. Nowadays, infestations of bedbugs are unusual and cause alarm among public health authorities, but until quite recently they were common in the houses of the poor.

Fleas, too, tend to be associated with animals that have permanent or semi-permanent homes or nests, which is why rabbits and birds are often flea-ridden. The human flea *Pulex irritans* is a true house-dweller which must have started its long association with man when caves were first used as shelters. The female requires a meal of blood before she lays eggs, but the larvae scavenge on human detritus, particularly on tiny fragments of shed skin. The pupae can lie dormant for many years in cracks in floors in unoccupied houses and are stimulated to hatch into adults by the vibrations caused by people walking about. There is little doubt that this species has flourished ever since man first used permanent dwellings, but the domestic cat flea *Ctenocephalides felis*, which also bites man, is now the more common flea in houses. Cats have been domesticated for thousands of years and the flea larvae are well-adapted to living in carpets and mats, feeding on detritus.

The existence of permanent or semi-permanent dwellings also accounts for the variety of scavengers and their predators, but probably equally important in tracing the association of these species with man is the history of the use of fire. It is not known for certain when or why fire was first used, but the evidence suggests that it was at least 400,000 years ago and that cooking relatively indigestible meat (man is really a plant-eater) and keeping warm were the most likely causes. A heated dwelling provides a totally new environment with new opportunities. All the animals now living indoors are related to similar species outdoors, suggesting that we are dealing with a varied assemblage of indoor opportunists that somehow were able to exploit the new circumstances. The silverfish and the firebrat *Thermobia domestica*, both members of the Thysanura, an order of primitive, wingless insects, are effectively confined to indoor-living where they scavenge from pieces of food dropped to the floor, but several related outdoor species live in more natural surroundings. Much the same is true of the cockroaches, such as *Blatta orientalis* and *Periplaneta americana*, both introduced to northern Europe long ago and now found almost exclusively in houses and buildings where they are scavengers.

Many species of house moths (Oecophoridae) and clothes moths also originated outside Europe. They were probably accidentally introduced by trading, since damaging clothes is only part of their omnivorous diet ranging from furs and carpets to dry seeds. It is unlikely that the larvae are attracted to the cloth itself, rather more to the dirt between the fibres, which in soiled clothes often contains proteins.

Spiders are perhaps the most obvious indoor opportunists. A remarkable number and variety now live in buildings and feed on the scavengers or on insects that accidentally enter through open windows. The spiders that suddenly appear in baths and sinks belong to the genus *Tegenaria*. Several house-living spiders are still extending their range of distribution. Thus, the long-bodied cellar spider *Pholcus phalangioides*, often found in cellars and attics, is currently spreading northwards in England.

Life in polluted waters

We have seen how, for certain birds in particular, the town and garden environment can provide better feeding than the countryside. But it would be wrong to give the impression that all is well. The growth of industry has led to the disappearance of many species, and nowhere is this more apparent than in waterways, which have become more and more polluted over the years.

Fish, waterfowl and aquatic invertebrates, which cannot stand high levels of water pollution, are especially affected. Rivers, streams, estuaries and harbours receive enormous quantities of waste material which is either deliberately discharged from towns and factories or enters as run-off following rainfall. This waste includes a variety of nasty chemical compounds known to be toxic, which can cause substantial decreases in the abundance and diversity of aquatic wildlife. Many large rivers have in the past few hundred years become gigantic drains which receive all the effluents of our affluent society. As a consequence, they support only a few species of animals that can somehow cope with pollutants in the water.

In the 1950s and 1960s, the realization that certain large rivers flowing through cities were effectively dead led to legislation and action towards cleaning up, in the hope that at least some species would come back. The story of how the River Thames was revitalized is remarkable, not only because it proved possible to do something effective despite the pressures of industry and the growth of consumerism, but also because of the rapid return of animals that had long since disappeared. The Thames is tidal through London, and by the 1950s was nothing more than a sewer carrying industrial and domestic waste into the North Sea. The black, smelly water contained no oxygen, but plenty of poisonous chemicals. In the 1960s, long overdue improvements were made to sewage works and new laws were introduced to restrict the discharge of industrial waste into the river. A rapid rise followed in the level of oxygen in the water and fish began to be found in places where they had long been absent. A further improvement occurred when biodegradable detergents replaced those not easily broken down, which for many years had been discharged into the Thames in such concentration as to do untold damage to the already depleted wildlife.

By 1976, about 90 species of fishes had been recorded in a stretch of the Thames that in 1957 had supported hardly any, apart from eels *Anguilla anguilla*. Various seaweeds began to colonize and there was even a return of so-called shipworms *Teredo*, which are actually bivalve molluscs and which, being wood-borers, can be damaging to moored boats. Even more spectacular was the reappearance of waterfowl, including large numbers of shelduck *Tadorna tadorna* and pochard *Aythya ferina*. Some of the ducks feed on river worms *Tubifex*, which live in mud and can stand high levels of pollution. Before the Thames was cleaned up, these particular worms became exceedingly abundant. The ducks could not dive for them because of poisonous hydrogen sulphide in the water and the presence of detergent which destroyed the waterproofing of their plumage. The worms have since decreased, presumably because they are once again available to diving ducks. At certain seasons, too, there are now plenty of dunlins *Calidris alpina* and redshanks *Tringa totanus*, and a sprinkling of other waders. Bird-watching along the Thames in London may not be quite the same as in the wild, open marshes, but the birds are back, showing that the river is once more an attractive habitat.

The transformation of the Thames is a story of successful action. Londoners are no longer appalled by the stench of the river and those interested can see for themselves how the birds have returned. Even salmon *Salmo salar* may be expected, and it may not be long before the banks once again attract keen anglers. There is no reason why the successful clean-up of London's waterway should not be copied elsewhere. What to do and how to do it are known; all that remains is the will to turn ideas into action.

The clean-up of the Thames has led to an increase in the number and variety of wintering ducks. In the Netherlands, Britain and Ireland in particular, ponds and lakes in town parks support many wintering ducks. The colder winters in eastern Europe and Fenno–Scandia result in regular freezing of open expanses of fresh water, and few ducks remain there.

Flight of ducks over the River Thames.

Some of the ducks in towns in winter are locally born and bred, others are migrants from the north and east. They find shelter in Britain and Ireland, and in towns they are relatively free from persecution: although it is still legal to shoot certain species of ducks, this is obviously not possible in urban areas. Many of the wigeon *Anas penelope* that spend the winter in Britain are from Scandinavia. In Sweden, wigeon often breed in the vicinity of ponds and lakes near towns and are fully protected by law; indeed, people construct artificial islands on which these ducks can breed. It is a pity that, when the birds arrive in Britain, they are liable to be shot; they are, after all, migrants in much the same position as the small song-birds that the south Europeans kill for food, a practice condemned by conservationists in the north.

Garden ponds

Once, if you wanted a small pond in the garden, you had to make it yourself with cement, but now ready-made plastic ones are easily bought and installed. The widespread disappearance of natural ponds, particularly in villages, and the common belief that those that remain are suitable places for dumping rubbish have led to serious reductions in numbers of many forms of wildlife. So the present profusion of garden ponds have become increasingly important as places where plants and animals can live in unpolluted and undisturbed surroundings.

Most garden ponds are small – no more than a few square metres – but, even so, offer good prospects for a variety of species. They are at first stocked

At first garden ponds may be carefully stocked with water-lilies and goldfish, but other plants and animals will establish themselves if allowed to do so.

with bought plants, such as water-lilies (Nymphaeaceae) and pondweeds *Potamogeton*, and with goldfish *Carassius auratus*, but are soon neglected and allowed to establish communities of their own. Fish caught in local rivers and streams by children are sometimes dumped in garden ponds; they rarely survive and, even if they do, there is insufficient space for them to grow properly and breed. Some garden ponds do, however, support small populations of wild species of fishes, especially three-spined sticklebacks *Gasterosteus aculeatus*, carp *Cyprinus carpio* and tench *Tinca tinca*.

A pond may become choked with living vegetation or with decomposing leaves from surrounding trees. Photosynthesis occurs in water plants, just as in those on land, and the quantity of plant material produced in a pond depends largely on the seasonal availability of light and on the temperature of the water. In winter, when plant production is at a minimum, most of the pond vegetation has died back and is decomposing. Water also supports teeming millions of microscopic green algae which, at the height of summer, contribute to the total richness of a pond. There is a rapid burst of plant growth in the spring: submerged plants and water-lilies spread their leaves over the surface, and the small animals that feed directly on the living plants exert little impact on the mass of vegetation produced. It is not until late autumn, when vegetation dies back and photosynthesis is much reduced, that the pond begins to clear again. Leaves that fall from trees sink and decay slowly; in limited quantity they add nutrients, but in excess they accumulate and create an oxygen deficiency that may lead to the disappearance of certain groups of small invertebrates, including many of the decomposers of dead vegetation.

Most of the animals that colonize ponds are very small. Those that are visible include small crustaceans, aquatic bugs, beetles and snails. Beetles and bugs fly considerable distances and are thus easily able to establish themselves in ponds. Snails and crustaceans are either accidentally introduced with plants or carried as eggs or young on birds and flying insects. For example, a close examination of one of the larger species of water beetle (Dytiscidae) may reveal snail eggs, and even tiny leeches (Hirudinea), attached to its body.

Several amphibians – for example, the common frog *Rana temporaria*, edible frog *R. esculenta*, common toad *Bufo bufo*, midwife toad *Alytes obstetricans*, smooth newt *Triturus vulgaris* and crested newt *T. cristatus* – may be found breeding in garden pools and sometimes hibernating in nooks and crevices among stones at the edge. Garden ponds are increasingly important as safe breeding places for amphibians, especially now that many natural waters are polluted, filled with rubbish, 'managed' or drained.

The recent history of the common frog in Britain illustrates this point well. Through the first part of the 20th century frogs were common everywhere, but during the 1940s and 1950s they decreased and disappeared from many places. In the 1960s, concern was expressed about the species' prospects. The decline is thought to have been made worse by excessive demand from biological laboratories, especially in schools and universities. In the 1940s and 1950s, the dissection of a frog was considered an important step in the education of young biologists; biological suppliers initiated large-scale frog hunts and hundreds of thousands were collected. Happily, the tradition of dissecting frogs has disappeared from the curricula of most educational establishments; but numbers are still used in research and even imported from France, Spain and Italy. Frogs have also declined because of changes in land use, especially drainage schemes, filling in small ponds, confining streams to concrete culverts, and developing rivers for commerce and leisure. Associated with these changes is an increased danger of pollution from industry and a run-off of pesticides and fertilizers used in farming. Other factors that may have contributed to the frog's decline include deaths on roads and the urbanization of previously rural areas. All this means that the garden pond may now be the most important stronghold of the frog in Britain. If you have frogs or newts in the pond, take care of them and consider disposing of the goldfish, which eat both spawn and tadpoles.

Wildlife in Icelandic towns and gardens

For many groups of animals, especially insects, there are fewer species in the whole of Iceland than in a well-established garden in England, France or Germany. This is because Iceland is an island in the far north and well isolated from the continental land mass, which means it has a relatively poor chance of colonization from overseas. Several species now common in Iceland were accidentally introduced by the Vikings, among them the wood mouse.

The visitor to Reykjavik will find most of the familiar European town birds missing. There are a few starlings, but the urban thrush is the redwing, not the song thrush. Redpolls are common in parks and gardens, whereas in most of the rest of Europe they are rarely seen in towns. It is almost as if the absence of many species of birds from Iceland has enabled the few that do exist to adopt urban habits.

Apart from occasional red admirals and painted ladies, there are no butterflies. Moths are common, but some of the more familiar town species of more southerly areas, such as the angle shades *Phlogophora meticulosa*, are no more than irregular migrants. The large yellow underwing *Noctua pronuba*, abundant farther south, exists only as an introduced species of cultivated land and gardens; even the vapourer, one of the most characteristic town moths in Britain, is rare in Iceland and found only in the countryside.

The hoverflies on flowers in Icelandic gardens are mostly the species to be seen throughout northern Europe, including the common and widespread *Platychirus albimanus*, *P. clypeatus*, *P. manicatus*, *P. peltatus*, *Melanostoma mellinum*, *Syrphus ribesii*, *Sphaerophoria scripta* and *Helophilus pendulus*. The seven-spot ladybird is probably introduced, as are one of the surface-casting earthworms, *Allolobophora rosea*, the garden worm *Lumbricus terrestris* and a woodlouse, *Porcellio scaber*.

Icelanders have made good use of the numerous hot springs in their country. Large greenhouses are heated entirely by natural hot water and provide fruit and vegetables, even a few bananas which could not otherwise be grown, as well as a plentiful supply of decorative flowers, popular in a country where, because of the climate, few species grow outdoors. As might be expected, the greenhouses support various introduced invertebrates and, if a detailed inventory were made of all the species, no doubt there would be additions to the Icelandic list. Summer gives almost continuous daylight and, provided it is warm, little restriction on photosynthetic activity: perhaps one day an enterprising naturalist will try the intriguing possibility of creating a subtropical environment in a large greenhouse there.

Nowadays, all Icelandic towns provide a source of food for several species of gulls and the fulmar *Fulmarus glacialis*. These birds are scavengers and have greatly increased in numbers during the past 50 years. They feed from refuse and the left-overs of the fishing and whaling industries. Gulls in particular are opportunists in the way they exploit fishing and fish-processing; as the development of marine fisheries is intensified, they may become more and more dependent on man. What will happen to their populations when fishing is no longer a commercial proposition, a likely possibility if the present rate of exploitation continues, is a matter of speculation.

Although the naturalist looking at wildlife in towns and gardens in Iceland is confronted with a much smaller diversity than in continental Europe, some of the species are immensely common. There are also some interesting adjustments to living in the far north: moths which in England fly only at night must do so in daylight during the short Icelandic summer, and the winter moth, which in England flutters around lights in December, appears as early as October.

Origins of cultivated plants

To understand the origins of the immense diversity of cultivated plants and trees now found in towns and gardens, we have to go back 10,000 years when, somewhere in western Asia, people gave up the hunting and gathering method of obtaining food and started to grow wild grasses for their grains. Seeds were selected from those plants yielding the best grain, the process was repeated season after season, and gradually the quality and quantity of the crop improved. As time passed, additional species were brought under cultivation – not only grasses, but many other plants that produced suitable food. No doubt mistakes were made and harvests lost, but over thousands of years what is essentially a process of trial and error has produced the rich variety of crops that now feeds the world. All crops are derived from wild species, although in some instances the wild ancestor has long since disappeared and we can only speculate on what it was like.

Plants were also cultivated for medicinal purposes. It is likely that most of those we now use to flavour food – sage, mint, thyme *Thymus vulgaris*, mustard *Brassica/Sinapis*, rosemary *Rosmarinus officinalis* and many others – were originally grown because they were believed to be of medicinal value. When and where plants were first cultivated for purely decorative purposes is uncertain, but in northern Europe it was probably not before the 15th century.

Today, horticulture and the breeding of ornamental plants are big business and there is seemingly no end to the variety that can be produced. Flowers for the herbaceous border, bulbs, shrubs and vegetables have received most attention from the plant-breeders. Trees have had less, perhaps because they take far longer to produce satisfying results, but, even so, there are plenty of specially selected varieties on the market.

Town trees are either natives, such as oak, birch and hawthorn *Crataegus*, or introduced species from other parts of the world. In other words, many are exactly the same as wild species and are simply grown in places where they would not normally occur. But, oddly enough, we appear to cultivate rather few species of native wild flowers in their unaltered state: it seems that we prefer artificial varieties and hybrids or exotic species from foreign countries.

This last point is exemplified by the well-known genus *Aster*, plants much loved by European gardeners but regarded as weeds in other parts of the world. The genus includes species and varieties commonly called asters, and also various kinds of Michaelmas daisies; at least nine separate species are widely cultivated and there are many hybrids. Thus *Aster sedifolius* has bright

Michaelmas daisies with feeding hoverfly and small tortoiseshell butterfly. Countryside flowers in North America, they are commonly planted in herbaceous borders in Europe.

mauve flowers and comes from southern Europe. From the Alps we get *A. alpinus*, a dwarf species with several different flower colours, and from Italy *A. amellus*, with purple or violet flowers. This last has also been crossed with *A. thomsonii*, a native of the Himalayas, to produce a distinct variety with abundant light blue flowers. *A. novi-belgii*, to which the name Michaelmas daisy is perhaps most widely applied, comes from North America: numerous hybrids have been developed to provide a wide array of flower colours and plant heights. All these species, varieties and hybrids of *Aster* may be grown with other flowers in a single herbaceous border and produce a more varied assemblage than ever occurs in the wild. What has been said about *Aster* is true of many other genera of cultivated flowers: for example, *Dahlia* and *Iris* offer even more possibilities, and we all know that the genus *Rosa* presents almost unlimited scope, satisfying the whims of even the most fastidious gardener.

Several plants are rare or local in the natural state but commonly grown in gardens. In Britain, the shrubby cinquefoil *Potentilla fruticosa* is rare in the wild, yet widespread as a garden plant; garden specimens are often identical with those in the wild, but additional varieties, with differently coloured flowers, have been developed. Another species in this category is mezereon *Daphne mezereum*, local on limestone and chalk, yet freely available from horticulturists and commonly grown in gardens, flowering in February before the leaves appear. Box *Buxus sempervirens*, an evergreen shrub or small tree rare on dry hillsides in Britain but rather more common in Belgium, France and Germany, is commonly planted in gardens as a screening bush or as part of a hedge, and there are now more box trees in gardens and parks than in the wild.

From the point of conservation, the establishment of rare or local plants in gardens is well worth while. Perhaps some of them also support rare insects in unexpected places. But no one should remove plants from the wild and transfer them to gardens. An increasing number of interesting species is becoming available from horticulturists and this is the way to obtain specimens. Removal of plants, particularly rare species, from the wild cannot be justified in the interests of conservation.

How the polluted town environment can alter species

We have seen how many of the plants grown in gardens and parks are different in appearance from their wild ancestors; some have been altered to such an extent that they can no longer survive in the wild. But what of the plants, and animals, that have successfully colonized our towns of their own accord? Is the rosebay willowherb on building sites the same in genetic make-up as that growing in the countryside, and are the yellow underwing moths in town gardens identical with their country cousins? In almost all instances the answer is that, although we have every reason to suspect genetic differences between town and country populations of the same species, we simply do not have the evidence. For one thing, the differences may be so slight as to be undetectable except by specialized techniques; for another, few people have actually looked.

The process of adaptation to the environment is brought about by natural selection, a well-understood phenomenon for which there is ample field and experimental evidence. All populations of plants and animals possess the ability to increase rapidly, but it is self-evident that their numbers do not go on growing indefinitely: we are not overrun by rosebay willowherb or yellow underwing moths. Somehow, populations are regulated at certain levels; this means that, given the high reproductive capacity of most species, only a tiny proportion of the individuals born manages to survive and reproduce. For many organisms, particularly insects, small invertebrates and plants, the death rate before reproducing is of the order of 99 per cent. Even among the familiar song-birds of our gardens, 70 per cent or more may die in the year following birth, before they have a chance to breed.

Individuals within a species vary – as among human beings, no two are exactly alike – and many, but not all, peculiarities are passed from parents to offspring. Individuals therefore differ from one another in their genetic make-up and, since death rates are high, the chances of survival depend on how well the particular animal or plant fits into its environment. This amounts to the same as saying that the probability of death before breeding is a non-random event, which is equivalent to the concept of natural selection. We are not, at present, concerned with causes of death, which vary with species, localities and times of year, but the result is that the survivors are the ones best able to cope with the pressures exerted by the environment in which they exist. If, however, the environment changes, other individuals with a different genetic make-up may become the survivors and, in time, even re-place the original stock. When this occurs, we have an evolutionary change within a population.

By any stretch of the imagination, the conversion of natural countryside to town and garden must constitute a major environmental change and we should therefore expect to find, for some species, evidence for evolutionary adaptation to the new circumstances. But has there been time? Evolution is usually considered a slow process, generally involving thousands of breeding generations over thousands of years. Another difficulty in seeking evidence for evolutionary adaptation is that most genes confer only small differences on the appearance of an individual, so small that it is difficult to see if changes are taking place. Thus, to find evidence for adaptation to town life, we have to search for species that respond quickly to environmental changes and show conspicuous differences in their appearance. There are only a few in this category, but they do exist; we shall discuss three of them on the understanding that similar alterations have probably occurred among many other species but as yet remain undiscovered.

The peppered moth *Biston betularia* has whitish wings peppered with black dots. It is common in towns, flying at night and resting by day on the trunks of trees – although it must be admitted that few have actually been found during the day-time. The colour and pattern blend well with the pale, speckled growth of lichens on trees and afford a considerable degree of pro-tection from predators that hunt by sight, particularly small birds assiduously searching the trunks for food items.

Lichens are extremely sensitive to pollution and have almost disappeared from trees in and around industrial towns in northern Europe, although they still flourish in unpolluted urban areas, as in northern Scandinavia, Finland and western Ireland. Tree trunks without lichens are dark, almost black, and peppered moths resting on them are conspicuous and easily found by birds. In the middle of the 19th century, mutant peppered moths started to appear in and around industrial centres in England, though not in the countryside. In their case, the dotted white pattern is replaced by uniform black, which makes them difficult to see on lichen-free tree trunks. This black form of the peppered moth is determined by a single gene difference and is a good example of an obvious change in appearance brought about in a simple way. The black form spread rapidly in and around towns, and today makes up more than 90 per cent of the individuals in some places. In truly rural areas, however, with little pollution and still plenty of lichens on tree trunks, the peppered moths are mainly or entirely of the original pale form.

The replacement of pale by dark peppered moths is an example of an evolutionary change brought about through natural selection by predators. Birds repeatedly find and eat moths that do not match the background: pale ones in towns, black ones in the countryside. Indeed, the frequency of pale and black moths in a locality may be used as an index of the level of pollution. In Manchester and a few other cities where the black form had reached a high frequency, there are signs of a slight decrease in recent years, attributable to cleaner industry resulting from public awareness of the dangers and unpleasantness of industrial pollution.

The story is slightly more complicated than this, because the caterpillars of a proportion of the black mutants are more resistant to leaves contaminated with chemicals. Peppered moth caterpillars feed on many kinds of broad-leaved trees, including those that grow in parks and gardens, and must often encounter chemical compounds deposited by airborne pollution. Some of the caterpillars that produce black moths have a better physiological tolerance of pollutants, and therefore survive better in a polluted environment.

The peppered moth is an excellent example of a species that has altered and adapted to life in towns, but it is not the only one. Other moths, almost all of them night-fliers that rest by day on tree trunks and comparable places, have been similarly affected and nearly always the black mutants first appeared and increased in or near centres of industry. Parallel events have occurred in the eastern United States: the moths involved have similar habits to those in Europe, the main difference being that black mutants first appeared there about 50 years later than in Europe, presumably because industrialization started later.

Male peppered moths are powerful fliers able to cover up to 5 km a night in search of females, which fly only infrequently. Another species that has produced a black form in industrial areas, the scalloped hazel *Odontopera bidentata*, flies only short distances, perhaps no more than 100 m a night. This moth does not rest on tree trunks but hides among bushes, usually with its wings closed over its back like a butterfly, and it bears a striking resemblance to a dead leaf. In some English cities, up to 80 per cent of the scalloped hazels are now black, but interestingly there are marked differences in frequency within a single town and even from street to street. In Liverpool, for example, the black form varies in frequency from 10 to 50 per cent as one crosses the city from west to east. The caterpillars of the scalloped hazel feed on the leaves of many plants, but especially privet. They are dark grey and look remarkably like blackened twigs. Black moths are less leaf-like than brown ones and it is difficult to interpret their increase in abundance as anything to do with selective predation by birds, so we are left with something of a mystery. In some industrial centres black forms have not appeared at all, which could perhaps be explained by the slow rate of dispersal among moths that fly such short distances.

There is no question of pollution actually causing black mutations in the first place; rather it has changed the environment in a way that, given they are capable of being produced, the mutants largely replace the paler forms in industrial areas.

The adaptive significance of the black form of our third example, the two-spot ladybird *Adalia bipunctata*, is a highly controversial subject. This species is typically red with two black spots, while the black form is variable but usually black with two red spots: the two look so different that we could be forgiven for thinking them separate species. Like all ladybirds, the two-spot is conspicuous and makes little attempt to hide itself from potential enemies; it has a strong scent and, when agitated, produces a yellow fluid from its leg-joints, which deters potential predators. It is rarely eaten and so the high frequency of the black form in large towns must be explained in another way.

It is now believed that the black form has a physiological advantage in polluted environments. In Birmingham, its frequency fell from 45 to 25 per cent during the period 1961–70, in which smoke pollution was reduced as the result of clean air policies. In some parts of northern Europe, the black form is more frequent in humid places. In Berlin, it has been shown that black two-spots die more often in winter and red ones in summer. Another experiment established that the black ones are the more active immediately after a spell of cooling, suggesting that their colour is a better absorber of heat than red. Finally, a correlation has been established between a high frequency of black two-spot ladybirds and relatively cloudy and overcast localities, which might perhaps explain why they are rare in London, a comparatively sunny city.

The occurrence of the black form of this ladybird is somehow associated with the town environment, and a correlation with high levels of smoke pollution seems established. There is probably more to the story than this, but in this case, as in those of the peppered moth and the scalloped hazel moth, there is no doubt that industrialization is largely responsible for initiating evolutionary changes which, although not always fully understood, show how some organisms can be altered by town life.

More effects of pollution

It is not easy to offer a precise definition of what is meant by pollution. Most of us think of chemical contaminants that originate from industry and traffic: we know that smog in autumn and winter results from a peculiar combination of climate with chemicals produced by factories and motor transport, and that noise is an increasing problem to town-dwellers. But how many of us

A night roost of starlings on ledges of the Admiralty Arch in Trafalgar Square, London.

realize that a large town can actually alter the local climate? A change in climate caused by a town and its urban activities can certainly be considered a form of pollution. Perhaps it is better to avoid a precise definition and be content with thinking of pollution as any event generated by man that affects the quality of the air, soil or water in a way that is potentially damaging to ourselves and wildlife.

The extent to which a built-up area exerts an effect on the climate depends on its size. Large cities are, on average, a little warmer than adjacent rural areas; they are slightly less humid; and there is considerably less wind, even though tall buildings create a complexity of updrafts and eddies. Cities may also have slightly more rain than the surrounding countryside, but, since much of it falls on roads and buildings, the evaporation rate is high and excess water is quickly drained into streams and rivers; as a consequence, it is possible that town gardens are actually more likely to dry up than rural ones. Towns are slightly more cloudy and much more foggy than country areas, which means that there is less sunshine. Precisely how these differences affect wildlife is a matter for conjecture. The well-known habit of starlings coming into towns to roost at night is probably to some extent associated with the need for warmth, but whether, for example, insects are influenced by a town's climate is not known.

Much more striking is the concentration of contaminants. There are ten times more dust particles in the air and the level of such pollutants as sulphur dioxide and carbon monoxide is substantially higher than in the countryside. But towns are less dusty than they used to be because of the decrease in the amount of ash in refuse. Surveys show that, a hundred years ago, refuse contained more ash than it does today and that we now dispose of more solids, including plastic and metal containers, glass and paper, all less polluting until they are burnt in refuse tips or incinerators.

Once soil is contaminated by pollutants, there is the likelihood of noxious materials being recycled accidentally by plants and animals. Indeed, it is difficult to put things right once a pollutant finds its way into soil. Large quantities of potentially dangerous materials originating from industry are returned to the earth by rainfall. Sulphur dioxide given off by coal-burning power stations combines with rain to form sulphuric acid and there is a serious danger of soil becoming more and more acid, which, in turn, affects what species of plants can grow.

One of the themes in this book is that towns are excellent habitats for many forms of wildlife and that some species are now thoroughly adjusted to urban living. But it would be wrong to give the impression that all is well. Gardens are usually located near roads, which are an important source of pollutants. Among the several impurities given off during the combustion of motor oil, the most dangerous is lead. There has been much publicity and controversy over dangers to human health from lead pollution, and in some countries lead has been banned as a petrol additive. Earthworms collected from soil near roads contain up to 20 times the amount of lead found in those collected from rural soils. Garden earthworms probably have more lead and other contaminants in their bodies than those living in open fields. Earthworms themselves can tolerate high concentrations of pollutants; the danger arises when they are eaten by birds and other animals.

The sulphurous pollutants produced by industry and released into the atmosphere may have harmful effects far beyond the source of the pollution. The prevailing wind in north-west Europe is from the west and much of the pollution produced by British power stations is carried out over the North Sea to Scandinavia, where it is deposited by rainfall, much to the annoyance of the Scandinavians. Apart from poisoning and inhibiting the growth of trees, pollution is resulting in large areas of countryside, including freshwater lakes, becoming more and more acid. This affects the survival of small organisms and produces changes in species composition. Measurements have shown that the rainfall in western Europe has become noticeably more acid in the last 20 years. In Britain, most of the acid rain falls in the south-east, the Midlands and East Anglia; the extreme south-west, Wales and Ireland are little affected, because of the prevailing wind.

Lichens appear to be the organisms most sensitive to the effects of sulphurous pollutants. These plants grow, or used to grow, on tree trunks and walls, but, as we have already seen, they have almost gone from many urban areas. Even relatively low levels of pollution can cause lichens to disappear. They accumulate nutrients from rainwater running down tree trunks and, as they do so, are exposed to sulphurous pollutants in solution. In contrast to most plants, they grow throughout the winter which, because of the inter-action of pollutant particles with rain, is the worst time of the year for acid rain. Lichens are sensitive indicators of pollution and their presence or absence is often used as a means of estimating the level of sulphurous com-pounds in the atmosphere. It is thought that about 90 species of lichens have disappeared from London's Epping Forest and that about 40, or 3 per cent of the total, have recently become extinct in Britain. Others are now rare and their future is uncertain; but, oddly enough, a few species are tolerant of pol-lution and have increased in abundance, sometimes filling the places of those that have gone. In general, heavy pollution, whether of soil or water, de-creases the diversity of plant and animal species, which can lead to an up-surge in the abundance of those that remain.

Despite disclaimers from manufacturers and retailers, pesticides and herbi-cides must ultimately be regarded as sources of pollution. Countless thou-sands of small insects and other invertebrates are killed accidentally in every garden where pesticides are used. Roughly speaking, there are two kinds of pesticides: those, such as pyrethrum, that are made from natural compounds found in plants of the daisy family; and synthetic ones. Mixtures of the two are frequently available. The synthetic kinds are persistent because there are no biological processes by which they are broken down to simpler, less harm-ful substances. Synthetic pesticides are thus transferred intact through food webs and, if we bear in mind the complexity of feeding relationships, it does not require much imagination to see that a compound applied in one place for a specific purpose can soon turn up in a different place in another organism.

For instance, many snails and slugs feed by grazing off living and dead vegetation; they do not always eat the actual plant material, but, instead, in-gest fungal spores and micro-organisms present on the surfaces of the leaves and stems. As they do so, they are especially liable to pick up quantities of pesticides and other pollutants present on the vegetation; some is lost by excretion, but much is stored and accumulated in their bodies. These gastro-pods are common in gardens and, if pesticides are used at all, they are bound to pick them up as they feed. In turn, snails and, to a lesser extent, slugs are eaten by birds, which thus also tend to accumulate pesticides from these and other sources.

There are indeed multiple pathways by which pesticides can move through food webs. Top predators suffer most, but bear in mind that, at the same time, the faeces of snails and similar creatures are decomposed by micro-organisms. It is the very complexity of feeding relationships that both distri-butes and concentrates pesticides and other pollutants. Thus, the use of chemical poisons to improve crop production is not without its dangers to wildlife. We are probably only just beginning to understand the extent of the changes initiated by poisoning the environment as a means of growing better crops, and it may be a long time before the full effects of what has already been done become apparent. Even if every gardener ceased using chemical poisons today, it would be many, many years before the compounds disappeared from the environment.

Refuse tips

Refuse tips might be seen as just another form of pollution resulting from increasing urbanization. But they occupy largely undisturbed and often open spaces with an assortment of rubbish, from plastics through organic waste to garden refuse, which is an attraction to a wide variety of animals and plants.

In the same way that the Oxford ragwort grows well in garden rubble and is replaced by other plants once a good layer of humus has become established, there is a succession of plant colonizers on rubbish dumps. The primary colonizers tend to be smallish annuals, such as shepherd's-purse *Capsella bursa-pastoris*, petty spurge *Euphorbia peplus* and groundsel *Senecio vulgaris*, although the taller fat-hen *Chenopodium album* is often very conspicuous. Some fairly tough annuals, common as well on the sides of paths and growing through cracks in pavements, are also found at this stage: annual pearlwort *Sagina apetala*, knotgrass *Polygonum aviculare* and annual meadow-grass *Poa annua*. Perennials with similar tolerance include procumbent pearlwort *S. procumbens*, docks *Rumex*, daisy *Bellis perennis*, dandelion *Taraxacum officinale* and greater plantain *Plantago major*. Where the soil is not compacted, common whitlowgrass *Erophila verna*, lesser chickweed *Stellaria pallida*, small toadflax *Chaenorhinum minus* and common cornsalad *Valerianella locusta* are typical.

As succession continues, rosette and cushion-forming plants, thistles *Carduus/Cirsium*, hawkweeds *Hieracium/Pilosella*, hawk's-beards *Crepis* and common chickweed *Stellaria media* replace the primary colonizers. The ability of creeping thistles *Cirsium arvense* to regenerate from fragments of roots is valuable if there is much disturbance on the dump. As a well-known perennial colonizer of wasteland, rosebay willowherb is often seen, as are common nettles *Urtica dioica*, indicators of nitrogen-rich soils typical of areas with much organic waste.

Large numbers of alien species become established, either through being transported in garden refuse or as garden escapes. For this reason, honesty *Lunaria annua*, Californian poppy *Eschscholzia californica*, opium poppy *Papaver somniferum*, evening-primroses *Oenothera*, sweet-william *Dianthus barbatus*, perennial sunflower *Helianthus rigidus* and several *Aster* species are not uncommon. Oxford ragwort, pineappleweed *Matricaria matricarioides* and *Buddleja* are non-natives with widespread success on any wasteland. The warmth of tips, a by-product of bacterial decomposition of the waste to

Herring gulls at a rubbish dump. Several species of gulls which obtain food from our refuse have become much commoner in towns.

humus, has also been held responsible for encouraging the germination of such exotics as sunflower *Helianthus annuus* and hemp *Cannabis sativa*, whose seeds have been traced to bird-cage refuse.

Unburied organic waste draws both vertebrate and invertebrate scavengers, from starlings and crows to winter gnats (Trichoceridae), hoverflies (Syrphidae), owl midges (Psychodidae), dung-flies *Scatophaga*, grey flesh-flies *Sarcophaga carnaria*, bluebottles *Calliphora*, greenbottles *Lucilia* and houseflies *Musca domestica*. Exposed tips with piles of rubble provide refuges in crevices for viviparous lizards *Lacerta vivipara* and slow-worms *Anguis fragilis*; these reptiles are also exploiting the tips' internal warmth. Mice have been known to overwinter within tips, and the warmth also attracts other indoor scavengers, such as common cockroaches *Blatta orientalis*, German cockroaches *Blatella germanica* and house crickets *Acheta domestica*, particularly in summer.

Refuse tips have even affected the habits and ranges of some animal species. Ever-increasing numbers of gulls are now seen inland during the winter. Great black-backed gulls *Larus marinus*, once exclusively maritime, have joined lesser black-backed *L. fuscus*, herring *L. argentatus* and black-headed gulls *L. ridibundus* on daily excursions to these sites. In fact, the habits of the lesser black-back have been so altered that, whereas it used to be a summer visitor, it is now at least partly resident in several areas of Britain.

Apart from bacteria, a range of invertebrates aids decomposition: earthworms, including *Eisenia*, *Dendrobaena* and *Lumbricus*; legions of minute white roundworms *Rhabditis*; and tiny springtails (Collembola).

Thus, a refuse tip containing a wide range of conditions attracts a diversity of organisms. All show the opportunism which is an important feature of their survival and success in towns. At the same time, the risk of the spread of disease from open tips cannot be ignored and, as more efficient means of disposing of rubbish are devised, this interesting agglomeration of plants and animals will disappear.

Decomposers and decomposition

Despite the many plant-feeding insects, most plants show little sign of extensive damage, but once a plant or part of a plant dies and falls to the ground, it quickly disappears through the actions of decomposers, which range from microscopic bacteria to relatively large earthworms. The surface of the ground and the soil support vast numbers of decomposers, most of them too small to see with the naked eye. If they did not exist, dead plant material would soon pile up; that it does not attests to their abundance and efficiency in disposing of dead vegetation.

There are various theories to account for the apparent under-utilization of living vegetation. Greenery may be deceptive: plants are not as edible as they may seem, and plant-feeders are unable to make use of the bulk of living vegetation because it is unpalatable or even toxic. This supposedly restricts consumption severely and inhibits the build-up of massive populations of plant-feeders which might otherwise destroy anything green as soon as it was produced. But possibly the plant-feeders are limited by predators and not by food; in other words, they never have a chance to reach numbers that could lead to wholesale destruction of plants. No one really knows why so little green vegetation is eaten, but we have every reason to be thankful for the present arrangement.

By disposing of dead vegetation, decomposers enable a recycling of nutrients: without them, there would be no soil rich in nutrients suitable for growing plants. We tend to take for granted this rich, dark soil and it is only when we dig deep and find clay or gravel lacking organic material that we appreciate the nature of topsoil and its supply of decomposing humus. People who move into newly built houses sometimes complain that there is no soil in the garden; they are really complaining about a lack of the organic topsoil which results from the decay of plant material. Most plants grow in the topsoil, and it is only the larger trees and bushes which push their roots down to the region where there is no organic matter.

Topsoil consists of mineral particles, resulting from the weathering of rocks, and organic material, resulting from the decomposition of dead plants. The bulk of this dead material enters the soil in autumn and winter, when leaves have fallen from trees and the summer growth has died back; a tiny proportion is derived from dead animals. Decomposition takes time, and dead vegetation is not converted into a form which can be re-used by living plants until it is completely broken down physically and chemically.

Examination of a small sample of soil with the aid of a microscope reveals countless hordes of small organisms, particularly mites, roundworms, springtails and fungi, as well as larger animals, such as earthworms, woodlice and a variety of insects. The abundance of these organisms is staggering. There may be tens of thousands of mites and up to 20 million roundworms in the top few centimetres of a square metre of soil. Most are decomposers, but, as would be expected, predators and parasites are also plentiful.

If left to its own devices, all the vegetation produced by a patch of land eventually dies and decays and is replaced by new growth. Not all plant material decomposes at the same rate. Wood takes longer than leaves, and some leaves, such as holly and beech *Fagus sylvatica*, remain intact longer than, for instance, birch and willow. Temperature is important, so is the amount of available moisture and the spectrum of decomposers that happens to be present.

As soon as a leaf falls to the ground, decomposition starts. There is a sequence of decay and each individual leaf is attacked by many different species of decomposers before it eventually disappears. If the ground is wet from rain or dew, and if fallen leaves are already lying around, bacteria and fungi establish themselves almost immediately and the first signs of decomposition appear. Decay is slower in dry weather, and in a drought there may be no significant decomposition for a long time.

Earthworms are the most obvious decomposers of dead vegetation. They are primarily responsible for the breaking down of dead leaves. One species, *Lumbricus terrestris*, pulls leaves from the surface into its burrow and then proceeds to eat them. It is easy to find leaves sticking out of holes in a lawn where they have been half pulled in by this garden worm. Other species of earthworms ingest soil containing tiny leaf fragments; they extract the nutrients they require and pass unwanted material through the anus back into the soil. As gardeners know, earthworms are especially common in damp compost heaps where they greatly accelerate the rate of rotting. In 1881, Charles Darwin wrote a book on earthworms and pointed out that all the topsoil in a garden is passed several times through the bodies of worms. Earthworms are thus not only important for decomposition, but, because they make holes, also help to aerate the soil.

The decay of wood is a much slower process. In northern Europe, few groups of insects are able to digest the cellulose in wood; the termites (Isoptera) which do this so effectively in the tropics are absent, and most decomposition is brought about by invisible bacteria and by fungi. A few insect larvae, mostly beetles, eat dead wood, but woodlice, despite their name and association with decaying wood, feed mainly on leaves. Millipedes (Diplopoda) may also be found near decaying wood, but most species feed on dead leaves or on living vegetation and roots.

In natural environments, dead vegetation is well scattered on the ground. Dead leaves may pile up in the beds of small streams, beneath hedges, and in nooks and corners in woodland. In towns, leaf-fall in autumn brings out the men with brooms, and the leaves are cleared from our streets and lawns. Our preoccupation with tidying up nature means that the process of decomposition is distributed in a most curious way. Quite exceptional numbers of decomposers occur in compost heaps. Earthworms and woodlice are the most obvious; indeed, there is a greater number of species of woodlice in gardens than in most more natural environments. But, of course, wherever we see these obvious decomposers, we can be sure that many other invisible species are abundant as well.

The British obsession with lawns

There are lawns of sorts everywhere. Some, such as golf courses and playing fields, are functional to a limited extent; those in parks have amenity value; but suburban lawns, usually tiny patches, seem to have little clearly identifiable use other than to provide sources of active work for their owners and pleasing vistas from houses. True, people may use lawns for picnics and outdoor games on a few occasions in summer, but, generally speaking, they exist because they are fashionable, neat-looking and, dare I add, a sign of affluence. In many ways, a garden lawn is a piece of land that the owner can afford to

An English suburban garden with a carefully tended lawn, surrounded by an enormous diversity of flowering plants.

leave uncultivated with useful crops. This statement may seem a little unfair, but, if we think of the amount of time, energy and money devoted to a lawn, we are quite close to the truth.

The lawn is the only place in the garden where grass is permitted to flourish; grass in a flower bed or vegetable patch is treated as a weed and removed. But, in terms of value to wildlife, it is not so much the presence of grass that is important as the uniform patch of closely mown turf adding a totally different environment to the garden.

We have seen how a compost heap results in an exceptional concentration of decomposers within a limited space. A lawn is almost the opposite: far from being concentrated, vegetation is constantly removed, usually to a compost heap. A lawn may be defined as a constantly mown and maintained area of grass, from which all plants, apart from one or two species of desirable grasses, are as far as possible excluded. It has many of the features of a field of wheat, but differs in that no crop is obtained. Natural lawns exist where there is intensive grazing by rabbits; they differ from man-made lawns in supporting more species of grasses and many more wild flowers. A garden lawn is a uniform patch of grass, preferably but not necessarily of one species, achieved by importing and laying specially prepared turf or by sowing selected seed. Other plants that appear are either removed by hand or killed with weed-killers: how effectively depends on the diligence of the gardener. In winter, there is often a substantial growth of moss, which is frequently killed by applying a mercury-based poison. Some plants, notably dandelions, daisies and greater plantains are beautifully adapted to colonizing lawns: they are able to produce flowers on extremely short stems and so escape the mower. Indeed, the daisy survives better in man-made lawns than anywhere else, and the greater plantain seems almost to 'enjoy' being mown and trampled.

Some people do not mind if non-grassy plants colonize the lawn; others are more fussy and remove everything that attempts to invade. For the keen botanist, there are all sorts of possibilities: the habitat is so unusual that almost anything may turn up, including species unlikely to establish themselves elsewhere in a garden. Common bird's-foot-trefoil *Lotus corniculatus*, bugle *Ajuga reptans*, yarrow *Achillea millefolium* and selfheal *Prunella vulgaris* are examples of plants that flourish in lawns if allowed to do so.

The removal of clippings means that much of the organic material produced by the lawn is not allowed to decompose where it is formed, and there is thus a steady loss of nutrients. This necessitates the application of fertilizers to restore and maintain the quality of the grass. Dead leaves from nearby trees are also removed and not allowed to decompose where they fall. There is, however, continued decomposition of dead roots, which cannot be removed.

Few animals feed directly on living lawn grass. They include one or two species of bugs and a few moth caterpillars, but these are inconspicuous. On

Country birds in the town. Rooks sometimes visit garden lawns to feed on earthworms and other invertebrates.

the other hand, many decomposers live on dead roots and various insects feed on living ones. People do not often dig up their lawns to see what is living below; if they did, they would be sure to find earthworms and the caterpillars of the yellow underwing and other moths.

We are all aware that birds feed on lawns and that they are usually seeking earthworms and insect larvae. Perhaps more important, lawns offer them open spaces well removed from shrubbery and herbaceous borders in which cats and other predators may be lurking. The song thrush and the blackbird are well-known on lawns, while flocks of starlings frequently poke about in the grass for insect larvae and leave behind hundreds of small but distinctive holes. Earthworms are much more easily removed in wet than dry weather, simply because they tend then to occur on or near the surface. Whenever a thrush takes a worm, there must be a small change in the rate of decomposition of dead roots in that part of the lawn, but the space created by the missing worm is soon filled by another. Certain birds are quick to exploit a newly mown lawn, for the disturbance and loss of cover can expose previously unobtainable worms: thus, the day after the first spring cutting may produce a temporary invasion of starlings.

For about the same amount of money and effort spent in maintaining a lawn, a gardener could produce a fine crop of vegetables. Most people know this perfectly well; they also know that some forms of energy, including oil-based fertilizers and petrol, are costly, yet they persist in the meticulous culti-

Oxford ragwort, an attractive weed quick to colonize a vacant space in even the most improbable places.

vation of their lawns. Now that both energy and vegetables are becoming more and more expensive, perhaps we may expect a decrease in the popularity of the garden lawn. In that case, there will be changes in the fauna and flora of gardens.

In praise of weeds
There is plenty of scope for a keen naturalist to keep an inventory of the wild plants which come up in the garden; whenever this has been tried, the results have been interesting. Thus, in one English garden, 95 species of 'weeds' were found over a period of 25 years: many of them were common for a short time and then became rare or disappeared; one or two were rare in the surrounding area. The best chance of finding unusual wild plants is to look closely whenever a piece of land is put to new use; if, for example, a lawn is dug up and the land cultivated, it may produce additional species, possibly because seeds remain dormant for a long time or perhaps because the new environment suddenly created is more suitable for colonization than anywhere else in the garden.

Most weeds, however, are not unusual or rare species, but abundant, aggressive and opportunist exploiters of patches of land left bare of cultivated plants. Many of us have been taught from childhood to exterminate them, not because they are necessarily harmful but because they are uninvited. Do weeds have a value? From the point of wildlife conservation, the answer is

A park in Helsinki. Lawns are quickly colonized by dandelions. If left alone, they can form a dense carpet in spring, especially where the lawn mower cannot easily reach.

yes, for many characteristic town insects need them for food. But do they have other uses?

It has always been the policy of farmers and gardeners to try to rid the land of weeds. The justification is that they take up space and compete with crops and flowers. Removal by hand is still the method adopted by most gardeners, but there is a growing tendency to use chemical herbicides, some of which may be harmful to insects and other animals.

In the 1960s, naturalists in Europe and North America conducted experiments to see whether weeds were really as harmful to agriculture as believed and, in particular, tried to find out if a limited growth of them was even beneficial to a crop. One experiment, which you can try in your own garden, involved growing cabbages in plots where weeds were either left alone or hoed out. Cabbages are often infested with the caterpillars of the small white butterfly, and in some seasons a crop may be badly damaged by them. The caterpillars, in turn, are attacked by numerous invertebrate predators and parasites, which collectively exert a considerable degree of control over their abundance. Some of these predators hunt at night and rest among ground cover during the day.

In the experiment, the caterpillars on the cabbages growing with weeds left between the rows were attacked more by invertebrate predators than those on the cabbages growing on bare ground. Among the predators were beetles of the family Carabidae, and these in particular seemed to benefit from the presence of weeds. About 20 species of Carabidae may be expected in an average English garden; their combined effect on plant-feeding caterpillars may be considerable, but they require ground cover and this is best provided by weeds. The results of this experiment, however, were not entirely conclusive: it was found, for example, that competition between the weeds and the cabbages led to a slightly reduced yield. Perhaps the best approach is to check weed growth a little: there is obviously a point at which weeds must be controlled, but it is by no means essential to remove them completely.

Weeds are useful indicators of the state of the soil. The presence or absence of certain species provides information on drainage, aeration and mineral deficiencies. Peasant farmers in the tropics know from experience that the occurrence of certain weeds indicates which crops are worth trying. Most farmers in northern Europe no longer possess such detailed knowledge, largely because of the development of mechanized techniques of cultivation, the need to produce extensive monocultures from which everything else is excluded, and the massive use of artificial fertilizers to boost crop production. The technology nowadays available to farmers, and especially the chemical aids to growing plants, are also available on a smaller scale to gardeners who, like farmers, rarely have the ability to judge the state of the soil by looking at the weeds.

A damp or badly drained soil is suggested by the presence of horsetails *Equisetum*, silverweed *Potentilla anserina*, creeping buttercup *Ranunculus repens* and a rich growth of moss. Acidity is indicated by sheep's sorrel *Rumex acetosella*, plantains *Plantago*, corn marigold *Chrysanthemum segetum*, sowthistles *Sonchus* and scentless mayweed *Tripleurospermum maritima*, to name but a few of the species. Scarlet pimpernel *Anagallis arvensis*, salad burnet *Poterium sanguisorba* and bladder campion *Silene vulgaris* grow best on soils rich in lime, while cornflower *Centaurea cyanus*, field bindweed *Convolvulus arvensis*, small nettle *Urtica urens*, shepherd's-purse, white campion *Silene alba* and a variety of other shallow-rooted species prefer lighter or more sandy soils.

Ironically, one of the most valuable weeds is the common nettle, a plant most gardeners hate and try to eradicate at all costs. It has a high nitrogen content and, when cut down, decomposes rapidly to enrich the soil. It is reported that yields of soft fruit have been much improved by allowing these nettles to grow among them. Common nettles also support a rich variety of insects and are valuable from this point of view as well.

Weeds with roots that penetrate deep into the soil accumulate trace elements and minerals and so are particularly useful if allowed to decompose on the soil surface. Colt's-foot *Tussilago farfara* is known to concentrate calcium, copper, iron, magnesium and potassium, and there are others with similar properties. Such weeds also prevent the surface of the soil from drying out during hot weather when evaporation from bare ground is high.

Thus, it is a curious thing that the weeds which gardeners dislike most –

the deep-rooted and persistent ones so difficult to eradicate – are often the most valuable. By penetrating deep into the soil, and bringing to the surface and accumulating minerals and trace elements that might otherwise remain unavailable to many cultivated plants, these species play an important part. The best policy is to keep them in check by cutting them down and either leaving the pieces on the ground to decompose or using them as compost.

We have looked at weeds in positive terms from the point of view of their value to wildlife and to gardening. Some are attractive plants, even though they come up of their own accord. No one would seriously consider eradicating selected species of wild flowers from a nature reserve and we can perhaps hope that more tolerance will be afforded to the wild flowers we choose to call weeds. Now that so many species have disappeared from arable fields, our gardens, wasteland and roadside verges offer the best hope for some of these.

Cucumbers among the weeds

As a plant community develops, there is competition between individuals and species for water and nutrients in the soil and for space and light, a statement just as true in a herbaceous border as in a natural area.

Certain plants – species of *Nicotiana* and *Brassica* are examples – release from their roots chemicals which inhibit the growth of other species, and this puts them at a competitive advantage in the struggle for survival. Recent research on cucumbers *Cucumis sativa* has demonstrated that the growing plants give out an unidentified substance which severely restricts weed growth. Cucumbers, like many crops, are immensely variable, with hundreds of genetic strains differing from one another in growth pattern, tolerance of climate and soil, and productivity. There is corresponding variation in the abilities of different strains to affect weeds: one was found to inhibit weed growth by 87 per cent and another 25 strains did so by 50 per cent or more, suggesting that the cucumber has some remarkable properties. It must be emphasized, however, that the experiments were conducted in a laboratory and that field trials have not yet been attempted. The substance released by the cucumbers can be leached out of the soil and applied to weeds, which soon begin to die back. If it could be extracted or synthesized, new possibilities for the natural control of weeds might emerge.

Old gardening books frequently recommend mixed assemblages of plants: marigolds among the roses, for example. A few gardens are still cultivated in accordance with the tradition of mixing flowers with vegetables, instead of allowing pure stands of a single species.

Peasants in the tropics also favour mixed assemblages; in some places, they grow melons *C. melo*, which are related to cucumbers, among maize and rice and yet do not use the melons. Is it possible that the ability of certain plants to produce toxic weed-killers has been known for a long time, but is nowadays forgotten by most modern gardeners? Modern research may reveal that ancient gardening practices had much to recommend them, even though exactly what was going on was not understood.

In an intriguing experiment in Russia, hemp was grown among tomatoes, potatoes and maize. Hemp, like many plants, produces chemical compounds which deter insects. The roots of these various crops had been suffering from attacks by mole-crickets *Gryllotalpa gryllotalpa*, but once the hemp was inter-planted the mole-crickets disappeared. In another experiment, this time in the United States, flea-beetles *Phyllotreta* became less abundant when cab-bages were grown mixed with tomatoes: each cabbage next to a tomato plant did better than those grown next to other cabbages. Cabbages produce mustard oil compounds which are attractive to certain insects, although they deter others. A pure stand of these vegetables not only provides an abundance of food, but also a concentration of scents, and is thus easily found by the insects. Tomato plants also have a powerful odour, which makes the location of the mustard oil scent more difficult.

Cabbages are perhaps more vulnerable to insect attack than any other gar-den plants. Why not try growing them mixed with tomatoes or other aro-matic plants? There is nothing to lose and you may end up with a better crop.

The old-fashioned herbaceous border, with its rich mixture of plants and complete ground cover, is the nearest parallel we have to the peasant cultiva-tor's way of growing crops. A well-established border contains, within a small area, a greater diversity of species of plants than ever occurs in the wild. Many of the flowers are attractive to insects and, as a refuelling centre, it has no equal among natural environments. Indeed, the herbaceous border may be the most efficient method of cultivation that exists: because of the diversity of plants and the confusing array of scents, there is rarely a build-up of pests and little need to use chemical sprays. Yet the gardening industry has suc-ceeded in persuading us to grow vegetables in single-species plots and rows, a system that seems to encourage pests and, in turn, to boost the sale of pesti-cides. There is no reason why flowers and vegetables should not be grown together: the ancient garden of the Château de Villandry in France is still organized according to an old plan by which the two are mixed, with excellent results, and the same approach could be tried in gardens everywhere.

Plant a tree

One of the recurring themes in this discussion of wildlife in towns and gar-dens is the more varied the vegetation the greater the variety of animal life. It looks as if, to encourage wildlife but at the same time discourage concen-trations of those we regard as pests, we should try to avoid pure stands and, instead, mix unrelated species together. If you have space, plant a young tree of a species not already present and watch what happens. If you already have a tree and no space for more, look after it and try to find out which animals are associated with it.

But what is best to plant? The first questions are the amount of space and the eventual size of the tree, for, although it is perfectly possible by judicious pruning to control its growth, the trunk and roots will tend to enlarge. Apart from this consideration, an effort should be made to plant a species native to the area: an oak in a region where oaks grow naturally supports hundreds of species of insects, while exotic conifers hold very few. Be guided especially by what already grows well locally: there is little point in introducing a species which is absent, because it has almost certainly been tried already and failed. Bear in mind, too, that most of the plant-feeding insects are each restricted to a few related species of plants, which means that, for example, although poplars and willows look different, they tend to support the same invertebrates because they are related and have many attributes in common.

From many points of view, willows and birches are best for gardens. Both grow quickly: willows do well in damp loams, while birches thrive in dry, acid soils but grow almost anywhere. There are several species of each and willows in particular have many ornamental varieties; one of the best is the weeping willow *Salix* × *chrysocoma*, which grows well in even a relatively dry garden, and has the added advantage that much of the foliage remains accessible and easier to inspect for caterpillars and other insects. In many parts of northern Europe, the best tree of all to plant is the silver birch *Betula pendula*, which grows quickly and is attractive to look at; its leaves provide food for many insects, especially the caterpillars of moths, yet are rarely damaged and unsightly, and it does not support vast numbers of aphids. It has a lot to offer and can be thoroughly recommended.

Some common town trees are not especially good for a wide variety of insects: limes and sycamores *Acer pseudoplatanus* support huge populations of aphids, but not a great deal besides, and are probably best avoided. Be cautious, too, about planting elms: the rapid spread of Dutch elm disease, caused by the fungus *Ceratostomella ulmi*, can be attributed partly to the abundance of elms lining roadways. The disease is usually transmitted from tree to tree by small beetles of the family Scolytidae, the larvae of which make radiating burrows just under the bark, but it is also passed on via the roots: a line of elms may be physically connected because each tree has originated from the growth of suckers from the one next to it. Severely infected elms die and decay, and are a hazard in built-up areas. All species and varieties of elms seem affected by the disease, but especially the English elm *Ulmus procera*, a common roadside tree in many parts of Britain. We do not know how long the disease will persist or whether any elms will become resistant.

The locust or false acacia *Robinia pseudacacia* was one of the first North American trees to be introduced to Europe: the original was planted about 1600 by Vespasien Robin (hence the generic name) in Le Jardin des Plantes in Paris. Not only is it now a characteristic tree of the boulevards, but it has spread widely, both by sucker shoots and seeds, and especially on light, sandy soils, colonizing railway cuttings much as the Oxford ragwort has taken to railway tracks in Britain. William Cobbett tried to popularize it as a timber tree in England about 1825, and it was planted extensively there and later in Denmark, Norway and Sweden, but the wood is not straight enough to be commercially successful.

Another aspect of tree-planting is the provision of cover for wildlife. The species best as food-plants for insects are almost all deciduous and bear leaves for only just over half the year. They are bare and leafless during winter and offer little cover, so try a few evergreens as well. Native pines and spruces are good, as is holly where it will grow. Apart from providing night roosts for birds, these trees are excellent wintering places for spiders and insects.

Trees are immensely valuable for the conservation of wildlife and there is everything to be said for encouraging them and planting more wherever space allows.

How to encourage wildlife

The way a town develops and the amenities it offers residents is largely in the hands of planners, who know – or ought to know – local needs in terms of housing, office blocks, factories, schools, parks, playing fields and roads. Most towns have a development plan of sorts, based on population predictions, job opportunities, and social and economic requirements. Town authorities are aware of the need for a pleasant environment, including parks, open spaces and trees; indeed, in some places it is now difficult for a developer to obtain permission to cut down well-established and attractive trees to make room for new buildings. The individual citizen can do little to change the general pattern of events: a piece of wasteland in the middle of a town may be a fascinating place for wild flowers and insects, but who is going to stand up and argue that it should not be used for much-needed housing? After all, the alternative might be further encroachment on countryside and farmland, and no one wants that to happen.

Local natural history societies and conservation groups exist in many European towns, and are usually able to offer advice or even protest about development plans that seem a threat to wildlife. One difficulty is knowing what interesting species occur in an area: it is no use protesting except from a position of knowledge.

The flora and fauna of northern Europe are better known than those of any other area in the world. An extraordinary number of people from all walks of life have taken, and still do take, a deep interest in observing and recording plants and animals. Birds, butterflies and wild flowers are understandably more popular than the 'difficult' groups, but there are experts on mosses, woodlice, earthworms, small parasitic wasps and, indeed, virtually everything. The depth of knowledge and interest, however, varies between groups: dedicated naturalists are now trying to map the distributions of birds, bumblebees, ladybirds, butterflies, moths and woodlice, but relatively few are interested in or capable of identifying certain other groups of insects, such as the parasitic Ichneumonidae. If a species of bird establishes itself – as the

A badger on a garden lawn at night. By putting out food, it is sometimes possible to attract even quite large mammals into gardens.

collared dove did – its presence is immediately detected and its progress meticulously documented by an army of bird-watchers: year-to-year extensions in range are mapped and recorded, and a clear picture emerges of the pattern of colonization. Unless it is a pest, a small beetle receives less attention; and an ichneumon fly none at all.

Experts on all groups of plants and animals agree that changes in the status of many species have occurred during the past few hundred years. Many of these changes are claimed to have been caused by variations in climate or by human alteration of the environment. Often, there is remarkably little evidence to substantiate these claims: we just know that species have become rare or locally extinct and that others have invaded or become common. On the other hand, the collared dove and the golden plusia moth have recently spread north and west and we know that both are intimately associated with towns and gardens; for these and a few other species, we can point out what it is that suits them and feel confident that we know part of the story of their success.

The collared dove and the golden plusia belong to groups which are popular with naturalists. What about the majority of species, mostly small invertebrates, about which so little is known, and whose presence is detected only if special sampling techniques are used?

The Ichneumonidae have already been mentioned: these are slender, parasitic wasps with a fidgety walk and what appears to be a 'nervous' disposition because they fly off at the least disturbance. The family is distinguished from other Hymenoptera by certain features of wing venation, but in practice they and the related Braconidae may be recognized in the field by their long, slender antennae. Most species are small, about 5 mm or less in length, but the few most often seen, because they are larger, may be up to 3 cm long. Females have conspicuous needle-like ovipositors and all species lay eggs in the immature stages of other insects. The adults are rarely found away from vegetation and they are especially common in dense and varied stands of plants, as in a herbaceous border. In Europe, and indeed in the world as a whole, there are more species of Ichneumonidae than all the mammals, birds, reptiles, amphibians and fish put together, and in those terms they are an important group of animals. Yet most people, including many professional biologists, are unaware of their existence.

A device known as a Malaise trap, after its inventor, is extremely good at catching Ichneumonidae and certain other groups of flying insects. It is an open-sided, tent-like construction of netting supported on poles, with internal baffles also of netting. Insects that wander into the trap tend to fly or walk upwards on encountering a baffle and eventually fall into a collecting jar containing alcohol, a useful preservative, attached at the apex. The trap's suitability for catching flying insects depends upon two attributes: no attractant is used, the insects caught being only those that fly into it of their own accord; and it can be operated continuously day and night in all weathers. Although the insects that enter the collecting jar are killed, the effect of the trap on the local fauna is negligible as it samples an area of only about 2·6 square metres up to a height of just over a metre. The trap is easily erected in a garden and, if operated for a year or, better still, a period of years, is an excellent means of monitoring small insects.

A Malaise trap in a garden at Leicester in the English Midlands produced 529 species of Ichneumonidae in three years, about a quarter of those known in Britain and far more than have been recognized on any of the national or regional nature reserves. No species was common, and many were found once only. It might be added that, if these little known and apparently rare species had been birds, butterflies or wild flowers, the Leicester garden would immediately have been declared a nature reserve or site of special scientific interest.

Lurking in the shrubbery, herbaceous border and vegetable patch, and among the dense plant cover of wasteland, are vast numbers of small insects which are hardly ever seen. They can be encouraged by allowing as much cover as possible to grow up and by leaving vegetation standing for as long as possible. Nothing more need be done, except of course to refrain from spraying with chemicals unless absolutely necessary.

The more conspicuous groups of insects, birds and mammals are also dependent on cover, and much good can be done by improving individually owned gardens. There should be plenty of flowers for the nectar-feeders and

A Malaise trap for sampling insects in a Leicester garden.

as many native plants as possible for the species that are dependent on leaves and stems. Experience will show which plants grow best and are most attractive, but, as a general rule, real exotics and especially those with complicated flower structures should be avoided.

Many people are interested in birds and not especially concerned about small insects. The simple approach to encouraging birds is to put out food in winter. But much more can be done, for, despite appearances, most birds depend not on the food we give them but on insects and other invertebrates, which, as we have seen, are in turn dependent on the variety and abundance of vegetation. Thus, by diversifying plants and encouraging insects, you automatically encourage birds. During late summer and autumn, too, some birds eat berries and fruit, so the provision of berry-bearing shrubs and trees will bring them into the garden. Birds also eat fallen fruit, especially apples, the juices of which serve too as foods for many species of noctuid moths and a few butterflies.

We started this book with a view from the air, then descended and looked more closely at plants and animals and at the intricacies of food webs. What we have found suggests that the town and garden environment is extremely rich in wildlife and worthy of our attention and respect. If you want to find out more, the best place to start is in your garden. Here, depending on what you grow and how you grow it, you will find a splendid panorama of predators, parasites and prey, interacting with plants in complex and interesting ways. Why not take a closer look?

Population map of Northern Europe
showing its limits and the division into ranges

GLOSSARY

abdomen segments immediately behind thorax (*qv*); especially apparent in insects

alternate leaves placed singly, at different positions along stem, *cf* opposite

apothecium flat or cup-shaped fruiting structure of fungi and lichens

awn long, stiff, bristle projecting beyond grain, *eg* some grasses

bract small, leaf-like structure from which flower-stalks arises

bulbil small bulb or tuber arising from angle between leaf and stem

calyx all the sepals; term often used when sepals are joined to form a tube

carapace in spiders, shield covering cephalothorax (*qv*)

carpel one of female parts of flower; contains seeds; fused carpels often form the fruit

cephalothorax in spiders, head and thorax fused, not clearly separate as in insects

cerci long or short projections from posterior of abdomen

clitellum in earthworms, saddle-like region secreting mucus

corm swollen, underground stem lasting 1 year; produces next year's on top

dioecious having fertile male and female flowers on different plants

elytra in beetles, hardened forewings covering abdomen

epiphyte plant growing on another plant for support, but not feeding from it

gemma small, bud-like body capable of reproducing the plant

gills wing-like structures beneath cap of fungi producing spores

inflorescence flower branch including bracts, flower-stalk and flowers

lanceolate spear-shaped; also compounds, *eg* linear-lanceolate

linear long and narrow, almost parallel-sided

mesonotum centre of thorax as visible from above

metamorphosis change in form; complete: young is totally different from adult, includes a pupal stage, *eg* caterpillar to butterfly; incomplete: young similar to

adult, always without pupal stage, *eg* aphid

microspecies groups of individuals differing only slightly from other groups of individuals but not interbreeding with them

monoecious having fertile male and female flowers on same plant

nerve strand of strengthening or conducting tissue running through leaf

ob- inverted; with broadest part of structure near apex in contrast to it being in normal position at base, *eg* obovate

opposite leaves arising at same level on opposite sides of stem

ovate shaped like a hen's egg, with broadest part near base

ovipositor egg-laying apparatus of female at posterior of body; in bees and wasps is modified into sting

palmate divided hand-like into lobes

panicle branched inflorescence

pinnae segments of pinnate (*qv*) leaf

pinnate regular arrangement of leaflets in 2 rows on either side of stalk (simply); each leaflet divided again (twice)

petiole leaf-stalk

pronotum front part of thorax as visible from above

rachis stalk-like part of pinnate (*qv*) leaf or inflorescence

reflexed bent back

rhizoids in mosses and liverworts, hair-like structures with same function as roots

saprophyte plant deriving its food wholly or partially from dead organic matter

scape leafless flower-stalk

sepal outer ring of petal-like structures; usually green; less conspicuous than petals

simple leaf not divided into segments; unbranched stem or inflorescence

sorus cluster of spore-cases on back of fern frond

species group of individuals showing similar features, and which can interbreed to produce viable offspring

stigma part of female organ of flower; receives pollen, *cf* style

stipule scale-like or leaf-like structure at

base of leaf-stalk; usually paired
stolon horizontal stem spreading above
or below ground; gives rise to new plant
by rooting at tip
style more or less elongated projection
from ovary; bears stigma (*qv*)
subspecies group of individuals, within
1 species, with distinct features which can
interbreed with other subspecies to
produce viable offspring
ternate leaf divided into 3 parts (simply);
each part may then be divided again (twice)
thallose like a thallus (*qv*)
thallus plant body undifferentiated into
leaf, stem etc; often flattened
thorax region between head and
abdomen, bearing legs and wings;
especially apparent in insects
umbel cluster of flowers whose stalks
radiate from top of stem resembling
spokes of an umbrella
variety group of individual plants of 1
species or subspecies possessing 1 or
more distinctive characteristics
viviparous giving birth to live young
whorls leaves or flowers arising in a
circle round stem

ABBREVIATIONS

The ranges in the order of their listing in
the field guide

n, s, e, w	north, south, east, west
W	widespread
T	throughout
Br	Britain; i.e. England, Scotland, Wales
Ir	Ireland
Ic	Iceland
Fr	France, north of the Loire
Lu	Luxembourg
Be	Belgium
Ne	Netherlands
De	Denmark
Ge	Germany
Cz	Czechoslovakia
Po	Poland
Fi	Finland
Sw	Sweden
No	Norway
FS	Fenno–Scandia; i.e. Norway, Sweden and Finland
SC	Scandinavia; i.e. Norway and Sweden
NE	Fenno–Scandia, Denmark, north Germany and north Poland
CE	Czechoslovakia, south Germany and south Poland
WE	Britain, Ireland, France, Luxembourg, Belgium and Netherlands

When the species is not native but
introduced and naturalized, the countries
concerned are put in brackets,
eg Fr, Ge, (Br, Ir).

esp	especially
fl(s); fl-head	flower(s); flowerhead
fr(s)	fruit(s)
inflor	inflorescence
juv	juvenile
lf (lvs); lflet	leaf (leaves); leaflet
microsp	microspecies
sp	species (singular)
spp	species (plural)
ssp	subspecies
var	variety

MEASUREMENTS

Scale in the plates: the relative sizes of
the animals and plants are preserved
whenever possible; the measurements in
the entries themselves must be referred to.

BL	body length; excludes tail in mammals; includes antennae in insects
EL	extended length, slugs; ear length, mammals
FA	forearm length
H	height
HF	hindfoot length
L	total length; includes beak, tail
SB	shell breadth
SH	shell height, snails; shoulder height, mammals
TL	tail length
U	underside
W	number of whorls
WS	wingspan
WT	weight

SYMBOLS

♀	female
♂	male
☿	worker
<	up to
>	more than
?	doubtful

88

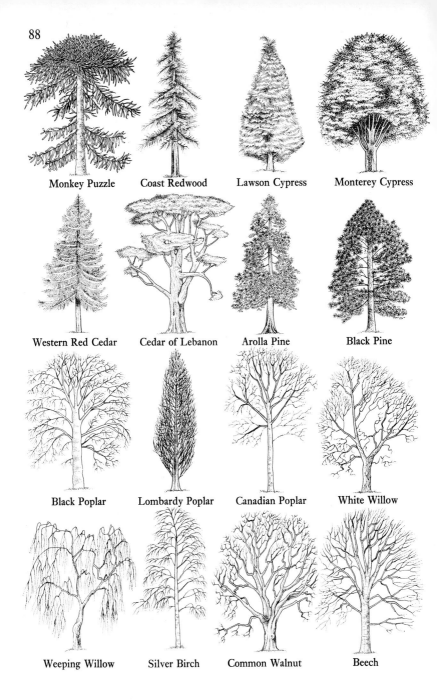

Monkey Puzzle Coast Redwood Lawson Cypress Monterey Cypress

Western Red Cedar Cedar of Lebanon Arolla Pine Black Pine

Black Poplar Lombardy Poplar Canadian Poplar White Willow

Weeping Willow Silver Birch Common Walnut Beech

Sweet Chestnut   Pendunculate Oak   Wych Elm   English Elm

Sweet Gum   London Plane   Swedish Whitebeam   Laburnum

Acacia   Sycamore   Horse Chestnut   Holly

Common Lime   Flowering Ash   Ash   Indian Bean

Rough-stalked Feather-moss
Brachythecium rutabulum HYPNACEAE
Creeping and irregularly branched,
forming large, loose tufts, bright green
with yellowish tinge. Lvs widely spreading,
oval, tapering to sharp point, with margins
finely toothed and nerve <$\frac{1}{2}$ length or
more. Spore capsules large, curved on
rough stalks, <25 mm. Ripe in spring.
Hedgerows, grassland; also woods, often
on lawns. T. [1]

Silky Feather-moss *Camptothecium
sericeum* HYPNACEAE Creeping and much
branched, forming large patches, very
glossy and silky; side branches curl
inwards on drying. Lvs close to stem,
narrow, triangular, tapering to fine point,
with margins toothed below and nerve
<$\frac{3}{4}$ length or more. Spore capsules large,
erect on rough stalks, <20 mm. Ripe in
spring. Trees, stone walls. T. [2]

Cypress-leaved Feather-moss *Hypnum
cupressiformae* HYPNACEAE Creeping,
irregularly branching, forming dense mats.

Lvs overlap and clasp stem; each lf oval,
narrowing to fine point, curved and
turned downward. Spore capsules slightly
curved, with beaked lid on red stalks,
<20 mm. Spores ripe in spring. Trees,
fallen logs, walls, bare earth. T. [3]

cushion-moss *Grimmia apocarpa*
GRIMMIACEAE H 15–25 mm. Growing in
dome-shaped, dark green tufts. Lvs
narrow, triangular, tapering to long, wavy,
silvery point into which nerve runs. Spore
capsules on very short stalks, almost
hidden by upper lvs, but show bright red.
Spores ripe Apr–Aug. Old walls.
T. [4]

beard-moss *Barbula unguiculata*
TORTULACEAE H 10–25 mm. Growing in
yellowish-green mats or cushions. Lvs
long, narrow, with blunt apex from
which short, sharp point protrudes. Spore
capsules on short, brownish-red or purple
stalks, <10 mm. Spores ripe in spring.
Wall tops, garden paths, bare earth. T,
but rare Ic. [5]

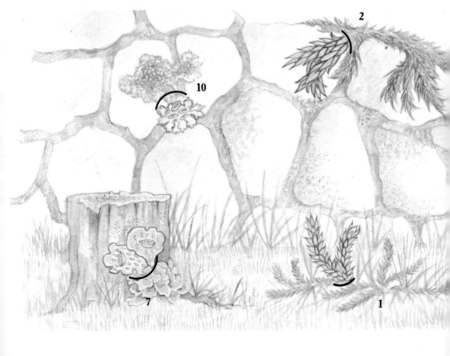

Wall Screw-moss *Tortula muralis*
TORTULACEAE H 10–15 mm. Growing in
small, dense, dull or bright green
cushions. Lvs long, narrow, with blunt
apex and silvery hair point ½ as long as lf.
Spore capsules on short stalks, yellow
when young, later purplish-red. Spores
ripe in spring. Walls. T, but rare
Ic. [6]

Crescent-cup Liverwort *Lunularia
cruciata* MARCHANTIACEAE Prostrate,
creeping, regularly branched. Lf-like
branches lobed, attached to ground by
long, white rhizoids; opening of air spaces
on upper surface indistinct. Reproduction
mainly by granular gemmae, produced in
crescent-shaped cups. Spore capsules
rarely formed. Garden paths, greenhouses.
(T, ex Ic, probably from Mediterranean.)
[7]

liverwort *Pellia epiphylla* CODONIOIDEAE
Prostrate, creeping, dark green, growing
in patches 30–60 cm across. Regularly
forked branches with broad, conspicuous

midribs. Spore capsules dark greenish-
brown or almost black, on long, thin,
almost transparent stalks. Spores ripe
early spring. Rich soil in shady, wet
places, *eg* banks of streams. T. [8]

Black-shields Lichen *Lecanora
conizaeoides* LECANORACEAE Crustose,
forming rather thick, grey-green, deeply
cracked thallus. Inconspicuous spore-
producing structures scattered like powder
over surface. Trees, wood, bricks.
Pollution-resistant, abundant in towns;
often only lichen on wood. T. [9]

Yellow-scales Lichen *Xanthoria
parietina* PHYSCIACEAE Thallose, circular
when young, but later dying at centre to
form open circle. Thallus usually bright
orange, but yellow-green in the shade.
Spore-producing apothecia darker,
crowded in centre. Walls, rocks, roofs,
trees, fences, esp where air enriched with
mineral salts, *eg* by sea. T. [10]
*The structures drawn within each semi-circle
are magnified.*

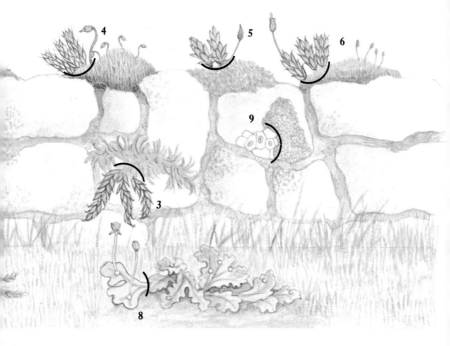

Maidenhair Spleenwort *Asplenium trichomanes* ASPLENIACEAE H 4–20 cm. Lvs simply pinnate with 15–40 oval pinnae, 3–7 mm, on each side of blackish rachis; lf-stalk short, $c\frac{1}{4}$ length of lf. Sori linear. Spores ripe May–Oct. Walls; ssp *quadrivalens*, with pinnae < 12 mm, on mortared walls. T. [1]

Black Spleenwort *Asplenium adiantum-nigrum* ASPLENIACEAE H 10–50 cm. Lvs 2–3 times pinnate with < 15 triangular to óvate pinnae, 2–6 cm, on each side of black rachis, decreasing in size upwards; lf-stalk about as long as lf. Sori linear. Spores ripe Jun–Oct. Rocks, hedge-banks, shady walls. T, ex Ic, Fi. [2]

Wall-rue *Asplenium ruta-muraria* ASPLENIACEAE H 4–15 cm. Lvs usually twice pinnate with 3–5 variously shaped pinnae, 1–3 cm, on each side of green rachis, decreasing in size from base; lf-stalk 1–2 times as long as lf. Sori linear. Spores ripe Jun–Oct. Lime-rich walls. T, ex Ic. [3]

Hart's-tongue *Phyllitis scolopendrium* ASPLENIACEAE H 10–60 cm. Lvs undivided, strap-shaped, with heart-shaped base, tapering to blunt apex; lf-stalk < $\frac{1}{2}$ as long as lf. Sori linear, in pairs, usually more than $\frac{1}{2}$ width of lf. Spores ripe Jul–Aug. Hedges, shady walls; also rocky woods. T, ex Ic, Fi. [4]

Male-fern *Dryopteris filix-mas* ASPIDIACEAE H 30–130 cm. Lvs simply or twice pinnate with 20–35 pinnae, < 15 cm, on each side, decreasing in length downwards, each having c30 oblong, toothed segments with 3–6 circular sori on undersides. Lf-stalk $\frac{1}{6}$–$\frac{1}{2}$ as long as lf, scaly. Spores ripe Jul–Aug. Rocks, woods, hedges, walls. T. [5]

Polypody *Polypodium vulgare* POLYPODIACEAE H 10–30 cm. Lvs pinnate with 5–25 pinnae, < 70 mm, on each side, many equal in length, each with two rows of oval to circular sori on undersides. Lf-stalk $\frac{1}{3}$–$\frac{3}{4}$ as long as lf. Spores ripe in spring. Rocks, hedge banks, walls; often as epiphyte on trees. T. [6]

Shaggy Ink-cap *Coprinus comatus* AGARICINEAE H 5–12 cm. White, cylindrical fungus, covered in shaggy scales when young; conspicuous ring on hollow stalk soon disappears. Gills white, then (beginning at bottom) pink and finally black, forming inky, fluid-containing spores. Apr–Dec. Roadsides, fields, dumps, in groups. Good eating when young. T. [7]

Fairy-ring Champignon *Marasmius oreades* AGARICINEAE H < 7 cm. Fungus with buff-coloured, convex cap, becoming paler and pinker when dry, 2–6 cm across. Stalk slightly downy at base. Gills broad and widely spaced. May–Oct. Lawns, short-grazed grassland; forms well-known 'fairy rings'. T. [8]

Sulphur-tuft *Hypholoma fasciculare* AGARICINEAE H 3–12 cm. Fungus with bright sulphur-yellow, convex cap, brownish in centre, 3–7 cm across. Stalk slender, colour of cap, but dirty brown below. Gills light green, becoming olive-green to chocolate. All year round. Large clumps on tree stumps. Tastes bitter. T. [9]

Coral-spot *Nectria cinnabarina* HYPOCREALES Flat fungus, forming small pinkish to dark red, granular cushions 3–4 mm across, minutely warted at maturity. Spores develop in tiny, flask-shaped cavities. All year round. Densely clustered and bursting through bark of damp, newly-fallen branches and twigs. T, ex Ic. [10]

Ginkgo, Maidenhair Tree *Ginkgo biloba*
GINKGOACEAE H <30 m. Slender,
deciduous tree. Lvs fan-shaped, 5–10 cm,
yellowish-green. Trees ♂ or ♀: most in Br
♂ with fls in hanging catkins, May; ♀ fls
green, acorn-like, inconspicuous. Frs
yellow, plum-like, foul-smelling, rarely
produced in N Europe. Parks, churchyards, occasionally large gardens. (W,
from China *c*1727.) [♂ 1]

Yew *Taxus baccata* TAXACEAE H <20 m.
Medium-sized, evergreen tree or shrub.
Lvs narrow, 20–30 mm, blackish-green,
spirally arranged. ♂ and ♀ fls normally on
separate trees, Mar–Apr. Frs scarlet,
fleshy, with single seed, Aug–Sep. Old,
large, spreading trees in churchyards;
young ones used in hedges. Saplings in
gardens from seeds dropped by birds. T,
ex Ic. [2]

Monkey-puzzle, Chile Pine *Araucaria
araucana* ARAUCARIACEAE H <25 m.
Evergreen tree, remarkable form:
horizontal branches point downward at
tips. Lvs dark green, stiff, spirally
arranged. ♂ and ♀ fls normally on separate
trees, autumn. ♀s produce globular cones,
11–18 cm, 2 years later. (W, from Chile.)
[3]

Coast Redwood *Sequoia sempervirens*
TAXODIACEAE H <40 m. Tall, evergreen
tree with fibrous, spongy, red bark. Lvs

1–2 cm, in 2 ranks but spirally arranged
on leading and cone shoots. Fls Jan–Feb.
Cones ripe Oct. Often planted by roadways
and in parks. (W, from California and
Oregon, USA.) [4]

Wellingtonia *Sequoiadendron giganteum*
TAXODIACEAE H <45 m. Superficially
similar to *Sequoia sempervirens*, but small,
narrow lvs all spirally arranged. Fls Feb–
Mar. Cones ripen following year. In
natural state, possibly largest tree in
world, growing to over 100 m. Commonly
planted by roadways and in parks. (W,
from California, USA.) [5]

Swamp or **Bald Cypress** *Taxodium
distichum* TAXODIACEAE H <40 m. Conical,
deciduous tree with reddish, peeling bark.
Stem lvs spirally arranged, bright green
in spring, yellow in summer, brown in
autumn. Fls Mar–Apr. Cones small and
round, ripe same autumn. Grows best in
damp places, esp near ponds; common
in some town parks. (W, from south
USA.) [6]

Caucasian Fir *Abies nordmanniana*
PINACEAE H <30 m. Conical, evergreen
tree; branches, with round scars where lvs
fallen, characteristic of *Abies*. Lvs 2–3 cm,
shiny green above, with 2 white bands
below. Fls spring. Cones ripe same
autumn. Does not grow well in polluted
environment. (W, from Caucasus.) [7]

Incense Cedar *Calocedrus decurrens*
CUPRESSACEAE H <25 m. Columnar,
evergreen tree. Lvs dark-green, arranged
in fan-like sprays, smell of turpentine
when crushed. ♂ and ♀ fls on same plant,
Jan–Feb. Cones ripe same autumn.
Planted in gardens and parks. (W, from
west USA.) [1]

Lawson Cypress *Chamaecyparis*
lawsoniana CUPRESSACEAE H <30 m.
Evergreen tree with numerous cultivars
differing chiefly in pyramidal or columnar
shape and lf colour. Lvs small, scale-like,
smell of parsley when crushed. ♂ fls
crimson, conspicuous, Mar. ♀ cones small,
berry-like, Sep–Oct. (W, from California
and Oregon, USA.) [2]

Nootka Cypress *Chamaecyparis*
nootkatensis CUPRESSACEAE H <30 m.
Conical, evergreen tree. Branchlets
drooping, with dark blue-green, nasty-
smelling, sharp-pointed, scale-like lvs. ♂
fls yellow, May. Scales of ♀ cones tipped
with pointed bosses, Sep–Oct. Widely
planted in parks and large gardens. (W,
from west N America, Alaska to Oregon.)
[3]

Leyland Cypress *Cupressocyparis* ×
leylandii CUPRESSACEAE H <30 m. Fast-
growing, evergreen tree with glaucous-
green foliage; originated in cultivation, a
series of hybrids between *Cupressus*
macrocarpa and *Chamaecyparis nootkatensis*.
Lvs similar to *Chamaecyparis*, but less
strong-smelling when bruised; general
form more like *Cupressus*, but cones
intermediate. Commonly grown in parks
and gardens; young trees used in hedges.
(W.) [4]

Monterey Cypress *Cupressus macrocarpa*
CUPRESSACEAE H <25 m. Fast-growing,
evergreen tree, conical or columnar when
young, becoming almost cedar-shaped
with age. Bright green foliage, smells of
lemons when crushed. Lvs scale-like,
swollen towards tips. Fls minute, May–
Jun. Cones ripe late summer of following
year. (W, from native region only 3 km
long, Monterey Bay, California.) [5]

Smooth or **Arizona Cypress** *Cupressus*
glabra CUPRESSACEAE H <12 m. Small-
medium, slow-growing, evergreen tree,
cone-shaped with ascending branches and
purplish bark which flakes readily. Lvs
grey-blue or grey-green, often white-
spotted, smelling of grapefruit when
crushed. Fls Mar. Cones ripe following
year. Often planted in parks and gardens;
also used in hedges. (W, from Arizona,
USA.) [6]

Chinese Juniper *Juniperus chinensis*
CUPRESSACEAE H <20 m. Medium-sized,
conical or columnar, evergreen tree. Lvs
greyish, awl-shaped when young,
becoming scale-like. Dioecious. ♂ fls
attractive yellow, early spring. Top-shaped
cones whitish, ripe following year. Several
cultivars exist: common one ('Aurea') has
golden foliage. (W, from China, Japan.) [7]

Western Red Cedar *Thuja plicata*
CUPRESSACEAE H <40 m. Fast-growing,
evergreen tree with shedding bark and
spreading branches. Lvs arranged in flat
sprays, glossy green above, streaked with
white below, smelling of pineapple when
crushed. Fls early spring. Upright cones,
1·5 cm, ripe same autumn. Used for
timber and hedging. (W, from west
N America 1853.) [8]

Cedar of Lebanon *Cedrus libani* PINACEAE
H <40 m. Large, evergreen, spreading tree often with more than one trunk. Lvs in erect clusters, dark-green. ♂ or ♀ fls on same tree, autumn. Cones upright, barrel-shaped, 8–10 cm, ripe 2 years later. Common at edges of lawns in parks, large gardens. (W, from Asia Minor, Syria.) [1]

Atlas Cedar *Cedrus atlantica* PINACEAE
H <35 m. Similar to *C. libani*, but young twigs hairy; grows rapidly when young, producing ascending branches. Lvs greyish-green. Cones flat-topped, 5–7 cm. Variety with bluish lvs ('Glauca') most often planted in parks. (W, from Atlas mountains in Morocco, Algeria.) [2]

Deodar *Cedrus deodara* PINACEAE
H <35 m. Similar to other *Cedrus*, but leading shoots pendulous. Lvs <50 mm, sharp-pointed. Cones rounded at apex, <12 cm. Commonly planted in large gardens and parks. (W, from west Himalayas.) [3]

Colorado Spruce *Picea pungens* PINACEAE
H <30 m. Medium-large, conical, ever-green tree. Lvs 4-angled, bluish-green, sharp-pointed (hence *pungens*). Fls in spring. ♀ cones pendulous, 6–10 cm, ripe same year. (W, from southwest USA.) [4] Several other *Picea* may be expected in towns, including Norway spruce or Christmas tree *P. abies*.

Canadian Hemlock *Tsuga canadensis* PINACEAE H <20–30 m. Large, evergreen, pyramidal tree, with horizontal branches, pendulous at tips; usually forks near base, unlike similar western hemlock *T. hetero-phylla* which normally has straight trunk. Lvs spirally arranged, narrow, with white bands beneath. ♂ and ♀ fls on same tree, spring. Cones small and pendulous, ripe same year. (W, from N America.) [5]

Arolla Pine *Pinus cembra* PINACEAE
H <25 m. Small-medium, conical or columnar, evergreen tree. Branches turn up at ends. Lvs <8 cm, shiny-green above, whitish below, arranged in 5s. ♂ and ♀ fls on same tree, May–Jun. Young cones blue, short-stalked, erect, 5–8 cm, ripe 2–3 years later. Seeds wingless, good to eat. (W, from Alps, NE Russia, N Asia.) [6]

Bhutan Pine *Pinus wallichiana* PINACEAE
H <50 m. Large, broad-headed, evergreen tree with horizontal lower branches. Lvs very long, <20 cm, grey-green, arranged in 5s, drooping with age. Cones 15–25 cm, banana-shaped, resinous, arranged singly or in groups. Splendid tree, commonly planted in large gardens and parks. (W, from Himalayas.) [7]

Black Pine *Pinus nigra* PINACEAE
H <40 m. Tall, evergreen tree with pyramidal crown. Several ssp, commonest *laricio* (Corsican pine) and *nigra* (Austrian pine). Lvs in 2s, grey-green in *laricio*, nearly black in *nigra*. Both common in parks and large gardens. (W, *laricio* from S Italy, Corsica, *nigra* from Austria to C Italy, Greece, Yugoslavia.) [8]

White Poplar *Populus alba* SALICACEAE
H <25 m. Suckering, deciduous tree, with
wide crown. Lvs 5-lobed, with additional
smaller lobes between main ones, silvery-
white on undersides; lf-stalks flattened.
Catkins of ♂ trees 4–8 cm, of ♀ 2–6 cm,
Mar. Well-established by roadsides in
many areas and common in parks. (W,
from S Europe.) [1]

Black Poplar *Populus nigra* SALICACEAE
H <35 m. Large, rough-barked tree, with
swollen bosses on trunks, branches arching
downwards. Lvs finely pointed, 5–10 cm.
Var *italica* (Lombardy poplar) unmistak-
ably columnar, common in many urban
areas, often planted in rows along
roadways. Var *betulifolia* (Manchester
poplar) more spreading in form; tolerant
of smoke pollution. Commonest in towns
are Canadian poplars *P.* × *canadensis*,
variable hybrids of *P. balsamifera* and
P. deltoides with bossless trunks and
branches ascending to form fan-like
crown. T, ex Ic, FS (planted forms more
widespread). [Black 2] [Lombardy 3]
[Canadian 4]

**Western Balsam Poplar, Black
Cottonwood** *Populus trichocarpa*
SALICACEAE H <35 mm. Large, fast-
growing poplar with relatively smooth
bark peeling from young trees. Lvs dark
green above, silvery-white and net-veined
beneath, balsam-scented when unfolding.
♂ catkins big, conspicuous in early spring.
(W, from west N America, Alaska to
Mexico.) [5]

Contorted Willow *Salix matsudana* var
tortuosa SALICACEAE H <5 m. Twisted,
contorted branches, twigs and lvs
unmistakable; planted essentially because
of peculiar growth-form. Lvs narrow,
long, slender-pointed, green above and
glaucous below. Catkins appear with lvs
in spring. (W. from Japan.) [6]

White Willow *Salix alba* SALICACEAE
H <25 m. Tall, conical tree with ascending
branches drooping at tips. Lvs 5–10 cm,
lanceolate, covered with white, silky hairs.
Catkins, ♂ yellow, ♀ greenish, appear with
lvs, Apr–May. Often planted by streams,
rivers. Br, Ir, Fr, Lu, Be, Ne, De, Ge,
Cz, Po. [7]

Weeping Willow *Salix* × *chrysocoma*
SALICACEAE H <20 m. Medium-sized,
wide-spreading tree, with vigorous,
arching, golden-yellow branches almost
reaching ground ('weeping'). Catkins
with both ♂ and ♀ fls. Hybrid between
S. alba ssp *vitellina* and *S. babylonica*, now
planted in preference to latter parent.
(W.) [8]

Silver Birch *Betula pendula* BETULACEAE
H <30 m. Medium-sized, silver-barked
tree changing to black at base; pendulous,
hairless, warty twigs. Lvs triangular,
prominently double-toothed. ♂ catkins 3–6
cm, Apr–May. Commonly planted in
towns; seedlings often in gardens.
Supports many insect spp, esp moth
caterpillars. T, ex Ic.

*Broadleaved trees are also scattered through
a number of other families, eg Rosaceae and
Leguminosae.*

Common Walnut *Juglans regia*
JUGLANDACEAE H < 30 m. Large,
deciduous tree with round head. Lvs
pinnate with *c*7 lflets; fragrant when
crushed. ♂ catkins 5–15 cm, late spring.
Frs smooth, globular, green, Sep–Oct.
Common in parks, large gardens;
regenerates naturally in southern areas.
(W, from SE Europe.) [1]

Black Walnut *Juglans nigra* JUGLANDACEAE
H < 50 m. Distinguished from *J. regia* by
lvs having 11–23 lflets with serrated edges.
Occasionally in parks, gardens; extensively
planted for timber in parts of central and
east Europe. (W, from east N America.) [2]

Beech *Fagus sylvatica* FAGACEAE
H < 40 m. Large, deciduous tree, with
smooth, grey bark. Lvs oval, pointed, with
wavy margins. ♂ catkins on slender stalks,
5–6 cm, Apr–May. Frs with prickly
covering containing triangular nuts, ripe
Sep–Oct. Var 'Purpurea', with copper-red
lvs, commonly planted in parks, large
gardens. Br, Fr, Lu, Be, Ne, De, Ge, Cz,
Po, Sw, No, (Ir).

Sweet Chestnut *Castanea sativa* FAGACEAE
H < 30 m. Large, deciduous tree, with
brownish-grey bark having conspicuous
spiral ridges. Lvs oblong-lanceolate, with
spines at edges. Catkins erect, ♂ above, ♀
below, 12–20 mm. Frs nuts, in pale green,
prickly husks, ripe Oct. Common in parks;
some trees hundreds of years old. (W,
from S Europe, Italy eastwards.) [3]

Red Oak *Quercus rubra* FAGACEAE H < 30
m. Fast-growing, broad-headed, deciduous
tree. Lvs 10–25 cm, mat green, with 8–10
lobes from which veins project as bristles;
turn red before falling. Fls May. Frs
acorns, 25 mm long, in saucer-shaped
cups, take 2 years to ripen. Parks, large
gardens. (W, from east N America.) [4]

Holm Oak *Quercus ilex* FAGACEAE
H < 25 m. Large, evergreen tree, with
corrugated bark and broad, dense crown.
Lvs like holly *Ilex aquifolium*, shiny dark
green above, pale brown and downy below.
♂ catkins 3–5 cm, May. Frs acorns, short,

almost hidden in cups when young, take 2
years to ripen. Common in parks, gardens.
(W, from S Europe.) [5]

Pedunculate Oak *Quercus robur*
FAGACEAE H < 45 m. Large, deciduous
tree, with massive trunk, spreading
branches. Lvs lobed, with ear-like flaps at
base, on very short petiole. ♂ catkins 2–4
cm, Apr–May. Frs acorns, on long stalks
2–8 cm, Sep–Oct. Supports more spp of
insects than any other tree. Also widely
planted. T, ex Ic.

Wych Elm *Ulmus glabra* ULMACEAE
H < 40 m. Broad, domed, deciduous tree,
with ascending branches, few suckers. Lvs
oblong, shortly petioled, rough to touch
above, occasionally 3-pointed. Fls before
lvs, Feb–Mar. Frs dish-like, with seed in
centre, May–Jun. Sometimes planted by
roadsides, in parks. T, ex Ic.

English Elm *Ulmus procera* ULMACEAE
H < 30 m. Erect, deciduous tree with few,
large, heavy branches suckering freely.
Lvs smaller, more rounded than *U. glabra*,
also hairier and less rough above, and on
longer petiole. Fls Feb–Mar. Frs May–
Jun, but rarely produce viable seed.
English population genetically uniform,
which may account for lack of resistance
to Dutch elm disease; planting no longer
advisable. Br, Fr.

Common Mulberry *Morus nigra*
MORACEAE H < 10 m. Small, gnarled,
deciduous tree, with crooked, widespread
branches. Lvs heart-shaped, rough above,
hairy below. Fls in unisexual, catkin-like
spikes, May. Frs like blackberries *Rubus
fruticosus*, acid until completely ripe, then
edible, Oct–Nov. Common in parks, large
gardens. (W, from C Asia.) [6]

Fig *Ficus carica* MORACEAE H < 10 m.
Small, spreading, deciduous tree or shrub.
Lvs large, 3–5 lobed. Fls produced inside
pear-shaped receptacles, May. Frs green,
edible, Jul–Oct. Introduced hundreds of
years ago; common in southern districts,
usually grown against south-facing walls.
(CE, from W Asia.) [7]

Common Nettle *Urtica dioica* URTICACEAE
H 15–30 cm. Perennial herb, dying back
in winter to leave pale buff stems. Lvs
toothed, with stinging hairs. Fls green, ♂
and ♀ on separate plants, Jun–Aug.
Abundant on wasteland, often in large
patches; vigorous garden weed. Young
shoots may be eaten like spinach. T. [1]

Pellitory-of-the-wall *Parietaria judaica*
URTICACEAE H 30–100 cm. Perennial herb
with densely hairy, spreading, red stems.
Lvs < 5 cm, each about 3 times as long as
petiole. Fls green, later reddish, ♂ or ♀,
Jun–Oct. Commonly growing on old walls.
Br, Ir, Fr, Lu, Be, Ne, Ge. [2] Larger,
more erect *P. officinalis* has lvs < 12 cm.
Fr, Ge, Cz, (Be, Ne, De, Po).

Mind-your-own-business *Soleirolia*
soleirolii URTICACEAE. Small, creeping,
perennial herb, forming dense, evergreen
mats. Lvs tiny, round, 2–6 mm. Fls green,
unisexual, ♀ below, ♂ above. Grows on
walls, often in dense mass, as escape from
rock-gardens; occasionally naturalized,
esp near coast. (Br, Ir, Fr, Ne, from
W Mediterranean islands.)

Knotgrass *Polygonum aviculare*
POLYGONACEAE H < 30 cm. Annual, erect
or spreading herb. Lvs lanceolate, on main
stem 2–3 times as long as on flowering
branches. Fls white or pinkish, Jul–Oct.
Common everywhere, esp weed of gardens,
wasteland. One of first plants to colonize
bare ground. T. [3]

Redshank *Polygonum persicaria*
POLYGONACEAE H 25–75 cm. Annual, upright herb with reddish stems swollen
above each lf-base. Lvs green, hairless,
lanceolate, often conspicuously black-
blotched. Fls pink or red, in cylindrical
spike, Jul–Sep. Common, spreading weed,
quick to colonize bare ground; often
appears in gardens among vegetables. T.
[4]

Black-bindweed *Polygonum convolvulus*
POLYGONACEAE H 30–120 cm. Climbing,
annual herb, somewhat mealy, with

angular stems. Lvs 2–6 cm, heart-shaped.
Fls arranged in spikes, greenish-pink, Jul–
Oct. Frs shiny black, enclosed in green
perianth. Common in gardens, wasteland.
Frs harmful to farm animals. T. [5]

Common Sorrel *Rumex acetosa*
POLYGONACEAE H 10–100 cm. Perennial
herb. Lvs arrow-shaped, < 10 cm, edible,
with vinegar taste. Fl-heads green, in
branching spikes. Frs vivid crimson,
May–Jun. Common everywhere, sometimes appearing in lawns. Used to flavour
sauces before lemons imported. T. [6]

Curled Dock *Rumex crispus* POLYGONACEAE
H 50–120 cm. Hairless, upright, perennial
herb. Lvs lanceolate, < 30 cm, with
undulate margins. Fls small, brown,
arranged in whorls clustered in dense
spikes, Jun–Oct. Common on wasteland,
sometimes appearing in gardens. When
dry, attractive in flower arrangements. T,
ex Ic.

Broad-leaved Dock *Rumex obtusifolius*
POLYGONACEAE H 60–100 cm. Similar to
R. crispus, but lvs broader with blunt
apex. Perennial, establishing itself in
dense clumps on wasteland, but rarely
allowed to grow in gardens. Common
everywhere. T. [7]

Good-King-Henry *Chenopodium bonus-*
henricus CHENOPODIACEAE H 20–50 cm.
Erect, perennial herb. Lvs < 10 cm,
angular, arrow-shaped, pale below, mealy
when young. Fls greenish-white, tiny, on
pyramidal, branching spike, May–Jul.
Introduced into gardens as vegetable and
frequently escaping. (T, ex Ic, from C and
S Europe.) [8]

Fat-hen *Chenopodium album* CHENOPODI-
ACEAE H 30–90 cm. Erect, mealy annual
herb, stem often red. Lvs variable in
shape, often long, rhomboid and toothed,
but always mealy-white or green. Fls
small, in greenish clusters. Abundant
weed in vegetable patches; can tolerate
drought. Seeds and leaves formerly eaten.
T, ex Ic. [9]

Love-lies-bleeding *Amaranthus caudatus*
AMARANTHACEAE H 60–90 cm. Upright,
half-hardy annual herb. Lvs ovate-
lanceolate, on long stalks. Fls in crimson
(sometimes green), drooping tassels, Jul–
Sep. Frequently grown in gardens;
sometimes escaping into wild. (W,
probably from S America.) [1]

Common Chickweed *Stellaria media*
CARYOPHYLLACEAE H 5–40 cm. Low-growing, annual herb. Stems round, with single
line of hairs. Lvs elliptical, <25 mm. Fls
small, white, with 5 strongly divided
petals giving impression of 10, all year.
Abundant everywhere, quick to colonize
bare ground in garden beds. T. [2]

Snow-in-summer *Cerastium tomentosum*
CARYOPHYLLACEAE H 15–30 cm. Prostrate,
mat-forming, perennial herb, densely
covered with silvery-white hairs. Lvs
linear-lanceolate. Fls white, 12–18 mm
across, with 5 notched petals. Vigorous

rock-garden and wall plant, often escaping
and becoming naturalized. (W, from SE
Europe, Caucasus.) [3]

Common Mouse-ear *Cerastium holoste-
oides* CARYOPHYLLACEAE H 25–30 cm.
Prostrate, somewhat hairy, perennial herb.
Lvs 10–25 mm, in pairs, blunt, without
stalks. Fls white, <15 mm, with 5 notched
petals, usually no longer than sepals, Apr–
Sep. Common weed of lawns, vegetable
patches. T. [4]

Annual Pearlwort *Sagina apetala*
CARYOPHYLLACEAE H 3–15 cm. Small,
annual herb, with procumbent to erect
stems. Lvs linear, with long, hair-like
points. Fls with petals tiny in 4s or absent,
May–Aug. Colonizes bare earth, gravel
paths, walls, cracks between stones. T,
ex Ic, Fi, No. [5]

Procumbent Pearlwort *Sagina procumbens* CARYOPHYLLACEAE H 3–20 cm.

Inconspicuous, low-growing, mat-forming, perennial herb. Lvs small, linear, narrowing abruptly to sharp point. Fls tiny, greenish-white, on long stalks. Sepals larger than petals, which sometimes absent, May–Sep. Bare, open places, grass verges, banks, streamsides; weed of lawns, rock-gardens. T. [6]

Sweet-William *Dianthus barbatus*
CARYOPHYLLACEAE H 30–70 mm. Ornamental, perennial herb with erect, hairless stems. Lvs lance-shaped, broadly elliptical. Fls scarlet, pink or white, in dense, compact heads of 3–30. Gardens everywhere, often escaping and occasionally becoming established. Fr, Cz, Po, (T, from S Europe).

Maltese-cross *Lychnis chalcedonica*
CARYOPHYLLACEAE H 30–60 cm. Erect, hairy, perennial herb. Lvs ovate, acute, clasping stem. Fls scarlet, sometimes pink or white, petals divided ⅓ of length, arranged in clusters of 10–50, Jun–Aug. Often cultivated for ornament. (W, from S Russia.) [7]

Stinking Hellebore *Helleborus foetidus*
RANUNCULACEAE H 8–15 cm. Tall, perennial herb, with stout, black, ascending stock and leafy, overwintering stems. Lvs palmately divided into narrow, toothed segments. Fls of yellow-green sepals with purple borders, petals absent, Mar–Apr. Whole plant smells fetid. Woods and scrub on calcareous soils; widely introduced into gardens, parks. Br, Fr, Lu, Ge. [8]

Winter Aconite *Eranthis hyemalis*
RANUNCULACEAE H 5–15 cm. Hairless, perennial herb. Lvs broad, palmately 3–5 lobed, produced after fls. Fls yellow, 20–30 mm, surrounded by leafy ruff, sensitive to temperature, only open < 10°C, Jan–Feb. Common in gardens, often growing wild. (W, from S Europe.) [9]

Hepatica *Hepatica nobilis* RANUNCULACEAE
H 5–15 cm. Perennial herb. Lvs apparently
arising directly from root stock, 3–lobed,
heart-shaped at base, purplish beneath,
effectively evergreen. Fls dark blue,
purple, pinkish or white, Mar–May.
Montane woods; naturalized beneath
trees in large gardens, parks. Fr, Ge, Cz,
Po, FS. [1]

Columbine *Aquilegia vulgaris*
RANUNCULACEAE H 50–100 cm. Perennial
herb, with erect, leafy, flowering stems.
Lvs twice-divided into 3-lobed segments,
bluish-green. Fls purple, blue or white,
single or double, with characteristic spurs
on sepals, May–Jun. Br, Ir, Fr, Lu, Be,
Ge, Cz, Po. [2] Other species also grown;
many hybrids with various flower colours
and long-spurred sepals.

Laurel or **Evergreen Magnolia** *Magnolia
grandiflora* MAGNOLIACEAE H < 25 m.
Evergreen tree, pyramidal or more
rounded. Lvs oval to oblong, tapering at
both ends, 15–25 cm. Fls 20–25 cm,
fragrant, white with yellow stamens, Aug–
Oct. Finest-flowered of evergreen trees,
often best grown against wall. (W, from
southeast USA.) [3]

Tulip Tree *Liriodendron tulipifera*
MAGNOLIACEAE H < 35 m. Tall, deciduous
tree with magnificent, columnar trunk.
Lvs large, saddle-shaped, with 4 distinct
points, long petioles. Fls greenish-white,
like tulips, with orange spots at bases of
petals, Jun–Jul. Common in parks, large
gardens, where golden, autumn foliage
much admired. (W, from east N America.)
[4]

Sweet Bay *Laurus nobilis* LAURACEAE
H < 15 m. Pyramidal, evergreen tree or
bush. Lvs long, leathery, dark green,
strong aromatic smell when crushed. Fls
greenish-yellow, small, arranged in clusters,
monoecious, Mar–Apr. True 'laurel' of
the ancients; used for flavouring puddings
and stews. (W, from S Europe.) [5]

Sweet Gum *Liquidamber styraciflua*
HAMAMELIDACEAE H < 25 m. Large,
pyramidal, deciduous tree with corky
wings on branches. Lvs alternate, like
maple *Acer* (but maple leaves are opposite),
15–20 cm across. ♂ fls in small, round
heads arranged in spikes, ♀ similar but
large and solitary, May. Prized for fine,
red, autumn foliage. (W, from east N
America.) [6]

Opium Poppy *Papaver somniferum*
PAPAVERACEAE H 30–100 cm. Erect, bluish-
green annual. Lvs 7–12 cm, lobed, oblong,
upper clasping stem. Fls white to purple,
with dark centres, Jun–Jul. Frs capsules,
$c7 \times 5$ cm. Cultivated since ancient times
for medicinal and narcotic latex obtained
from capsules; colonizes wasteland and
can become garden weed. (T, ex Ic, Be,
De, Fi.) [7]

Californian Poppy *Eschscholzia
californica* PAPAVERACEAE H 20–60 cm.
Annual or perennial, bluish-green herb.
Lvs much divided into linear segments.
Fls orange, yellow, red or white, 50–75
mm across. Frs capsules, narrow, long,
< 10 cm. Escapes from gardens and
naturalized. (Br, Fr, Ne, Ge, Cz, from
southwest USA.) [8]

Welsh Poppy *Meconopsis cambrica*
PAPAVERACEAE H 30–60 cm. Sparsely
hairy, perennial herb. Lvs divided into
toothed, ovate segments. Fls yellow, 50–75
mm across, on long stalks, Jun–Aug. Frs
ellipsoid capsules, < 3 cm long. Damp,
shady, rocky places; commonly cultivated
and often established as escape. Br, Ir,
Fr. [9]

Yellow Corydalis *Corydalis lutea*
PAPAVERACEAE H 15–30 cm. Hairless,
perennial herb. Lvs delicate green, much
divided, fern-like. Fls yellow, with 4
petals, upper ones spurred, arranged in
spikes of 6–10, May–Aug. Widely
cultivated, often naturalized on walls. (W,
from Alps.) [10]

Flixweed *Descurania sophia* CRUCIFERAE
H 30–80 cm. Erect, annual or overwintering herb. Lvs greyish-green, hairy,
much divided into linear segments. Fls
pale yellow, 4-petalled, c3 mm across,
Apr–Sep. Frs long, slender, cylindrical
pods, 15–25 mm, making angles with
spreading, slender stalks. Common weed
of roadsides, waste places. T. [1]

Wallflower *Cheiranthus cheri* CRUCIFERAE
H <90 cm. Biennial to perennial herb.
Lvs 2–10 cm, oblong, lanceolate, covered
with branched hairs flattened against them.
Fls c25 mm across, variable, yellows and
reds predominating, arranged in leafless
spikes. Frs 2-valved pods, <7 cm long.
Widely cultivated and naturalized on
walls, cliffs, rocks. (Br, Ir, Fr, Lu, Be, Ne,
Ge, Cz, from S Greece, Aegean islands,
where has yellow fls.) [2]

Garden Rock-cress *Arabis caucasica*
CRUCIFERAE H 15–35 cm. Perennial, mat-
forming herb. Lvs grey-green or whitish,
with 2–3 blunt teeth on each side. Fls
white, 15 mm across, Mar–May. Frs 2-
valved pods, <60 mm long, each with
prominent midrib. Widely cultivated on
rock-gardens, walls, occasionally escaping.
(Br, Fr, Be, Ne, Ge, from SE Europe.) [3]

Aubretia *Aubretia deltoidea* CRUCIFERAE
Prostrate, mat-forming, perennial herb.
Lvs hairy, variable, tongue-shaped to
rhomboid, with 1–2 teeth on each side.
Fls reddish-purple to violet, rarely white,
Apr–May. Frs short, elliptical pods, <1
cm. Widely cultivated on rock-gardens,
walls, occasionally escaping. (Br, Fr, Ne,
from S Greece, Aegean region.) [4]

Honesty *Lunaria annua* CRUCIFERAE H 30–
100 cm. Biennial or short-lived perennial
herb, with stiff, hairy stems. Lvs heart-
shaped, coarsely toothed, lower ones long-
stalked. Fls lilac, purple or white, c3 cm
across, Apr–Jun. Frs large, rounded,
conspicuous pods, often used for
decoration. Much grown in gardens,
escaping and colonizing wasteland. (W,
from SE Europe.) [5]

Golden Alyssum *Alyssum saxatile*
CRUCIFERAE H 10–40 cm. Perennial herb,
rather woody at base. Lvs greyish,
obovate to lanceolate, 7–10 cm. Fls yellow,
arranged in clusters, Apr–Jun. Frs
hairless, valves almost flat. Rocks and
stony places; commonly cultivated and
sometimes escaping to wasteland. Ge, Cz,
Po, (Br). [6]

Sweet Alison *Lobularia maritima*
CRUCIFERAE H 10–30 cm. Low-growing,
annual or perennial herb, branching from
base. Lvs narrow, greyish-green, 2–4 cm
long. Fls small, white, arranged in dense
clusters, Jun–Sep. Frs obovate, with two
1-veined valves. Widely cultivated as
bedding plant, often naturalized. (W, from
S Europe.) [7]

Common Whitlowgrass *Erophila verna*
CRUCIFERAE H 2–20 cm. Low-growing,
annual weed, with leafless stem. Lvs 10–
15 mm, elliptical, arranged in basal
rosette. Fls small, white, Feb–May. Frs
rounded to elliptical pods, on long stalks,
very variable in shape. Common on
rocks, walls, sandy and disturbed ground.
T. [8]

Shepherd's-purse *Capsella bursa-pastoris*
CRUCIFERAE H 3–40 cm. Erect, annual or
biennial herb, hairless or with unbranched
hairs. Lvs of basal rosette lanceolate,
deeply lobed; upper ones less divided,
clasping stem. Fls white, 2·5 mm across,
all year. Frs pods, shaped like triangular
purses. Garden beds, paths, waysides,
waste ground everywhere. T. [9]

Garden Cress *Lepidium sativum*
CRUCIFERAE H 20–40 cm. Annual herb
with single, erect stem. Basal lvs deeply
cut into toothed lobes; upper linear,
stalkless. Fls small, white, 6 mm across,
Jun–Jul. Frs hairless, 5–6 mm, elliptical
with narrow wings. Commonly grown in
gardens, often escaping and widely
naturalized. Seed-lf, eaten in 'mustard
and cress', deeply 3-lobed. (T, ex Ir, Ic,
from Asia.) [10]

House-leek *Sempervivum tectorum*
CRASSULACEAE Perennial herb, with
rosettes of fleshy, short- or unstalked,
hairless lvs, 3–4 cm across. Fls star-like,
pale reddish, clustered on stout stems,
30–60 cm, Jun–Jul. Grown in gardens,
esp on old walls, roofs. Fr, Ge, (W, from
S Europe). [1]

Biting Stonecrop *Sedum acre*
CRASSULACEAE H 2–10 cm. Hairless,
creeping, yellowish-green, evergreen
perennial. Lvs small, 3–5 mm, fleshy,
triangular, blunt, without stalks. Fls
yellow, star-like, <12 mm across, in
branched inflor, Jun–Jul. Tastes hot and
acrid. Often cultivated. T. [2]

White Stonecrop *Sedum album*
CRASSULACEAE H 7–15 cm. Hairless,
creeping, bright green, evergreen
perennial. Lvs 6–12 mm, fleshy, oblong,
blunt, without stalks. Fls white, <9 mm
across, in much-branched, reddish-
stemmed, flat-topped inflor, Jun–Aug.
Rocks, walls; commonly planted in
gardens, can form dense covering on old
walls. T, ex Ic, (Ir). [3]

stonecrop *Sedum spectabile* CRASSULACEAE
H <60 cm. Erect, hairless, perennial herb.
Lvs large, fleshy, oval, whitish-green. Fls
rosy-purple, arranged in dense heads,
Aug–Oct. Grows well on old walls where
plenty of lime. Excellent for attracting
butterflies, bees and hoverflies in late
summer, autumn. (W, from China.) [4]

Reflexed Stonecrop *Sedum reflexum*
CRASSULACEAE H 5–15 cm. Creeping,
succulent, evergreen perennial. Lvs
cylindrical, linear, <20 mm, on ascending
stems. Fls yellow, in clusters on reddish
stems, Jun–Aug. Common on rocks,
walls; often planted in rock-gardens. T,
ex Ic, (Br, Ir). [5]

London Plane *Platanus* × *hybrida*
PLATANACEAE H <35 m. Large, deciduous
tree with bark flaking to reveal big, yellow

patches. Lvs <25 cm, with 3–5 pointed
lobes. Fls in unisexual, spherical heads,
May. Fr-heads *c*25 mm across, usually
paired. Possible hybrid between Oriental
plane *P. orientalis* and American plane
P. occidentalis, originated S Europe *c*1700.
Common in town parks, remarkably
resistant to pollution and city life. (W.)
[6]

Willow Spiraea or **Bridewort** *Spiraea*
salicifolia ROSACEAE H 1–2 m. Rather
small, deciduous shrub with erect,
suckering stems. Lvs 3–7 cm, elliptical.
hairless, sharply or sometimes doubly
toothed. Fls pink, *c*8 mm across, densely
aggregated in terminal heads, Jun–Sep.
Naturally in scrub; commonly grown in
gardens for decoration, planted in hedges.
Cz, Po, (W, from C Europe). [7]

Bramble, Blackberry *Rubus fruticosus*
ROSACEAE H<4 m. Woody perennial with
biennial, trailing, prickly stems. Lvs 3- or
5-lobed. Fls white to deep pink, <3 cm
across, in terminal clusters, May–Sep. Frs
edible, in fleshy, juicy segments, black
when ripe. Extremely variable: *c*2000
microspp recognized in Europe; cultivars
grown in gardens for fruit. Abundant as
wild plant, except far north. T, ex Ic. [8]

Shrubby Cinquefoil *Potentilla fruticosa*
ROSACEAE H <1 m. Deciduous, much-
branched, woody shrub. Lvs with,
usually, elliptical lflets 1–2 cm long. Fls
bright yellow with 5 petals, solitary or few
in terminal cluster, Jun–Jul. Several vars
commonly grown in gardens, one with red
flowers. Native on damp rocks in some
mountain areas. Br, Ir, Fr, Sw. [9]

Hawthorn *Crataegus monogyna* ROSACEAE
H <10 m. Prickly, woody shrub or tree.
Lvs <3·5 cm, obovate to rhomboid, 3- to
7-lobed. Fls single or double, white or
pink, <15 mm across, May–Jun. Frs red
berries, autumn, much eaten by birds.
Widespread hedging plant, also grown as
trees in gardens. T, ex Ic.

Quince *Cydonia oblonga* ROSACEAE H 1·5–6 m. Deciduous shrub or small tree. Lvs <10 cm, oval, hairless above. Fls pink, 4–5 cm across, Apr–May. Frs <10 cm, pear-shaped, woody, green becoming yellow on ripening. Cultivated most of Europe for frs, edible when cooked; naturalized Fr, Ge, Cz, (W, from Asia.) [1]

Pear *Pyrus communis* ROSACEAE H <15 m. Deciduous, broadly pyramidal tree. Lvs <6 cm, oval, rather shiny green. Fls white, <3 cm across, in umbel-like clusters, Apr–May (earlier than apple *Malus domestica*). Frs <15 cm, brownish, sweet-tasting. Common in suburban gardens, cultivated in orchards since ancient times; many vars developed. (T, native distribution unknown.) [2]

Apple *Malus domestica* ROSACEAE H <10 m. Deciduous tree, with dense, round crown. Lvs oval, downy, 3–4 cm long. Fls white, <4 cm across, in umbel-like clusters, May. Frs >5 cm, varying in colour, taste acid to sweet. Widely cultivated, often escaping, occasionally naturalized; many vars developed with different tasting and textured frs. (T.) [3]

Swedish Whitebeam *Sorbus intermedia* ROSACEAE H <10 m. Deciduous tree. Lvs simple, toothed, dark yellowish-green above, grey and hairy beneath. Fls white, 10–15 mm across, May. Frs scarlet berries, longer than broad, 12–15 mm. Genus includes common whitebeam *S. aria*, with simple, often lobed leaves, and rowan *S. aucuparia*, with pinnate leaves; many species introduced into towns and gardens, but this one of the commonest in parks, by roadways. Po, FS, (W.) [4]

Plum *Prunus domestica* ROSACEAE H 2–6 m. Deciduous tree, suckering freely. Lvs elliptical, <10 cm. Fls white, <2·5 cm, appearing with lvs, Apr–May. Frs edible, <8 cm in cultivated forms, very variable, including bullace and greengage. (T, ex Ic, native distribution unknown, probably always derived from cultivated sources.) [5]

Almond *Prunus dulcis* ROSACEAE H <8 m. Deciduous tree or shrub. Lvs lanceolate, <12 cm, hairless, with toothed margins. Fls pink, c4 cm across, in pairs, appear before lvs, Mar–Apr. Frs grey-green, covered with velvety down. Cultivated for edible seeds S Europe, for decorative fls farther north. (W, from Asia, N Africa.) [6]

Dwarf Cherry *Prunus cerasus* ROSACEAE H <7 m. Shrub or small tree, suckering freely. Lvs <8 cm, elliptical, finely and often doubly toothed, hairless. Fls white, in groups of 2–6, often double, Apr–May. Frs round, bright red, sour. Cultivated for fruit, sometimes planted for hedges. (W, from SW Asia.) [7]

ornamental cherry *Prunus sargentii* ROSACEAE H <15 m. Round-headed tree. Lvs lanceolate, <15 cm, long-pointed, sharply toothed, bright red when young. Fls pink, <5 cm across, single, in clusters, Mar–Apr. Frs small, black. Cultivated for mass of early flowers and red autumn foliage. (W.) [8]

Laurel *Prunus laurocerasus* ROSACEAE H <6 m. Vigorous, spreading, evergreen shrub. Lvs <13 cm, elliptical-oblong, leathery, dark shining green. Fls white, c15 mm across, fragrant, on erect, short spikes, Apr–Jun. Frs c8 mm, egg-shaped, purplish-black. Commonly planted for screening. (W, from Balkans.) [9]

Serviceberry *Amelanchier grandiflora*
ROSACEAE H 9 m. Deciduous shrub or
small tree. Lvs broadly elliptical, 7 cm,
heart-shaped at base, finely toothed. Fls
white, 2 cm, wide-spaced petals in slender,
nodding clusters, Apr–May. Frs red-
purple, fleshy, sweet. Of garden origin,
often cultivated for ornament. (Br, Fr,
Be, Ne, Ge.) [1]

cotoneaster *Cotoneaster microphyllus*
ROSACEAE H < 1 m. Evergreen, dwarf,
spreading shrub. Lvs small, 5–8 mm,
blunt, glossy. Fls white, $c1$ cm across,
May–Jun. Frs bright red berries, autumn.
Grown for ornament; bird sown and
naturalized, esp on limestone near sea.
(Br, Ir, from Himalayas.) [2]

firethorn *Pyracantha coccinea* ROSACEAE
H < 6 m. Densely branched, spiny, evergreen shrub or tree. Lvs elliptical,
hairless, 2–4 cm, toothed. Fls white, $c7$
mm across, in downy clusters, Jun. Frs
bright red berries, 7–10 mm, in dense
bunches. (Br, Fr, from S Europe.) [3]

Tree-of-Heaven *Ailanthus altissima*
SIMAROUBACEAE H < 20 m. Deciduous
tree, with smooth, grey bark, suckering
freely. Lvs 45–60 cm, pinnate, with 13–25
ovate lflets, red later green. Fls small,
greenish, Jul–Aug. ♀ trees produce large
bunches of red-brown, 'key'-like fruits.
Planted as ornamental, widely naturalized.
(Br, Fr, Lu, Be, Ge, Cz, from China.) [4]

Sycamore *Acer pseudoplatanus* ACERACEAE
H < 30 m. Large, spreading, fast-growing,
deciduous tree. Lvs with 5 coarsely
toothed lobes, red stalks. Fls yellowish-
green, $c6$ mm across, in long, pendulous
spikes, Apr–Jun. Frs with 2 membranous
wings, hanging in bunches. Widely
naturalized. Fr, Ge, (T, ex Ic, Fi, No). [5]

Ash-leaved Maple, Box-elder *Acer
negundo* ACERACEAE H < 20 m. Small,
deciduous tree. Lvs pinnate, with $c7$ oval
lflets. Fls greenish, without petals,
opening before lvs, Mar–Apr. Frs
hairless, in long clusters, pairs of wings
diverging at acute angle. Widely planted,
esp variegated var with white and green
lvs. (W, from east N America.) [6]

Smooth Japanese Maple *Acer palmatum*
ACERACEAE H < 6 m. Small, round-topped
tree. Lvs with 5–9 lobes, bright green,
occasionally purple. Fls purple, in erect,
stalked clusters, Apr–May. Frs winged,
$c15$ mm long. Commonly grown for
ornament; cultivated vars have red, orange
or yellow foliage. (W, from Japan, China,
Korea.) [7]

Horse-chestnut *Aesculus hippocastanum*
HIPPOCASTANACEAE H < 30 m. Erect,
domed, deciduous tree, with resinous
'sticky' buds. Lvs palmate, with 5–7 ovate
lflets. Fls clustered in white 'candles',
May. Frs shiny brown nuts (familiar as
'conkers') in prickly, green husks.
Common in parks, gardens. Hybrid with
red flowers ($\times$ *hybrida*) also widely
grown. (Br, Ir, Fr, Ge, Cz, from S
Europe.) [8]

Holly *Ilex aquifolium* AQUIFOLIACEAE
H < 10 m. Evergreen tree or shrub. Lvs
prickly, dark shiny green above, paler
beneath. Fls white, small, < 8 mm across,
Jun. ♀ trees produce bright red berries,
late autumn–winter. Native; also planted
in gardens, parks, hedges, including
cultivars with less prickly or variegated
lvs. Br, Ir, Fr, Lu, Be, Ne, De, Ge, No.

flowering currant *Ribes sanguineum*
GROSSULARIACEAE H < 2 m. Deciduous
shrub. Fls red or pink, in pendulous
clusters, Mar–Apr. Frs small, black,
inedible, late summer. Lvs and growth
form similar to red/black currant
R. rubrum/nigrum, grown for edible frs.
Common in suburban gardens, sometimes
naturalized. (W, from W America.)

Box *Buxus sempervirens* BUXACEAE H < 6
m. Evergreen shrub or small tree. Lvs
small, oval, shiny dark green. Fls without
petals, in clusters, ♀ at top, ♂ below,
greenish-white, Apr–May. Frs papery
capsules, Sep. Dry soils; also commonly
planted in gardens, used in hedges. Br,
Fr, Lu, Be, Ge. [9]

Laburnum *Laburnum anagyroides*
LEGUMINOSAE H <7 m. Small tree, with
smooth bark. Lvs of 3 elliptical lflets,
long-stalked, hairy beneath. Fls yellow,
*c*20 mm, in long, pendulous panicles,
May–Jun. Frs pods, 3–5 cm, remain on
tree through winter; seeds black. Whole
plant poisonous. Mountains; planted for
ornament, occasionally as hedges. Fr, Ge,
(Br, Ir). [1]

garden lupin *Lupinus polyphyllus*
LEGUMINOSAE H <150 cm. Silky-haired,
robust, perennial herb. Lvs palmate, with
10 or more lflets. Fls 16 mm, blue, yellow,
purple or pink, arranged in large spikes.
Frs hairy pods, 30–50 mm. Popular
herbaceous border sp, often escaping to
wasteland. (Fr, Ne, Ge, Cz, Po, SC, from
west N America.) [2]

False Acacia, Locust *Robinia pseudacacia*
LEGUMINOSAE H <25 m. Deciduous tree,
with coarsely fissured bark, suckering
freely. Lvs pinnate, with 3–10 pairs of
elliptical lflets. Fls white, *c*20 mm, in long,
hanging spikes, Jun. Long, hanging seed-
pods conspicuous in winter. Several vars,
notably 'Frisia' with beautiful orange-
yellow foliage. Extensively naturalized.
(Br, Fr, Lu, Be, Ne, Ge, Cz, from N
America.) [3]

Bladder-senna *Colutea arborescens*
LEGUMINOSAE H <6 m. Much-branched,
deciduous shrub. Lvs pinnate, with 4–5
pairs of broadly elliptical lflets. Fls yellow,
*c*20 mm, in 2–8 flowered spikes. Frs much
inflated pods, <7 cm. Dry woods; grown
in gardens, often escaping. Used as
substitute for senna pods. Fr, Ge, Cz, (Br,
Lu, Be). [4]

Everlasting Pea *Lathyrus latifolius*
LEGUMINOSAE H <2 m. Robust, climbing
perennial with winged or angled stems
and lf-stalks. Lvs with 2 ovate lflets, <15
cm, 5-veined. Fls 2–3 cm, bright, deep
pink. Frs hairless pods, 5–11 cm. Scrub,
woodland margins; grown as ornamental
in gardens. Fr, Ge, Cz, Po, (Br). [5]

White Clover *Trifolium repens*
LEGUMINOSAE Low-growing, creeping,
hairless, perennial herb, rooting at nodes.
Lvs of 3 elliptical lflets, usually marked
with white band on upperside. Fls white
or pink, in globular heads, <3 cm, Jun–
Sep. Abundant on grassland everywhere;
often in lawns. T. [6]

Red Clover *Trifolium pratense*
LEGUMINOSAE H <60 cm. Spreading or
erect, somewhat hairy perennial. Lvs of 3
elliptical lflets, with white, crescent-
shaped spot near base. Fls purplish-pink,
in globular heads, <3 cm, May–Sep.
Abundant in grassland everywhere. T.

Yellow-sorrel *Oxalis corniculata*
OXALIDACEAE Creeping, hairy perennial
herb, rooting at nodes. Lvs purplish, on
long stalks <8 cm, of 3 lflets *c*10 mm.
Fls yellow, small, <15 mm, Jun–Sep. Frs
cylindrical, hairy capsules. Garden weed,
spreading by overground stems and seed.
Dry, open habitats. (Br, Ir, Lu, Be, Ne,
Ge, Cz, Po, FS, from S Europe.) [7]

Pink Oxalis *Oxalis corymbosa* OXALIDACEAE
H 5–15 cm. Hairy, perennial herb,
produced from subterranean bulb which
develops into mass of bulbils. Lvs of 3
lflets, lobes rounded with deep, narrow,
terminal notch. Fls purplish-pink, <3 cm,
Jul–Sep. Frs unknown in Europe; bulbils
enable rapid spread over bare earth. (Br,
Fr, from S America.) [8]

Petty Spurge *Euphorbia peplus*
EUPHORBIACEAE H 10–30 cm. Hairless,
erect, annual herb; cut stems produce
milky latex. Lvs oval, blunt, <3 cm. Fls
green, in clusters, lack petals and sepals:
single 3-styled ♀ fl and several 1-anthered
♂s, all on green bract. Common garden
weed. T, ex Ic. [9]

Virginia Creeper *Parthenocissus quinquefolia* VITACEAE H <30 m. Common wall climber, with long tendrils, grown for scarlet and orange autumn foliage. Lvs large, 5–10 cm, 3- to 7-lobed. Fls in terminal clusters, Jul–Aug. Frs black, globose, c6 mm. Common on older buildings, walls, surrounding gardens. (W, from east USA.) Now largely replaced on houses by 'Boston ivy' *P. tricuspidata*, with 3-lobed leaves. (W, from Japan, China, Korea.) [1]

Lime *Tilia* × *europaea* TILIACEAE H <45 m. Spreading, deciduous tree. Lvs heart-shaped at base, pointed above, <10 cm long. Fls yellow-white, in pendulous clusters, fragrant, Jun–Jul. Frs rounded, pubescent, slightly ribbed. Hybrid between 2 native European trees, large-leaved lime *T. platyphyllos* and small-leaved lime *T. cordata*. Commonest lime in towns, often grown in long rows beside roads. In summer, leaves and shoots support many aphids and become covered with sticky honeydew. (W.) [2]

Rose-of-Sharon *Hypericum calycinum* GUTTIFERAE H <60 cm. Extensively creeping, evergreen shrub. Lvs elliptical, 5–10 cm, scented when crushed. Fls yellow, solitary, each with 5 petals and sepals, many stamens, Jul–Sep. Common ornamental in gardens, sometimes escaping to wasteland. (Br, Ir, Fr, from Bulgaria, Turkey.) [3]

Common Rock-rose *Helianthemum chamaecistus* CISTACEAE H 5–30 cm. Low-growing, perennial herb. Lvs <2 cm, oblong, green above, white and hairy below. Fls yellow, with 5 petals, c25 mm across, Jul–Sep. Vars grown in rock-gardens are hybrids, may be single- or double-flowered, and white, pink, scarlet or crimson. T, ex Ic, No.

Large-flowered Evening-primrose *Oenothera erythrosepala* ONAGRACEAE H 50–100 cm. Biennial herb; erect, robust, leafy stem covered in long hairs with red, bulbous bases. Lvs elliptical, stalked, strongly crinkled. Fls yellow, <7 cm across, opening suddenly at dusk, Jun–

Sep. Frs capsules, <4 cm, tapering upwards. Weed of gardens, wasteland; now naturalized. (Br, Fr, Lu, Be, De, Ge, Cz, Po, from N America.) [4]

Rosebay Willowherb *Epilobium angustifolium* ONAGRACEAE H 30–120 cm. Robust perennial, with long, spreading roots, producing erect, leafy stems. Lvs alternate, long, narrow, 5–15 cm. Fls pink, 2–3 cm across, arranged in long, dense spikes, Jul–Sep. Frs capsules, <8 cm, splitting to release white-plumed, wind-borne seeds. Persistent weed in gardens, wasteland. T. [5]

Cornelian Cherry *Cornus mas* CORNACEAE H <8 m. Shrub or small tree with greenish-brown twigs. Lvs in opposite pairs, ovate, <10 cm. Fls yellow, *c*5 mm across, arranged in flat-topped clusters, Feb. Frs ellipsoid, scarlet, edible. Woods, scrub; cultivated for ornament and edible frs. Fr, Lu, Be, Ge, Cz, (Br). [6]

Red-barked Dogwood *Cornus alba* CORNACEAE H <3 m. Shrub with crimson young stems. Lvs elliptical, 4–8 cm. Fls yellowish-white, *c*10 mm across, Jun. Frs ellipsoid, *c*8 mm, white. Common in gardens, parks, where cultivated for autumn foliage and winter stem colour; occasionally naturalized. (Br, Sw, No, from Korea, N China.) [7]

Spotted Laurel *Aucuba japonica* CORNACEAE H <6 m. Evergreen shrub, forming dense, round bush. Lvs tough, toothed, usually spotted with yellow in ♀ plants. Fls dark purple, 8 mm across, in axillary clusters, Apr. Frs red berries. One of commonest shrubs used for winter screening in gardens. (W, from E Asia.) [8]

Ivy *Hedera helix* ARALIACEAE H 30 m. Woody evergreen, either spreading across ground or climbing trees and walls. Lvs of 2 kinds: of non-flowering shoots 3- to 5-lobed, of flowering shoots elliptical. Fls yellowish-green, <10 mm across, arranged in umbels, Sep–Nov. Frs black berries, with 2–3 seeds. Many vars in cultivation. T, ex Ic, Fi.

Coriander *Coriandrum sativum*
UMBELLIFERAE H 20–70 cm. Erect, annual
herb with ridged, hairless stems. Lvs
simply or twice pinnate, with ovate
segments. Fls white or pink, in umbels
1–3 cm across with 3–5 rays, Jun. Frs
hard, red-brown, globose. Cultivated for
aromatic frs; widely naturalized in S
Europe. (Fr, Ge, Cz, Po, from N Africa,
W Asia.) [1]

Ground-elder *Aegopodium podagraria*
UMBELLIFERAE H 40–100 cm. Hairless,
low-growing perennial with far-creeping,
underground stems. Lvs simply or twice
ternate, segments 4–8 cm. Fls white, in
umbels 2–6 cm across with 15–20 rays,
May–Jul. Frs 4 mm, oval. Common in
woods and hedges; often forms dense
patches, difficult to eradicate once
established in gardens. T, (Ic, Br, Ir). [2]

Fool's Parsley *Aethusa cynapium*
UMBELLIFERAE H 5–200 cm. Hairless,
annual, sometimes biennial herb. Lvs like
parsley *Petroselinum crispum*. Fls white, in
umbels, with long, green, downward-
pointed bracts, Jul–Aug. Frs 3–4 mm,
ovoid, ridged. Weed of cultivated land,
river banks, gardens. T, ex Ic. [3]

Garden Parsley *Petroselinum crispum*
UMBELLIFERAE H 30–75 cm. Erect, hairless,
biennial herb, with ascending branches.
Lvs crisped, much divided, with characteristic aroma. Fls yellow, in umbels 2–5 cm
across with 8–15 rays, Jun–Aug. Frs
$c2 \cdot 5$ mm, oval. Commonly grown as herb
for flavouring food; occasionally garden
escape, colonizing old walls. (T, ex Ic,
Ne, Fi, from SE Europe, W Asia.) [4]

Wild Parsnip *Pastinaca sativa*
UMBELLIFERAE H 30–150 cm. Erect, hairy,
biennial herb with characteristic smell.
Lvs simply pinnate into oval, lobed,
toothed segments. Fls yellow in umbels
3–10 cm across with 5–15 rays, Jul–Aug.
Frs 5–8 mm, oval. Widespread and
common. Vars with sweet, fleshy roots
grown as vegetables. T, ex Ic, but only
escape from cultivation in far north.
[5]

Giant Hogweed *Heracleum mantegaz-
zianum* UMBELLIFERAE H 2–5 m. Very
large, robust, biennial or perennial herb,
with stems < 10 cm thick, red-spotted.
Lvs < 1 m, pinnate. Fls white, in umbels
< 50 cm across with 50–150 rays, Jun–
Jul. Frs c13 mm, elliptical. Sometimes
grown as curiosity in town parks, large
gardens; naturalized in wasteland, often
near rivers. When touched, sensitizes skin
to sun, causing blistering. (Br, Ir, Fr, Ne,
De, Ge, Cz, FS, from SW Asia.) [6]

Fennel *Foeniculum vulgare* UMBELLIFERAE
H 60–250 cm. Erect, hairless, biennial or
perennial herb. Lvs feathery, with
characteristic strong smell. Fls yellow, in
umbels 4–8 cm across with 10–30 rays,
Jul–Oct. Frs 4–6 mm, ovoid. Grown in
gardens as flavouring for food. Wasteland,
as escape from cultivation. (T, ex Ic, FS,
probably native only near coasts of S
and SW Europe.)

Azalea *Rhododendron luteum* ERICACEAE
H 2–3 m. Medium-sized, deciduous shrub,
belonging to largest genus of woody plants
grown in parks, gardens. Lvs oblong, 7–10
cm, turning crimson, orange and purple
in autumn. Fls yellow, funnel-shaped,
< 5 cm across, arranged in rounded
clusters, May. Wet, coniferous woods;
one of commonest species in cultivation
for fls and lvs. (W, from E Europe.) [7]

Ash *Fraxinus excelsior* OLEACEAE H <40 m. Deciduous tree, with smooth, grey bark when young. Lvs opposite, pinnate, <13 lflets, black buds. Fls purplish, without petals or sepals, appearing before lvs, Apr–May. Frs winged 'keys', <5 cm. Cultivars, including weeping 'Pendula', common in town parks, large gardens. T, ex Ic, Fi.

Mana, Flowering Ash *Fraxinus ornus* OLEACEAE H <20 m. Deciduous tree, with smooth, blackish bark. Lvs opposite, pinnate, <7 lflets, brownish buds. Fls white, with petals and sepals, appearing with lvs, May. Frs <25 mm. Native rocky woods; introduced long ago, now common in gardens, parks. Cz, (W, from S Europe). [1]

Lilac *Syringa vulgaris* OLEACEAE H <7 m. Deciduous tree or shrub, suckering freely. Lvs opposite, heart-shaped, 5–12 cm. Fls lilac or white, arranged in large, pyramidal clusters, fragrant. Many vars grown: variable colours, double or single fls. Common in suburban gardens and parks, sometimes established on wasteland. (Br, Ir, Fr, Be, Ge, Cz, from Balkans.) [2]

Privet *Ligustrum vulgare* OLEACEAE H <5 m. Partially evergreen shrub. Lvs opposite, lanceolate, 3–6 cm. Fls white, short-stalked, 4–5 mm, fragrant. Frs berries, 6–8 mm, black. Woodland margins and scrub, esp on limy soils. No longer common privet of garden hedges, having been replaced by broad-leaved privet. T, ex Ic, De.

Broad-leaved Privet *Ligustrum ovalifolium* OLEACEAE H <5 m. Similar to native *L. vulgare*, but more persistent evergreen. Lvs broader and larger; yellow-leafed var commonly grown in hedges. In many areas, now commoner privet, remarkably tolerant of pollution and town life. (W, from Japan.) [3]

Greater Periwinkle *Vinca major* APOCYNACEAE H <30 cm. Low-growing, trailing, evergreen shrub; spreads by forming new roots from tips of downward-pointing shoots. Lvs shiny green, opposite, ovate, 2–7 cm. Fls purplish-blue, solitary, 4–5 cm across, Apr–Jun. Frs of 2 spreading carpels. Common in parks and large gardens, occasionally escaping. (Br, Ir, from S Europe.) [4]

Large Bindweed *Calystegia sylvatica* CONVOLVULACEAE H 1–3 m. Hairless, climbing, perennial herb, with far-creeping, underground stems. Lvs lanceolate, <15 cm. Fls white or purplish, solitary, trumpet-shaped, 5–9 cm, Jul–Sep. Frs capsules, 7–12 mm. Attractive weed, often difficult to eradicate. Common, esp in old gardens, wasteland. (Br, Ir, Fr, from S Europe.) [5]

Common Comfrey *Symphytum officinale* BORAGINACEAE H 30–120 cm. Hairy, perennial herb, with wings from lvs running down stem. Lvs lanceolate, <25 cm. Fls cream or carmine, 12–15 mm, in terminal clusters, May–Sep. Native of damp, grassy places. T, ex SC. Plant cultivated in gardens, source of nitrogen-rich compost, is Russian comfrey *S.* × *uplandicum*, hybrid between *S. officinale* and *S. asperum*. [6]

Soft Comfrey *Symphytum orientale* BORAGINACEAE H <70 cm. Erect, softly hairy, branched, perennial herb. Lvs oblong, <14 cm, shortly stalked. Fls white, funnel-shaped, 15–17 mm, in terminal clusters, Apr–May. Native of damp, shady places; in gardens, sometimes escaping to wasteland. (Br, Fr, from Turkey, SW Ukraine.)

Wood Forget-me-not *Myosotis sylvatica* BORAGINACEAE H 15–45 cm. Erect, hairy perennial. Lvs <8 cm, lower ones long and narrow, forming rosette, stem lvs lanceolate. Fls pale blue, <8 mm across, arranged in long spikes which elongate after flowering, May–Jun. Woodlands; commonly grown in herbaceous borders and rock-gardens. T, ex Ic, Ir, Fi. [7]

Cat-mint *Nepeta cataria* LABIATAE
H 40–100 cm. Erect, hairy, much-
branched, perennial herb. Lvs 3–7 cm,
strongly scented, silvery-grey, with
coarsely serrate margins. Fls white with
small purple spots, c12 mm long, Jul–Sep.
Banks, roadsides, wasteland; usual plant
of garden borders is hybrid with pale
lavender flowers. T, ex Ic. [1]

Henbit Dead-nettle *Lamium amplexicaule*
LABIATAE H 5–25 cm. Finely hairy, square-
stemmed, annual herb. Lvs opposite, round,
blunt-toothed, <25 mm; upper lvs clasp
stem. Fls purplish-pink, c15 mm long, Apr–
Aug. Also produces small, self-pollinated
fls which do not open. Common weed in
garden beds, gravel paths. T, ex Ic. [2]

Spotted Dead-nettle *Lamium maculatum*
LABIATAE H 15–80 cm. Hairy, erect,
perennial, square-stemmed, extensively
creeping underground. Lvs 2–5 cm,
greenish or purplish, spotted white. Fls
pinkish-purple, 10–18 mm long, May–
Oct. Woods; cultivated for decorative
foliage in rock-gardens, but soon spreads
as weed. T, ex Br, Ir, Ic, SC. [3]

Spear Mint *Mentha spicata* LABIATAE
H 30–90 cm. Erect, branched, hairless,
perennial herb with characteristic mint
smell. Lvs lanceolate, short-stalked, <9
cm. Fls pale lilac, in long, slender, cylindrical spikes, 3–6 cm, Aug–Sep. Widely
cultivated as herb; commonest mint
grown in gardens; widely naturalized. (T,
ex Ic, Fi, origin unknown.) [4]

Duke of Argyll's Teaplant *Lycium
barbarum* SOLANACEAE H <3 m. Spiny,
deciduous shrub; arching, greyish-tinged
branches. Lvs lanceolate, <6 cm, grey-
green. Fls rose-purple, turning pale
brown, <1 cm across, funnel-shaped,
solitary or in small clusters, May–Sep.
Frs scarlet berries, <2 cm. Widely
grown as hedges, naturalized in much of
Europe. (T, ex Ic, Fi, from China.) [5]

Bittersweet *Solanum dulcamara*
SOLANACEAE H <2 m. Scrambling, woody

perennial. Lvs <8 cm, ovate, with 1–4
deep lobes on stalked segments at base.
Fls purple with yellow centres, c1 cm
across, Jun–Sep. Frs red berries, tomato-
like, many-seeded, c1 cm. Native of
shingle beaches, hedges, wet woods;
can reach top of 10 m tree. T, ex Ic.

Black Nightshade *Solanum nigrum*
SOLANACEAE H <70 cm. Somewhat hairy,
prostrate or erect, annual herb. Lvs ovate
or rhomboid, <7 cm. Fls white with
yellow centres, 10–14 mm, Jun–Sep. Frs
conspicuous berries, at first green, black
when ripe. Frequent garden weed, quick
to colonize bare spaces. T, ex Ic.

Thorn-apple *Datura stramonium*
SOLANACEAE H <1 m. Erect, almost
hairless, annual herb. Lvs elliptical,
toothed or lobed, <18 cm. Fls white or
purple, trumpet-shaped, <10 cm, Jul–
Oct. Frs spiny capsules, many-seeded, 4–5
cm long, splitting into 4 valves. Very
poisonous. Seeds can remain dormant for
many years, plants sometimes appearing
unexpectedly in gardens. Widely
naturalized except far north. (T, ex Ir, Ic,
Fi, from America.) [6]

Small Tobacco *Nicotiana rustica*
SOLANACEAE H <1·5 m. Erect, hairy,
sticky, annual herb. Lvs heart-shaped,
<15 cm. Fls greenish-yellow, 12–17 mm,
arranged in dense, many-flowered terminal
clusters, Jun–Aug. Frs capsules, 7–16 mm.
Formerly cultivated for tobacco, locally
naturalized. (Fr, Be, Ne, Ge, Cz, from
S America.) [7]. Other *Nicotiana* spp
common herbaceous border plants.

Butterfly-bush *Buddleja davidii*
BUDDLEJACEAE H 1–5 m. Fast-growing,
deciduous shrub. Lvs lanceolate, toothed,
dark green above, grey and hairy beneath,
<25 cm. Fls blue, purple, red-purple or
white, in dense, many-flowered panicles,
10–30 cm, very attractive to butterflies,
Jun–Oct. Widely cultivated, frequently
escaping and naturalizing. (Br, Ir, Fr, Lu,
Be, Ne, Ge, from China.) [8]

Snapdragon *Antirrhinum majus*
SCROPHULARIACEAE H 30–80 cm. Erect,
short-lived perennial, often woody at
base. Widely grown, many cultivars
developed; naturalized. (Br, Ir, Lu, Be,
Ne, Ge, Cz, from SW Europe.) [1]

Purple Toadflax *Linaria purpurea*
SCROPHULARIACEAE H 30–90 cm. Erect,
hairless, bluish-green perennial, branched
above. Lvs narrow, <45 mm. Fls
spurred, purple-violet, $c8$ mm, in dense
spikes, Jun–Aug. Frs capsules, longer than
calyx. Cultivated; naturalized old walls,
wasteland. (Br, Ir, from Italy, Sicily.) [2]

Ivy-leaved Toadflax *Cymbalaria muralis*
SCROPHULARIACEAE Trailing, hairless
perennial, with stems <60 cm. Lvs like
ivy *Hedera helix*, 5-lobed, alternate, <25
mm. Fls lilac and yellow, short-spurred,
8–10 mm, May–Sep. Frs spherical capsules.
Cultivated; widely naturalized old walls.
(T, ex Ic, Fi, from S Europe.) [3]

Blood-drop Emlets *Mimulus luteus*
SCROPHULARIACEAE H 20–50 cm. Hairless
perennial, with trailing stems. Lvs
opposite, shiny green, ovate, toothed, 1–7
cm. Fls 2-lipped, with long tube, hairy in
throat, yellow with red 'blood drops',
Jun–Sep. Cultivated; naturalized locally,
by streams. (Br, from Chile.) [4] Monkey-
flower *M. guttatus*, yellow with smaller
red spots, widely naturalized.

Ivy-leaved Speedwell *Veronica
hederifolia* SCROPHULARIACEAE H 10–60 cm.
Hairy, annual herb. Lvs shaped like ivy
Hedera helix, <15 mm. Fls pale lilac,
solitary, 4–9 mm across, Apr–May.
Common in cultivated ground, except
arctic. T, ex Ic. [5] *Veronica* spp
have opposite lvs, 4 petals, usually 4
sepals.

Common Field-speedwell *Veronica
persica* SCROPHULARIACEAE H 10–60 cm.
Trailing annual, branching from base,
with hairy stems. Lvs oval, coarsely
toothed, light green, hairy on veins below.
Fls blue, solitary, 8–12 mm across, all
year. Frs capsules, divergent lobes. Widely
naturalized. (T, from SW Asia.) [6]

Slender Speedwell *Veronica filiformis*
SCROPHULARIACEAE. Slender, creeping
perennial, often forming dense mats. Lvs
kidney-shaped with shallow lobes, $c5$ mm.
Fls pale lilac-blue, solitary, <15 mm
across, Apr–Jun. Frs rare. Grown in rock-
gardens, widespread weed in lawns. (T,
ex Ic, Fi, No, from W Asia.) [7]

Fairy Foxglove *Erinus alpinus*
SCROPHULARIACEAE H 5–15 cm. Tufted
perennial, with ascending hairy stems.
Lvs oval or tongue-shaped, toothed, lower
ones forming basal rosette. Fls pink
with 5 almost equal petal lobes, May–
Oct. Grown in rock-gardens, escaping.
(Br, Ir, from S Europe.) [8]

Indian Bean *Catalpa bignonioides*
BIGNONIACEAE H <15 m. Round-headed,
wide-spreading, deciduous tree. Lvs
broadly ovate, heart-shaped at base, <25
cm, hairy beneath, with unpleasant odour
when crushed. Fls white with yellow and
purple spots, <4 cm, Jul–Aug. Frs pods,
<35 cm, pencil-shaped. Planted in parks,
gardens. (W, from east USA.) [9]

Ribwort Plantain *Plantago lanceolata*
PLANTAGINACEAE H <40 cm. Usually
hairless, perennial herb. Lvs in rosette,
lanceolate, ribbed, <15 cm. Fls brownish,
4-petalled, $c4$ mm, in spike on long stalk,
Apr–Aug. Grassland except far north;
common garden weed, esp on old lawns,
and important fodder plant. T. [10]

Greater Plantain *Plantago major*
PLANTAGINACEAE H <15 cm. Short,
usually hairy, perennial herb. Lvs
elliptical, with 3–9 prominent longitudinal
veins, <20 cm, in rosette. Fls yellow-
white, $c3$ mm, in spike on short stalk,
May–Sep. Weed of lawns. T. [11]

Hoary Plantain *Plantago media*
PLANTAGINACEAE H 10–30 cm. Finely
hairy, perennial herb. Lvs in rosette,
elliptical, with 5–9 prominent longitudinal
veins, <15 cm. Fls white, <2 mm, with
prominent, purple stamens in dense,
cylindrical spikes <6 cm, on stout,
smooth stalk, May–Aug. Dry, often limy
grassland, also lawns. T, ex Ic, (Ir). [12]

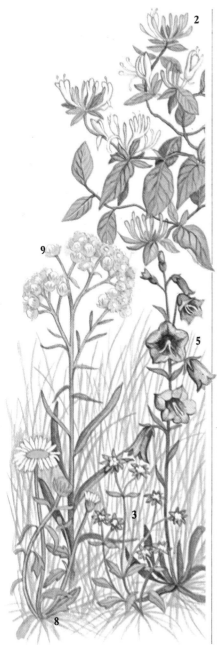

Snowberry *Symphoricarpos rivularis*
CAPRIFOLIACEAE H 1–3 m. Small shrub,
with yellow-brown twigs, suckering freely,
spreading underground. Lvs oval, 2–4 cm,
those of sucker shoots often lobed. Fls
pink, bell-shaped, in clusters of 3–9, Jun–
Sep. Frs large, white berries. Commonly
grown in parks, suburban gardens, for
decorative frs; widely naturalized. (Br,
Ir, Fr, Lu, Be, De, Ge, Cz, SC, from
west N America.) [1]

Japanese Honeysuckle *Lonicera japonica*
CAPRIFOLIACEAE H 6–9 m. Rampant, semi-
evergreen, woody climber. Lvs oval, lobed,
on young shoots. Fls white, tinged purple,
tubular, <5 cm, strong scented, Jun–Oct.
Often planted in gardens; naturalized.
(Br, Fr, Ge, from E Asia.) [2] Native,
deciduous honeysuckle *L. periclymenum*,
with red berries conspicuous in autumn,
more commonly planted in gardens. T.

Common Cornsalad *Valerianella
locusta* VALERIANACEAE H 7–40 cm.
Slender, hairless, erect, overwintering,
annual herb. Lvs oblong, unstalked, 2–7
cm. Fls whitish-lilac, tiny, funnel-shaped,
in clusters. Bare ground, dunes; cultivated
as substitute for early lettuce, persisting
as self-sown seed. T, ex Ic. [3]

Red Valerian *Centranthus ruber*
VALERIANACEAE H 30–80 cm. Erect,
hairless, perennial herb. Lvs ovate, lower
ones with short stalks, <10 cm. Fls
pinkish-red or white, *c*5 mm across, in
pyramidal, terminal clusters, Jun–Aug.
Widely cultivated for ornament, often
naturalized on walls. (T, ex Ic, Ne, Cz,
Po, SC, from Mediterranean.) [4]

Canterbury-bells *Campanula medium*
CAMPANULACEAE H <60 cm. Stout, erect,
roughly hairy, biennial herb. Lvs toothed
lower ones oblong, stalked; upper ones
lanceolate. Fls white, pink, blue or mauve,
solitary, 5-lobed, bell-shaped, 30–40
mm, May–Jun. Popular garden plant;
naturalized. (Br, Ge, from Italy, SE
France.) [5] *Campanula* spp have bell-
shaped fls; often cultivated as dwarfs in
rock-gardens or in herbaceous borders.

Canadian Goldenrod *Solidago canadensis*
COMPOSITAE H 60–250 cm. Erect, hairy,
perennial herb, with spreading, underground stems. Lvs lanceolate, 3-veined,
<13 cm, 40–110 per stem, basal ones
soon falling. Tiny fls in fl-heads, yellow,
<3 mm, arranged in pyramidal clusters,
Aug–Oct. Common in gardens, often
escaping to wasteland; widely naturalized.
(T, ex Ic, SC, from N America.) [6]

Daisy *Bellis perennis* COMPOSITAE
H <12 cm. Low-growing, hairy, perennial
herb, spreading by short, overground
stems. Lvs rounded at end, narrowed into
short, broad stalk, <4 cm, in basal
rosette. Fl-heads white with yellow centres,
16–25 mm across, on hairy stems, Mar–
Oct. Abundant in lawns, short grassland.
Rare in far north. T. [7]

Michaelmas Daisy *Aster novi-belgii*
COMPOSITAE H 40–120 cm. Erect, almost
hairless, perennial herb. Lvs ovate to
lanceolate, slightly toothed, <20 cm. Fl-
heads usually mauve with yellow centres;
also light blue, rosy-crimson or white,
Sep–Oct. Widely cultivated in herbaceous
borders, escaping, often established on
banks, wasteland. (T, ex Ic, Fi, from N
America.)

Mexican Fleabane *Erigeron karvinskianus*
COMPOSITAE H 10–50 cm. Slender, hairy,
branched, perennial herb, somewhat
woody below. Lower lvs ovate, often 3-
lobed, <35 mm; upper lvs linear. Fl-
heads white, like daisy *Bellis perennis*, 15
mm across, on branching stems 3–8 cm
long. Cultivated for ornament, naturalized
on rocks and walls in south and west. (Br,
Fr, from Mexico.) [8]

pearly everlasting *Anaphalis
margaritacea* COMPOSITAE H 30–100 cm.
Robust, woolly, erect, perennial herb. Lvs
grey, elliptical, woolly below, <10 cm.
Fl-heads appear pearly white, 9–12 mm
across, in terminal clusters, petals of
florets yellow, Aug. Cultivated for decoration, stems dried for flower arrangements;
naturalized. (Br, Fr, Ne, De, Ge, Cz, Po,
SC, from America, NE Asia.) [9]

coneflower *Rudbeckia laciniata*
COMPOSITAE H 50–250 cm. Erect, hairless,
perennial herb, with branched, creeping,
underground stems. Lvs various: lower
ones undivided, middle ones simply or
twice pinnate, with acute lobes. Fl-heads
yellow with green centres, 7–12 cm across,
Jul–Oct. Cultivated in gardens, but
escaping and naturalized. (Fr, Be, Ge, Cz,
Po, from N America.) [1]

Sunflower *Helianthus annuus* COMPOSITAE
H 75–300 cm. Rough, erect, annual herb,
often unbranched. Lvs broadly ovate,
stalked, spirally arranged, <40 cm. Fl-
heads enormous, <30 cm across, yellow,
brown-centred, Aug–Oct. Cultivated for
oil-yielding frs, in gardens for bird seed
and ornament; locally naturalized in
C Europe. (W, from N America.) [2]

Jerusalem Artichoke *Helianthus
tuberosus* COMPOSITAE H 100–250 cm.
Perennial herb, overwintering by
underground stems irregularly swollen at
tips. Lvs strongly toothed. Fl-heads 4–8
cm across, erect, Sep–Nov. Much grown
for tubers, containing a special starch
(inulin); often escaping from cultivation
and locally naturalized in Ne, Ge, Cz.
(W, from N America.) [3]

Lavender Cotton *Santolina chamae-
cyparissus* COMPOSITAE H 10–50 cm. Hairy,
evergreen shrub, with branching, woody
stems. Lvs grey, linear in outline, divided
into 4 rows of crowded, blunt lobes, each
1–2 mm. Fl-heads dark yellow, 10–15 mm
across, globular, solitary, Jul–Aug.
Commonly grown in gardens for
attractive, much-divided foliage. (W, from
S Europe.)

Yellow Chamomile *Anthemis tinctoria*
COMPOSITAE H 20–60 cm. Erect or
ascending, biennial or perennial, with
woody stems. Lvs feathery, 4–7 cm,
hairless above, white and woolly below.
Fl-heads yellow, 25–40 mm across,
solitary, on long stalks, Jul–Aug. Native
of dry places; cultivated for silvery-grey
leaves. T, ex Br, Ir, Ic, Fi. [4]

Yarrow *Achillea millefolium* COMPOSITAE
H 8–45 cm. Creeping, aromatic perennial
with erect, furrowed, woolly stems. Lvs
dark green, feathery, 5–15 cm. Fl-heads
white or pink, 4–6 mm across, numerous
in dense terminal clusters, Jun–Aug.
Native in grassland; forms dense, non-
flowering mats in lawns, looking like moss.
T. [5]

Feverfew *Tanacetum parthenium*
COMPOSITAE H 25–60 cm. Aromatic,
perennial herb, with erect, hairy stem.
Lvs yellow-green, <8 cm, simply or
twice pinnate, with toothed or lobed
segments. Fl-heads white, yellow-centred,
<20 mm across, long-stalked, Jul–Aug.
Cultivated for ornament and medicine,
becoming weed, often escaping and
naturalized. (T, ex Ic, Fi, No, from
Balkan mountains.) [6]

Pineappleweed *Matricaria
matricarioides* COMPOSITAE H 8–45 cm.
Erect, rather fleshy, pineapple-scented
annual. Lvs much-divided into linear
segments. Fl-heads greenish-yellow,
without rays, 5–8 mm across, Jun–Jul.
Widespread as introduction; common
garden weed, esp paths, gateways.
(T, ex Ic, probably from NE Asia.)
[7]

Mugwort *Artemisia vulgaris* COMPOSITAE
H 60–120 cm. Tufted, aromatic,
perennial herb, with erect stems. Lvs <8
cm, dark green, hairless above, whitish
and hairy beneath, much-divided into
lanceolate segments. Fl-heads red-brown,
<2·5 mm across, numerous in branched
spikes. Wasteland, roadsides. Once used
in herbal remedies. T, ex Ic. [8]

Colt's-foot *Tussilago farfara* COMPOSITAE
H <15 cm. Creeping perennial with long,
white, scaly, prostrate stems. Lvs <20
cm across, roundish-polygonal (like colt's
foot), appear after fls. Fl-heads yellow,
15–35 mm across, solitary, terminal, on
erect, scaly, woolly shoots 5–15 cm.
Damp places, esp clay soils; occasional in
gardens. T. [9]

Groundsel *Senecio vulgaris* COMPOSITAE
H 8–45 cm. Annual or overwintering herb.
Lvs hairless or cottony, with irregularly
toothed lobes, variable. Fl-heads yellow,
<5 mm across, with or without rays, in
dense terminal clusters, all year.
Cultivated ground, sand dunes, wasteland;
common garden weed. T. [1]

Common Ragwort *Senecio jacobaea*
COMPOSITAE H 30–150 cm. Erect, biennial
or perennial herb. Lvs dark green, simply
or twice pinnate, variously toothed and
lobed. Fl-heads <25 mm across, in dense,
flat-topped clusters, Jun–Oct. Weed of
wasteland, grassland, esp overgrazed
pastures; rare in far north. T, ex Ic, Fi.

Oxford Ragwort *Senecio squalidus*
COMPOSITAE H 20–30 cm. Annual, biennial
or short-lived perennial. Lvs hairless,
deeply divided into distinctly toothed
lobes, variable. Fl-heads yellow, <20 mm
across, in loose clusters, May–Dec.
Woodland, scrub; naturalized in
wasteland. Ge, Cz, (Br, Ir, Fr, De). [2]

Pot Marigold *Calendula officinalis*
COMPOSITAE H 20–50 cm. Erect, much-
branched, annual or perennial herb. Lvs
oblong, <14 cm, hairy, somewhat fleshy.
Fl-heads orange and yellow, 4–7 cm
across, Jun–Oct. Vars with yellow or
dark-centred fl-heads; widely cultivated
for ornament. Locally naturalized in
W Europe. (W, origin unknown.) [3]

Spear Thistle *Cirsium vulgare*
COMPOSITAE H 50–150 cm. Erect, biennial
herb with winged, spiny stem. Lower lvs
pinnate, lobed, spiny and hairy beneath,
<30 cm. Fl-heads pink-purple, often
solitary, 3–5 cm across, Jul–Oct. Widespread weed of fields, roadsides, wasteland,
often invading gardens. T, ex Ic. [4]

Creeping Thistle *Cirsium arvense*
COMPOSITAE H 30–90 cm. Far-creeping,
perennial herb, with erect, flowering and

non-flowering shoots. Lvs oblong or
lanceolate, divided into triangular,
variously cut segments. Fl-heads pale
purple, 15–25 mm across, solitary or in
small clusters, Jul–Sep. Weed of
wasteland, gardens. T, (Ic). [5]

Globe Artichoke *Cynara scolymus*
COMPOSITAE H 50–200 cm. Erect, hairy,
perennial herb; stems ribbed. Lower lvs
in rosette, <80 cm, much-divided into
linear segments, greyish, very hairy beneath. Fl-heads blue, spherical, <15 cm
across, spreading leathery bracts, fleshy at
base, Jul–Aug. Cultivated for edible
young fl-heads; often naturalized in Fr,
Be, Ne, Cz. (W, origin unknown.) [6]

Perennial Cornflower *Centaurea montana*
COMPOSITAE H <80 cm. Creeping
perennial; erect, winged stems. Lvs ovate,
<10 cm, hairy beneath. Fl-heads blue
with violet centres, 10–15 mm across,
Jun–Sep. Native in open woods and
meadows on limy soils in mountains;
widely grown in herbaceous borders. Fr,
Lu, Be, Ge, Cz, Po, (Fi). [7]

Nipplewort *Lapsana communis*
COMPOSITAE H 10–125 cm. Erect, annual
herb, with ascending branches above. Lvs
hairy, lower ones with large terminal lobe
and few small lateral lobes, upper ones
lanceolate. Fl-heads yellow, 15–25 mm
across, in clusters of 15–20, on slender
stalks, Jul–Sep. Common weed of hedges,
woodland, wasteland, gardens. T, ex Ic. [8]

Dandelion *Taraxacum officinale*
COMPOSITAE H <40 cm. Includes
aggregation of similar microspp, difficult
to separate. Perennial herbs, with deep
tap-roots. Lvs coarse, variously divided,
<40 cm, in basal rosette. Fl-heads
yellow, <6 cm across, solitary, terminal,
Apr–Oct. Frs familiar 'clocks'. Cut
leaves and stems produce milky sap.
Roadsides, wasteland; also woods,
meadows. T. [9]

Prickly Sow-thistle *Sonchus asper*
COMPOSITAE H 20–150 cm. Erect, hairless,
annual or biennial herb. Lvs glossy-green,
lobed, stem lvs with rounded ear-like flaps
at base. Fl-heads golden-yellow, 20–25 mm
across, in irregular clusters, Jun–Aug. Frs
distributed on fluffy pappus. Cut stems
produce copious milky sap. Abundant in
gardens, wasteland. T, ex Ic. [1]

Smooth Sow-thistle *Sonchus oleraceus*
COMPOSITAE H 20–150 cm Erect, hairless,
annual or biennial herb, very similar to
S. asper but lvs greyish-green, softer
prickles on margins, lvs of stem with
pointed ear-like flaps at base. Cultivated
ground, wasteland. T, ex Ic. [2]

Smooth Hawk's-beard *Crepis capillaris*
COMPOSITAE H 20–90 cm. Erect,
branching, annual or biennial herb. Basal
lvs <25 cm, variably dissected; stem lvs
lanceolate, without stalks, with spear-
shaped base. Fl-heads yellow, often
reddish beneath, <15 mm across, in lax
clusters, Jun–Sep. Abundant weed of
grassland, gardens, wasteland. T, ex Ic,
Fi, No. [3]

Orange Hawkweed *Hieracium
aurantiacum* COMPOSITAE H 20–40 cm.
Hairy, perennial herb, spreading by
creeping runners above and below ground.
Basal lvs hairy, pale-green, obtuse to
acute, in rosettes; stem lvs few. Fl-heads
deep orange, <10 mm across, in compact,
terminal clusters, on stems covered in
long, black hairs, Jun–Sep. Grassy areas,
wasteland; commonly grown in rock-
gardens, occasionally escaping. Fr, Ge,
Cz, Po, FS, (Br, Ic, Be, Ne, De). [4]
Hieracium includes several other spp and
many microspp difficult to separate, some
of them grown in rock-gardens.

Dog's-tooth Violet *Erythronium dens-
canis* LILIACEAE H 15–20 cm. Perennial
herb. Lvs 2, basal, broadly elliptical,
spotted with brown. Fls violet-pink, <6
cm across, with petals curved back,
pendant, solitary, on stems <15 cm,
Mar–May. Mountains; common

ornamental in parks, gardens. Fr, Cz, Po,
(W). [5]

Asparagus *Asparagus officinalis* LILIACEAE
H 30–150 cm. Erect, hairless, perennial
herb with extensive, creeping, underground stem. Lvs reduced to small scales,
bearing in axils feathery, lf-like shoots.
Fls green or yellow, bell-shaped, 3–8 mm
long, solitary or in pairs, Jun–Jul. Frs red,
globular berries. Grassy areas, wasteland;
cultivated for edible young shoots and for
foliage. T, ex Ic.

Spanish Bluebell *Endymion hispanicus*
LILIACEAE H 20–50 cm. Hairless, bulbous,
perennial herb. Lvs linear, glossy, <45
cm. Fls blue, bell-shaped, almost erect, in
terminal spikes on long, leafless scape
<50 cm, May. Garden vars also white,
purple or pink. Distinguished from
common bluebell *E. non-scriptus* by blue
anthers, broader lvs. (W, from SW
Europe.) [6]

Lily-of-the-valley *Convallaria majalis*
LILIACEAE H 10–25 cm. Hairless, creeping,
perennial herb. Lvs in pairs, broadly
elliptical, glossy, acute, <20 cm. Fls
white, bell-shaped, *c*8 mm, nodding on
1-sided, terminal spikes, fragrant, May–
Jun. Frs red berries. Native in woods,
thickets; often grown in gardens, parks.
T, ex Ic.

Adam's-needle *Yucca gloriosa* LILIACEAE
H <120–250 cm. Shrub or small tree,
with stout, usually unbranched stem. Lvs
long, stiff, greyish-green, spine-tipped,
<60 cm, in terminal rosette. Fls white,
bell-shaped, 8–10 cm, on erect, crowded,
cone-shaped spike 1–2 m high, Jul–Sep.
Commonly grown for ornament. (W,
from southeast USA.) [7]

Cabbage-palm *Cordyline australis*
AGAVACEAE H <15 m. Small, evergreen
tree. Lvs <65 cm long, <3 cm across.
Fls white, small, in large terminal clusters,
fragrant, May–Jun. Planted along roadsides
in seaside towns. (Br, Ir, Fr, from New
Zealand.) [8]

Snowdrop *Galanthus nivalis* AMARYL-LIDACEAE H 15–25 cm. Bulbous, hairless perennial. Lvs grey-green, long, narrow, <25 cm. Fls white, with inner petals tipped green, 20–25 mm long; nodding, solitary, on long, lfless stalks, Jan–Mar. Frs ovoid capsules. Native or naturalized in woods, plantations; widely cultivated in gardens, parks. T, ex Ic. [1]

Hoop-petticoat Daffodil *Narcissus bulbocodium* AMARYLLIDACEAE H 5–30 cm. Erect, bulbous perennial. Lvs long, narrow, channelled, <20 cm. Fls yellow, <4 cm long, with conspicuous inner trumpet, solitary, erect or inclined, Feb–Mar. Widely grown for ornament among grass in parks, gardens. (W, from rocky mountain meadows in SW Europe.) [2]

Jonquil *Narcissus jonquilla* AMARYL LIDACEAE H 20–30 cm. Bulbous, perennial herb. Lvs narrow, 3–4 mm across, grooved, half-cylindrical in cross-section. Fls golden-yellow, <3 cm across, sweetly scented, 2–6 in terminal cluster, on hollow round stem, Mar–Apr. Widely cultivated; produces oil used in scents. (W, from S Europe, NW Africa.) [3]

Pheasant's-eye Narcissus *Narcissus poeticus* AMARYLLIDACEAE H 40–50 cm. Erect, bulbous perennial. Lvs grey-green, long, narrow, <40 cm. Fls white, <7 cm across, fragrant, with short, yellow corona, crinkly and red at edge, giving 'pheasant eye' appearance, solitary, Apr–May. (W, from damp meadows in S Europe.) [4]

autumn crocus *Crocus nudiflorus* IRIDACEAE H 10–20 cm. Hairless perennial; corms develop stolons in spring. Lvs long, thin, appearing in spring, dying back before fls in autumn. Fls deep-purple,

<5 cm long, solitary, Sep–Oct. Widely
grown in parks, gardens; naturalized. (Br,
Fr, from Pyrenees.) [5]

spring crocus *Crocus vernus* IRIDACEAE
H 10–25 cm. Hairless perennial; flattened
corms not stoloniferous. Lvs long, thin,
appearing with fls in spring. Fls lilac,
white, deep purple, golden-yellow or
mauve with dark stripes, <5 cm long,
solitary, Feb–Apr. Cultivated and
naturalized in parks, gardens everywhere.
(W, from S Europe.) [6]

Montbretia *Crocosmia* × *crocosmiiflora*
IRIDACEAE H 30–90 cm. Erect, hairless,
perennial with corm <2 cm across. Lvs
long, slender, pointed, <50 cm. Fls deep
orange, funnel-shaped, 25–50 mm across,
clustered in long, 1-sided spikes, Jul–Aug.
Hybrid of garden origin raised in France
*c*1880; naturalized on hedge banks,
wasteland, by water, in Br, Ir, Fr. (W.) [7]

Garden Iris *Iris germanica* IRIDACEAE
H <1 m. Robust perennial, with branched
stems. Lvs long, stout, greyish-green,
<50 cm. Fls violet with 3 yellow-bearded
outer petals, several erect and slightly
twisted inner petals, <10 cm across,
May–Jun. Widely grown in gardens,
parks; naturalized in wasteland. (Br, Fr,
Be, Ne, Ge, Cz, Po, perhaps from
Mediterranean area.) [8]

Freesia *Freesia refracta* IRIDACEAE
H <60 cm. Perennial herb, with branched
stems and round corms. Lvs long, thin,
<30 cm. Fls creamy-yellow, funnel-
shaped, in 1-sided terminal sprays, fragrant, May–Oct. Hybridization has produced wide range of colours: cream, yellow,
orange and crimson. Grown under glass for
winter decoration. (W, from S Africa.) [9]

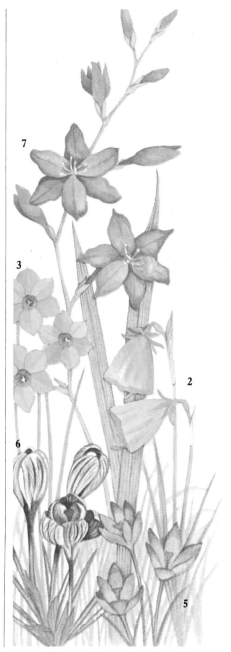

Soft-brome *Bromus mollis* GRAMINEAE
H <5–80 cm. Lvs flat, grey-green, 2–7
mm wide. Fls awned, with rotund spikelets 1–2 cm long, May–Aug. Meadows,
wasteland, dunes, gardens. T. [1]

Barren Brome *Bromus sterilis* GRAMINEAE
H 30–100 cm. Lvs flat, green or purplish,
softly hairy, 2–7 mm wide. Fls awned, in
spikelets of 4–10, 6 cm long, in loose,
open, nodding inflor, May–Jul. Gardens,
hedgerows, wasteland. T. [2]

Common Couch *Agropyron repens*
GRAMINEAE H 30–100 cm. Lvs flat, <13
mm wide, sparsely hairy above. Fls awned,
with erect, overlapping spikelets 1–2 cm
long; in spike-like inflor 5–30 cm. Cultivated ground, difficult to control. T. [3]

Red Fescue *Festuca rubra* GRAMINEAE
H 10–70 cm. Lvs of sterile shoots rolled,
of flowering stems flat, <3 mm wide. Fls
curved in spikelets of 3–9, 5–14 mm long;
loose, nodding inflor, May–Jul. Grassland,
lawns, salt marshes, mountains. T. [4]

Crested Dog's-tail *Cynosurus cristatus*
GRAMINEAE H 5–75 cm. Lvs flat, smooth,
<2 mm wide. Fls in dense, narrowly
oblong spike *c*5 cm long. Stems persistent.
Acid or limy grassland. T, ex far north. [5]

Smooth Meadow-grass *Poa pratensis*
GRAMINEAE H 10–90 cm. Lvs flat, abruptly
contracted at tip. Fls in spikelets of 2–5,
4–6 mm long; pyramidal inflor, often nodding, May–Jul. Lawns, grassland. T. [6]

Annual Meadow-grass *Poa annua*
GRAMINEAE H 3–30 cm. Lvs flat, slightly
keeled, <5 mm wide, crinkled when young.
Fls in spikelets of 3–10, 3–10 mm long;
loose, triangular inflor, all year. Gardens,
grassland, paths, roadsides. T. [7]

Perennial Rye-grass *Lolium perenne*
GRAMINEAE H 10–90 cm. Lvs shining green,
hairless, folded when young, <3 mm
wide. Fls in spikelets of 4–14, <20 mm
long, overlapping on either side of stiff,
terminal spike 4–30 cm long, May–Aug.
Cultivated for pasture, hay. T, ex Ic. [8]

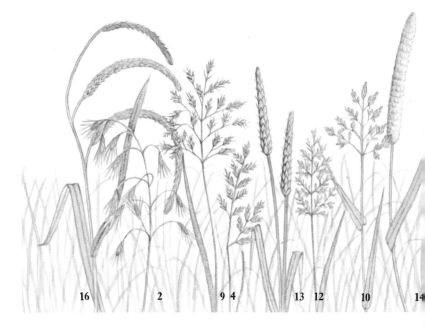

16   2   9 4   13 12   10   14

Yellow Oat-grass *Trisetum flavescens* GRAMINEAE H 20–80 cm. Lvs flat, hairy above, 2–4 mm wide. Fls tiny, awned, in spikelets of 2–4, 5–7 mm long, clustered in yellow panicle, May–Jun. Drought resistant; wide range of soils. T, ex Ic. [9]

Yorkshire-fog *Holcus lanatus* GRAMINEAE H 20–100 cm. Lvs flat, grey-green, <1 cm wide. Fls in spikelets of 2, 4–6 cm long; dense, oblong, erect or nodding panicles, pale grey, pinkish or purple, Jun–Sep. Meadows, woods, wasteland. T. [10]

False Oat-grass *Arrhenatherum elatius* GRAMINEAE H 60–150 cm. Lvs flat, green, rough, loosely hairy or hairless. Fls large, awned, <1 cm, in spikelets of 2; loose, erect to nodding panicles, Jun–Jul. Roadsides, ungrazed or waste land. T, ex Ic. [11]

Creeping Bent *Agrostis stolonifera* GRAMINEAE H 8–40 cm. Lvs flat, hairless, tapering to point. Fls tiny, in spikelets of 1; dense, much-branched panicles, Jul–Aug. Grassland on many soils. T. [12]

Black-grass *Alopecurus myosuroides* GRAMINEAE H 20–80 cm. Lvs flat, green or purplish, <8 mm wide. Fls awned, in dense, tapering, cylindrical spike 2–12 cm long, Jun–Jul. Arable, wasteland. T, ex Ic. [13]

Timothy *Phleum pratense* GRAMINEAE H 50–150 cm. Lvs flat, green, hairless, <9 mm wide. Fls awned; dense, narrow, spike-like, green or purplish panicles, 6–15 cm long, Jun–Jul. Grassland; cultivated for hay, grazing. T. [14]

Pampas-grass *Cortaderia selloana* GRAMINEAE H <2 m. Lvs long, arching, <2 m, narrow, with saw-like edges. Silky fl-heads 80–100 cm long, Aug–Oct. Ornamental in gardens. (Br, Fr, from Argentina.) [15]

Pendulous Sedge *Carex pendula* CYPERACEAE H <60–150 cm. Lvs long, yellow-green, with rough margins, keeled, broad, <20 mm. Fls clustered in separate ♂ and ♀ stalked spikes, drooping from slender, smooth stem, May–Jul. Native in woods; cultivated for ornament. T, ex Ic. [16]

15

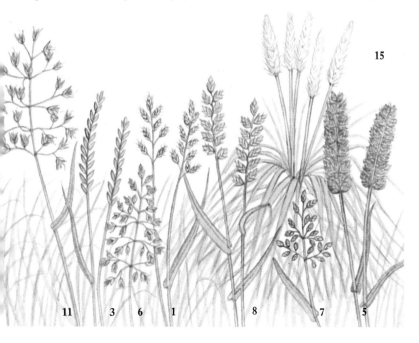

11 3 6 1 8 7 5

Shelled Slug *Testacella haliotidea*
TESTACELLIDAE EL 80–120 mm. Medium-sized burrower; in motion, has conspicuously tapering front end; whitish to dull greyish-yellow; tiny, brown or white shell, 7 × 5 mm, on back at rear. Gardens, shrubberies. Feeds at night, on or near surface of ground, on earthworms, centipedes, other slugs. Br, sIr, Fr, Be. [1]

Large Red Slug *Arion ater* var *rufus*
ARIONIDAE EL <150 mm. Large, broad, with conspicuous mantle shield; contracts into hemisphere, rocks from side to side if touched; brick-red to yellow-red, sometimes brown or black within colour range of large black slug (var *ater*); cream, yellow or grey underneath. Mucus orange or colourless. Ubiquitous, but red form more in gardens, hedgerows, near buildings. Omnivorous. T. [2]

Garden Slug *Arion hortensis* ARIONIDAE
EL 25–30 mm. Small, slender, cylindrical; dark brown-grey with yellow-brown dots; yellowish to orange underneath; groove on side, with thick black line above. Mucus yellow. Gardens, parks, wasteland, fields, woods. Burrows, feeding on underground parts of plants, bulbs, tubers; serious pest of crops. T, ex nFS. [3]

Great Grey Slug *Limax maximus*
LIMACIDAE EL 10–20 cm. Very large when full-grown; posterior $\frac{1}{3}$ of back keeled; whitish, grey or grey-brown with dark-spotted mantle shield at front, $\frac{1}{3}$ of total length; keel and underside pale. Mucus colourless. Gardens, parks, cellars; also woods. Feeds at night, on fungi, dead vegetation; not pest. T, ex nFS.

Yellow Slug *Limax flavus* LIMACIDAE
EL <9 cm. Tentacles distinct steely blue; body yellowish-grey, mottled; yellow underneath. Mucus colourless. In damp, decaying matter, *eg* compost heaps. Feeds on fungi. T, ex Fi, nSC. [4]

Netted Slug *Agriolimax reticulatus*
LIMACIDAE EL 35 mm. Small, usually in contracted, humped position, more elongate when moving; short keel on back at hind end; whitish or brown-yellow to blue-black, mottled with dark brown spots and streaks; yellowish-white underneath; mantle shield at front, $\frac{1}{3}$ of total length. Mucus white. Ubiquitous. Omnivorous, esp young shoots, flowers, soft fruits, tubers; common garden pest. T. [5]

Keeled Slug *Milax sowerbyi* LIMACIDAE
EL 70–75 mm. Conspicuous, pale-coloured keel on back; otherwise, pale to dark brown or grey with darker markings; pale underneath. Mucus yellow. Gardens, cultivated land, esp compost heaps. Lives underground, feeds on roots, damages potatoes. Br, Ir, Ne, Fr, Be. [6]

Cellar Glass Snail *Oxychilus cellarius*
ZONITIDAE SH 5 mm, SB 10–11 mm, W $5\frac{1}{2}$–$5\frac{3}{4}$. Shell yellowish-grey and partly transparent, white underneath; snail slate-grey, darker above; smells unpleasant. Cellars, buildings, greenhouses, also backyards, gardens, fields, woods. Feeds on fungi. T, ex Ic, nFi, most SC. [7]

Garlic Glass Snail *Oxychilus alliarius*
ZONITIDAE SH 2·5 mm, SB 6·5 mm, W 4–$4\frac{1}{2}$. Resembles *O. cellarius*, but smaller, shell darker horn, pale underneath; snail blue-black; smells of garlic when irritated. Rock-gardens, walls, wasteland, fields, woods. T. [8]

Strawberry Snail *Trichia striolata*
HELICIDAE SH 6–9 mm, SB 11–13 mm, W $5\frac{3}{4}$–$6\frac{1}{4}$. Shell whitish-grey, yellowish-grey or reddish, paler near opening; snail ash-grey. Gardens, hedges, fields, wood edges, esp damp places, rank herbage. Grazes off vegetation, including strawberries. T, ex Ic, De, FS. [9]

Garden Snail *Helix aspersa* HELICIDAE
SH 35 mm, SB 35 mm, W $4\frac{1}{2}$–5. Shell large, thick, yellowish-brown to buff with 5 dark brown spiral bands broken by zigzag streaks of the paler colour; dark grey, spotted yellow-grey on mantle. Commonest large snail of gardens in W Europe; also hedges, banks, old walls. Grazes off vegetation; often pest. Usually has fixed 'home', returning after foraging. Hibernates in old walls, under stones, often in groups. Br, Ir, Fr, Be, Ne. [10]

Brandling *Eisenia foetida* LUMBRICIDAE
L 35–130 mm. Red, purple or brown with
red-brown and yellow bands, first few
segments pink; clitellum orange. Ejects
yellow fluid with fetid smell when
irritated. Gardens, in compost heaps,
manure, dead leaves, rich organic soil;
fields, forests. At night often on surface
where compost recently spread. T, ex Ic. [1]

Long Worm *Allobophora longa*
LUMBRICIDAE L 90–150 mm. Long, thin,
cylindrical, with flattened rear end; brown
or grey, dirty-looking, first few segments
light to dark brown. Gardens, fields,
woods, also near rivers and lakes. T, ex Ic.
[2] Other *Allolobophora* spp, some pinker,
bluer, greener or yellower; 1 or more in
most gardens, producing conspicuous
earth casts on lawns.

Cockspur Worm *Dendrobaena mammalis*
LUMBRICIDAE L 30–65 mm. Rather short,
flattened; red-violet; clitellum usually
pale. Gardens, fields, marshy meadows, by
rivers, in rich organic soil, under moss,
stones, wood, dead leaves. Br, Ir, Fr, [3]
Other *Dendrobaena* spp also in gardens.

Eisen's Earthworm *Bimastos eiseni*
LUMBRICIDAE L 30–65 mm. Small, thin,
cylindrical; reddish or violet above, paler
below; clitellum red. Associated esp with
dead leaves, decaying wood, moss; also
moorland, bogs. T, ex Ic. [4]

Garden Worm *Lumbricus terrestris*
LUMBRICIDAE L 30–90 mm. Large,
cylindrical with flattened rear end; dark
brown-red to violet above, yellow-orange
underneath; clitellum orange-red.
Gardens; also fields, woods, by rivers, esp
clay soils. Lives in burrow, pulling dead
leaves in for food; leaves stuck in holes in
lawns characteristic. T. [5] Other
Lumbricus spp also in gardens.

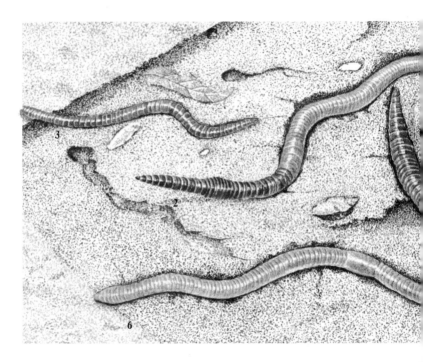

Blue Worm *Octolasion cyaneum*
LUMBRICIDAE L 65–180 mm. Rather large,
cylindrical; blue-grey, often with lilac
line along back, tail segments yellow;
clitellum red or red-orange to yellow.
Common in some gardens, among damp
plants; otherwise in moist soils, under
stones, moss, occasionally by ponds.
Br, Ir, Fr, De, Ge, Cz. [6] Related milky
worm *O. lacteum*, L 35–160 mm, more
variable, milky-white, grey, blue or
pinkish, with pink or orange clitellum;
habitats similar, but the 2 seldom occur
together. T.

potworms *Enchytraeus* ENCHYTRAEIDAE
L *c*25 mm. Genus of small, almost white
worms, sometimes mistaken for young
Lumbricus or *Allolobophora*. Compost
heaps, gardens, damp places, by water;
also fields, woods. Do not burrow;
squeeze through cracks in soil. T.
[7]

Roundworms, eelworms and other
Nematoda forms include an enormous
array of parasitic and non-parasitic
species, mostly too small to see with
the naked eye.

roundworms *Rhabditis* RHABDITIDAE
L <2 mm. Free-living worms. Larvae may
live in earthworms (Lumbricidae), dirty-
white, become obvious when host dies.
Adults among decaying vegetation and
animal remains. T.

eelworms *Heterodera* TYLENCHIDAE L ♂
<2 mm, ♀ <1 mm. ♂ slender, ♀ drop-
shaped. Eggs laid in soil or in roots.
Larvae penetrate and feed on rootlets; root
knots of scar tissue form round them. T.

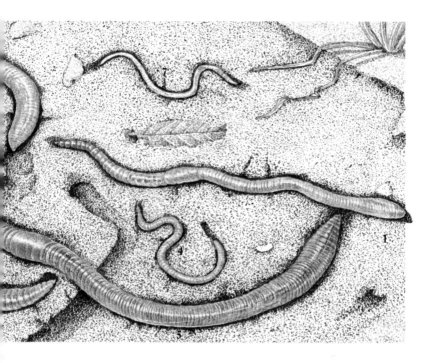

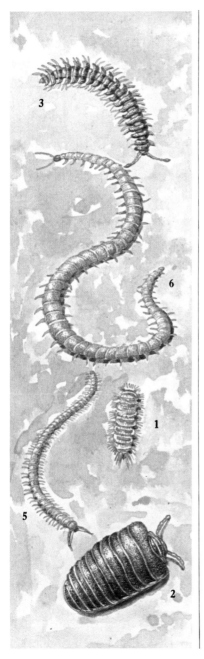

Millipedes (Diplopoda) have 2 pairs of legs on each body segment; centipedes (Chilopoda) have one. The number of pairs of legs varies with the species: some centipedes have 100 or more, others have only 15. Centipedes are usually predators and have a pair of poison claws attached to the first body segment; millipedes are mostly plant-feeders and move more slowly. Both classes include species that have been widely introduced as a result of gardening activities.

aberrant millipede *Polyxenus lagurus* POLYXENIDAE BL 1–3 mm. Small and, unlike typical millipede, quite soft; body with tufts of bristles. Under stones and bark, also in nests of ants (Formicidae), but easily overlooked. T, ex Ic. [1]

Pill Millipede *Glomeris marginata* GLOMERIDAE BL 17–20 mm. Shiny, dark grey with conspicuous segments and dorsal plates. When disturbed, rolls into ball like woodlouse. Common among vegetation, even in dry places. T, ex Ic, Po, Fi. [2]

flat-backed millipede *Polydesmus angustus* POLYDESMIDAE BL 17–25 mm. Pale brown; dorsal segments strongly sculptured; body rather flattened. Mostly in damp places, feeding on roots. Br, Ir, Fr, Be, Ne, wGe. [3]

Greenhouse Millipede *Oxidus gracilis* STRONGYLOSOMIDAE BL 16–20·5 mm.

Reddish to brown with lateral keels. Range extended by transport of plants; cosmopolitan in greenhouses. (T.) [4]

Spotted Snake Millipede *Blaniulus guttulatus* BLANIULIDAE BL 7·5–18 mm. Pale brown, with reddish spots along sides. Lives in soil, burrowing deep in dry weather. Feeds on roots, esp destructive to potatoes; mouthparts relatively weak, often enters root through hole bored by another animal. T, ex Ic. [5]

burrowing centipede *Haplophilus subterraneus* HIMANTARIIDAE BL 50–60 mm. Rather large, long, slow-moving. Yellow to light brown, head darker. Damp soil and under stones, habitat varying from suburban areas, grassland to sea shores. Unusual in feeding on plant material as well as small invertebrates. T, ex Ic. [6]

stone-dwelling centipede *Lithobius forficatus* LITHOBIIDAE BL 18–30 mm. Common, active centipede of gardens, most often seen because it enters buildings. Poison claws well-developed, used to catch slugs, earthworms, insects. Will bite if handled, but does little harm. T. [7] Other *Lithobius* spp also in gardens, including *L. variegatus* in Br only.

House Centipede *Scutigera coleoptrata* SCUTIGERIDAE BL <30 mm. Long-legged, fast-moving. Feeds on insects and other small animals in or near buildings. Rare Br, but common C Europe southwards. T, ex Ic, FS. [8]

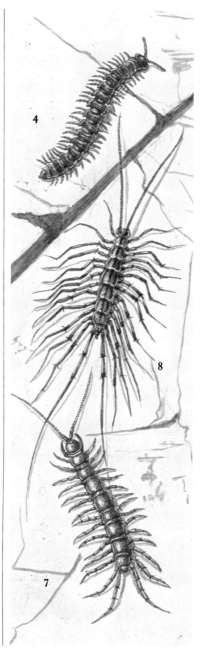

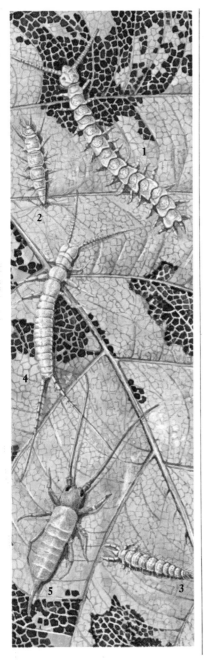

symphylans *Scutigerella* SYMPHYLA
BL <5 mm. Resemble small centipedes,
but lack poison glands; white to colourless.
Abundant in soil, among dead leaves.
Feed on living roots; generally regarded
as pests. Several spp in gardens. T. [1]

pauropods *Pauropus* PAUROPODA
BL <2 mm. Similar to *Scutigerella*;
distinguished by forked antennae. In
decaying vegetation, compost heaps. T. [2]

Insects include the only flying invertebrates, but not all have wings. 3 pairs of
legs, 1 pair of antennae, body divided into
head, thorax, abdomen. Most diverse class
of animals with up to 1 million known
spp. Life histories of 2 distinct types:
(1) young (nymph) similar to adult, always
without pupal stage (metamorphosis
incomplete); (2) larva (caterpillar, maggot)
totally different from adult, always with
pupal stage (metamorphosis complete).

proturans PROTURA BL <2 mm.
Wingless, tiny, white; no antennae, eyes,
tails or rear bristles; front legs extend
forward, probably used like antennae.
Among decaying leaves, leaf litter, damp
soil. T. [3]

two-pronged bristletails *Campodea*
DIPLURA BL <5 mm. Wingless; less
tapered than three-pronged bristletails
(Thysanura), with 2 bristles at rear. In
soil, under stones, rotten wood. Feed on
decaying vegetation. T, ex Ic. [4]

springtails COLLEMBOLA BL 1–6 mm.
Wingless, but jump when disturbed, using
forked springing organ at rear; some spp
globular, others more elongate. In leaf
litter, soil surface; also on snow, glaciers
(hence 'snow worms'). Biting mouthparts;

feed on organic debris, *eg* plant remains. Abundant, sometimes pests, *eg* Lucerne flea *Sminthurus viridis* damaging crops. T. [5]

Silverfish *Lepisma saccharina* THYSANURA: three-pronged bristletails BL 10 mm. Wingless; 3 long tail bristles; fine scales give shiny, silvery colour. Common in houses, esp kitchens; active, nocturnal, often seen when light switched on. Feeds on organic dust on floors, under skirting boards; can be destructive to book bindings, backings of pictures. T. [6]

Firebrat *Thermobia domestica* THYSANURA: three-pronged bristletails BL 12 mm. Wingless; longer antennae and tail bristles (lateral bristles protrude more) than *Lepisma saccharina*. Houses, kitchens, bakeries, outdoors farther south; active, nocturnal. Feeds on scraps of food, esp near ovens. T, ex Ic. [7]

White-shouldered House Moth *Endrosis sarcitrella* OECOPHORIDAE WS 14–20 mm. Conspicuous white head and thorax. Nocturnal, Apr–Oct; houses, warehouses. Caterpillar whitish, head red-brown; lives under skirting boards, between floor boards, all year; constructs silk galleries among its food, all kinds of vegetable matter. T. [8]

Brown House Moth, False Clothes Moth *Hofmannophila pseudospretella* OECOPHORIDAE WS 19–23 mm. Brown with black spots on wings. Nocturnal, attracted to light, May–Sep; houses, other buildings. Caterpillar whitish, head red-brown; feeds on organic dust between floorboards, damages fibre carpets, polythene, polystyrene, also outdoors in old birds' nests, most months. T. [9]

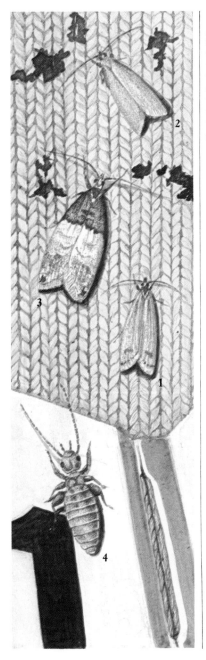

Case-bearing Clothes Moth *Tinea pellionella* TINEIDAE WS 10–14 mm. Pale, shining yellow-brown with fringe on outer margin of hindwings. In houses, shops. Caterpillar lives in case which it carries with it; feeds on wool, feathers, damages clothing, manmade fibres, also eats through polythene bags to reach wool; signs of damage are silk webbing and black spots (frass, excreta). Less common now. T. [1] Adult clothes moths do not feed on fabrics, so 'moth-eaten' should strictly be 'caterpillar-eaten'.

Common Clothes Moth *Tineola bisselliella* TINEIDAE WS 11–15 mm. Shining golden, similar to *Tinea pellionella* but paler. May–Sep, but season varying in centrally heated buildings. Caterpillar small, whitish, no case; feeds on raw or soiled wool (rather than clean garments), hair, feathers, stored cereals, also eats through polythene bags to reach food; leaves webbing and frass on food. T, ex Ic. [2]

Tapestry Moth *Trichophaga tapetzella* TINEIDAE WS 16–21 mm. Larger than 2 previous spp; whitish forewings with dark bases. Jul–Oct, but season varying in centrally heated buildings; often seen resting on walls. Caterpillar damages fur, woollens. Less common now. T, ex Ic. [3]

Common Booklouse *Troctes divanatorius* PSOCOPTERA BL <6 mm. Not a true louse. Soft-bodied, wingless, relatively large protruding eyes, long antennae, biting mouthparts, conspicuous swelling on hindlegs. Feeds on paste used in bookbinding; can be very destructive. Presence in new building indicates dampness; easily cleared by drying atmosphere. T. [4] Outdoor psocids, winged, may occur in immense swarms; feed on pollen, algae, fungi, and many live on tree bark (hence 'barklice'). T.

Chicken or **Shaft Louse** *Menopon gallinae* MALLOPHAGA: biting lice BL 2 mm. Mallophaga are wingless, flat-bodied, external parasites, mostly of birds; chew fragments of skin and feather; often numerous on hosts in poor condition; eggs (nits) attached to feathers. *M. gallinae* one of several found on poultry; heavy infestation may cause chicken to cease feeding and die. T, ex Ic. [5]

Human or **Body Louse** *Pediculus humanus* ANOPLURA: sucking lice BL 1–3·5 mm. Anoplura are wingless, external parasites of mammals; mouthparts adapted to pierce skin and suck blood. 2 forms of *P. humanus* infest man, smaller associated with head hair [6], larger with body hair [7]. Eggs (nits) attached to hair, clothing; nymphs mature in 1–2 weeks. Everywhere in dirty, crowded conditions; vector for typhus and other diseases. T.

Pubic or **Crab Louse** *Phthirus pubis* ANOPLURA: sucking lice BL *c*1 mm. More compact shape than *P. humanus*. Lives in perianal and pubic regions of man. T.

Fleas (Siphonaptera) are small, wingless, laterally flattened, blood-sucking insects, parasitic on birds and mammals; each sp confined to narrow range of hosts. White eggs produce tiny, white, legless larvae, which feed on fragments of skin and other detritus in hair, feathers and nests.

Human Flea *Pulex irritans* PULICIDAE BL *c*2 mm. Primarily parasite of hole-dwelling mammals. Adults transmit several diseases, *eg* 'black death'. Less common now on man. T. [8] [larva 9]

Domestic Cat Flea *Ctenocephalides felis* PULICIDAE BL *c*2 mm. Sp most seen in houses; readily bites man. T.

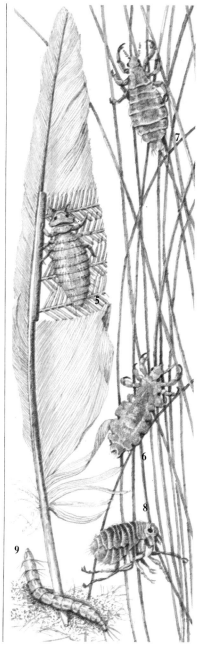

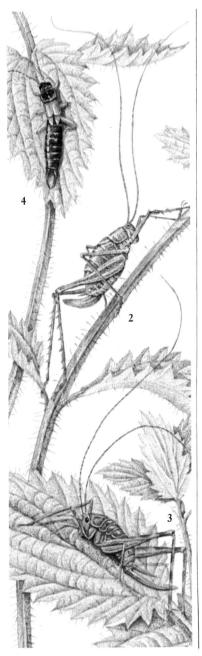

Crickets (Orthoptera) are stout-bodied, large-headed insects, with elongate hind-legs for jumping; ♂s 'sing' by stridulation which involves rubbing the wings together. Metamorphosis is incomplete.

House Cricket *Acheta domestica* GRYLLIDAE BL 15–21 mm. Brown; long antennae, 2 long cerci, wings flat over back at rest; large hindlegs, but runs, seldom jumps. ♂ chirps at dusk in summer. Active at night in houses, at rubbish dumps; not esp common. Scavenges on refuse. (T, ex Ic, from N Africa.) [1]

Speckled Bush-cricket *Leptophytes punctatissima* TETTIGONIIDAE BL 10–18 mm. Short, fat, mainly green; long, spiny legs; very long, thin antennae. Walks in flowerbeds in gardens. Feeds on leaves. Distribution patchy; mainly in more southerly parts. T, ex Ic, Fi. [♀ 2]

Greenhouse Camel-cricket *Tachycines asynamorus* RHAPHIDOPHORIDAE BL 11–15 mm. Yellowish mottled with brown; medium-sized, wingless, very long antennae; ♀ has long, curved ovipositor. In heated greenhouses, where introduced; hides in warm, damp crevices. Nocturnal. (T, from Asia.) [♀ 3]

Earwigs (Dermaptera) are elongate, with short elytra (hard forewings), ear-shaped hindwings, and stout, curved pincers at rear for offence and defence.

Common Earwig *Forficula auricularia* FORFICULIDAE BL 11–15 mm. Dark brown body; yellowish elytra. Only sp common in towns. Feeds on fl-heads, ripe fruit; scavenges widely. ♀ looks after and feeds young. Nocturnal, hiding by day in fl-heads; rarely flies. No truth in belief that earwigs enter and damage human ears. T. [♀ 4]

Cockroaches (Dictyoptera) are rather flattened, with long thin antennae, long spiky legs, and shield-like head covering.

Common Cockroach *Blatta orientalis* BLATTIDAE BL 18–30 mm. Beetle-like; poorly developed wings, conspicuous legs, long antennae; ♂ dark reddish-brown, wings not reaching tip of abdomen; ♀ black-brown, wider body, vestigial wings. Egg cases contain 14–16 eggs. Old buildings, esp where dirty; rubbish dumps in summer. Feeds on scraps, contaminated food, rubbish. Nocturnal. Transmits diseases, *eg* dysentery, anthrax. (T, from tropics.) [♂ 5]

American Cockroach *Periplaneta americana* BLATTIDAE BL 28–45 mm. Large, reddish-brown; fully-developed wings, large spiny legs, long antennae. Egg cases contain 12–16 eggs, hatch in 3–12 weeks. Common scavenger in buildings, esp dirty bakeries, restaurants, also sewers. Nocturnal. (T, from tropics.) [6]

German Cockroach *Blatella germanica* BLATTIDAE BL 10–15 mm. Small, pale yellow-brown with 2 dark brown stripes on thorax; fully-developed wings; ♀ more rounded than ♂. Egg cases contain 30–40 eggs. Houses, bakeries, restaurants; rubbish dumps in summer. Mainly nocturnal. (T, from tropics.) [7]

thrips, thunderflies THYSANOPTERA BL 0·5–5 mm. Small, elongate, flattened; 2 pairs of feathery wings (some spp wingless). Mostly seen in clusters on flowers, esp Compositae. In thundery weather may fly in large swarms; frequently get in eyes. ♀ lays eggs on or in plant tissue; larvae feed on sap, causing silvery spots on leaves where cell contents sucked out. Some spp predatory on smaller insects, including other thrips; few are destructive pests of crops. T.

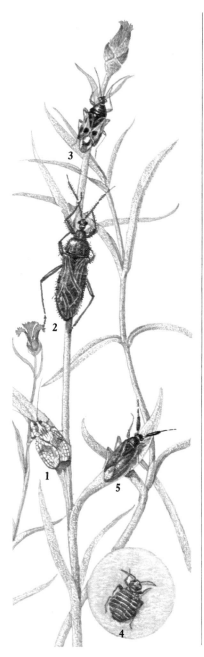

Bugs (Hemiptera) are extremely variable in shape and size. Many superficially like beetles (Coleoptera), but piercing, sucking, beak-like mouthparts distinctive: these are inserted into plant or animal tissues for liquid food. Usually 2 pairs of wings (some spp wingless); forewings often form a shield. Young stages resemble adults but have reduced wings. 2 major divisions: (1) Heteroptera (land and water bugs) with apical third of forewings membraneous, rest hardened; folded flat over body at rest; (2) Homoptera (leafhoppers, spittlebugs, plant lice, aphids) with forewings uniformly membraneous or hardened; held roof-like over body at rest.

Rhododendron Bug *Stephanitis rhododendri* TINGIDAE BL 5 mm. Tingidae are small bugs with lace-like wings, feeding on plants, moss. *S. rhododendri* lays eggs in rows on rhododendron; nymphs disfigure the leaves. Extends range wherever food-plant introduced. T, ex Ic, No. [1]

Kissing Bug *Reduvius personatus* REDUVIIDAE BL 15–18 mm. Reduviidae are robust, fast-moving, predatory. No sp common in towns. *R. personatus*, red-brown, lives in buildings. Feeds on flies (Diptera), other insects; also bites man, esp on lips when asleep. T, ex Ic, Fi. [2]

Common Flower Bug *Anthocoris nemorum* CIMICIDAE BL 4–6 mm. Small, dark with pale forewings. In gardens, on flowers. Feeds on aphids, small insects. Adults Jun–Jul; 2nd generation Sep, hibernates among litter, under bark. T, ex Ic. [3]

Bedbug *Cimex lectularius* CIMICIDAE BL 5–6 mm. Red-brown, globular; no obvious wings. In houses. Sucks human

blood. Nocturnal, hiding in nooks by day.
Dramatic decline due to insecticides and
greater hygiene. T. [4] Related spp found
on birds, bats; these also occur indoors.

mirid bug *Heterotoma merioptera* MIRIDAE
BL 4–5 mm. Grey-brown; middle parts
of antennae swollen; position of wings at
rest make rear look pointed. Common
among vegetation in some gardens. Feeds
on aphids, fruit. T, ex Ic, Fi, No. [5]

European Tarnished Plant Bug *Lygus
rugulipennis* MIRIDAE BL 6–8 mm. Dark
with pale head, legs; thorax with 2 dark
lines laterally. Abundant on fl-heads; eggs
laid on buds. May be destructive to crops,
fruit bushes; frequently blemishes leaves.
Adults overwinter. T, ex Ic, No. [6]

Common Green Capsid *Lygocoris
pabulinus* MIRIDAE BL 4–6 mm. Green,
darker posteriorly. Eggs laid in woody
plants, overwinter, hatch early spring.
Nymphs move to herbaceous plants;
damage currants, plums, apples. Abundant
mid-summer; 2nd generation Sep.
T, ex Ic. [7]

Potato Capsid *Calocoris norvegicus*
MIRIDAE BL 7–9 mm. Similar to *Lygocoris
pabulinus*, but wings dark-marked, thorax
with 2 black spots. Abundant in gardens.
Feeds on buds, flowers, fruit, esp nettle;
may become pest. 1 generation a year in
N Europe. T, ex Ic. [8]

Lucerne Plant Bug *Adelphocoris
lineolatus* MIRIDAE BL 7–9 mm. Mainly
green; forewings with distinct, broad, dark
stripe. Adults Jul–Aug; eggs laid on stems,
esp Leguminosae, overwinter, hatch early
spring. 1 generation a year in N Europe.
Occasionally pest of clover and flowers.
T, ex Ic. [9]

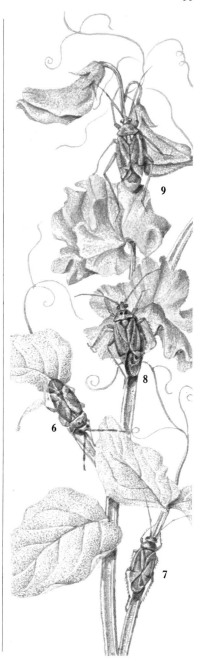

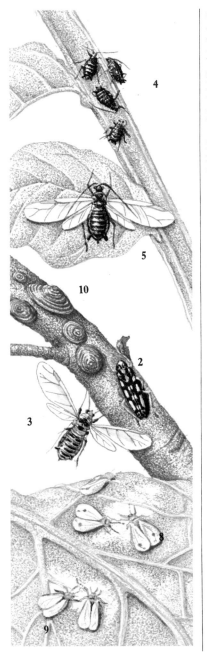

spittlebug, froghopper *Philaenus spumarius* CERCOPIDAE BL 5 mm. Variable colour, pattern: upperside pale buff, darker brown markings; sometimes mainly black or black and white. Adult rather frog-like; jumps when disturbed. Nymph lives in mass of own foam. On wide variety of non-woody plants. Commonest of Cercopidae in gardens, wasteland. T, ex Ic. [1]

leafhopper *Eupteryx aurata* CICADELLIDAE BL <5 mm. All leafhoppers are small, colour variable. Abundant in gardens, on leaves. All suck sap of plants; some are pests. *E. aurata* on potatoes, causes pale patch where feeding. T, not Ic, Fi. [2]

Aphids (Aphididae), also known as greenfly, blackfly, can muster 30–40 spp in average garden, but most difficult to distinguish. Many confined to narrow range of related plant spp. Root, stem and leaf feeders. Life histories complicated, varied: in many spp, winged adults lay eggs which overwinter, hatch into winged individuals in spring; several generations follow, some parthenogenetic, others viviparous, building up vast populations in favourable summers. Important in foodwebs: without them, animal life in gardens would be less diverse.

Cabbage Aphid *Brevicoryne brassicae* APHIDIDAE BL 2–2·5 mm. Dark grey-green. In dense clusters on cabbage. T. [3]

Blackfly *Aphis fabae* APHIDIDAE BL 2–3 mm. Black. Feeds on beans and many other plants in summer. Overwinters in trees, *eg* spindle tree. T. [wingless 4] [winged 5]

Rose Aphid *Macrosiphon rosae* APHIDIDAE BL 2–3 mm. Pear-shaped, stubby; green, sometimes pink; long, black siphuncles (pair of tubes near tip of abdomen). Common on roses, spring; 2nd generation on teasel and other Dipsacaceae, summer. With pruning of roses and growth of new shoots, some aphids remain on roses throughout summer. Eggs overwinter. T, ex Ic. [wingless 6] [winged 7]. Other aphid spp lack black siphuncles.

whiteflies ALEYRODIDAE BL *c*1 mm. Tiny, white, covered with powdery wax. Dense clouds of cabbage whitefly *Aleyrodes proletella* rise when cabbages disturbed, then immediately settle. T. [8] *Trialeurodes vaporariorum*, introduced pest of greenhouse crops and indoor pot-plants which cannot survive outdoors, sucks plant sap. T. [9]

scale insects, mealy bugs COCCIDAE ♂ with 1 pair of wings; ♀ wingless, effectively legless, often living under protective waxy scale. Many reproduce live young (vivipary) without mating (parthenogenesis). Capable of rapid build-up of numbers, like aphids. Remain attached to food-plant throughout life. T. Some commoner spp introduced, *eg* San José Scale *Quadraspidictus pernicosus*, BL 2 mm, pest of greenhouse crops. [♀ 10]

Lacewings (Neuroptera: Chrysopidae) have 2 pairs of transparent, gauze-like wings; often metallic-golden eyes. Best-known spp bright green; others brown. Slow fliers.

green lacewing *Chrysopa septempunctata* CHRYSOPIDAE WS 28–40 mm. Green body, transparent wings with network of green veins, metallic eyes; gives off offensive smell. Nocturnal, attracted to lights, often enters buildings. Feeds on aphids. Eggs laid on stalks fastened to plants. T, ex Ic. [11] [eggs 12] [larva 13]

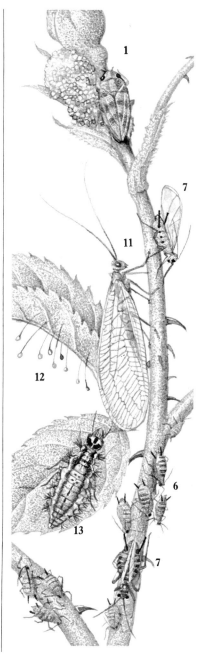

Butterflies and moths (Lepidoptera). In general, butterflies have clubbed antennae, close wings vertically, and have chrysalises with no cocoons; moths have variable antennae, close wings horizontally, have chrysalises with cocoons, or mud cells if pupation underground.

Large White *Pieris brassicae* PIERIDAE ws 56–66 mm. Upperside white, with black apical border; underside yellower, esp hindwings. ♀ with 2 black spots, black bar on upperside of forewings. 2–3 broods, Apr–Oct. Caterpillar conspicuous, greenish blue-grey, yellow lines, dotted all over with black, slightly hairy; feeds gregariously on Cruciferae, chiefly cultivated *Brassica*. T, but rare north of 62°N; partial migrant from south. [♀ 1] [♂ 2]

Small White *Pieris rapae* PIERIDAE ws 46–54 mm. Like *P. brassicae*, but smaller with black apical border not extending down outer margin of wings. 2–3 broods, Apr–Oct. Caterpillar green, solitary; feeds on Cruciferae, esp cultivated *Brassica*, usually hiding among leaves. Commonest town butterfly, though numbers vary markedly from year to year. T, but rare far north; partial migrant from south. [♀ 3] [♂ 4]

Green-veined White *Pieris napi* PIERIDAE ws 36–44 mm. Distinguished from previous 2 by dark pigmentation along veins on underside of hindwings; extremely variable. 2–3 broods, Apr–Sep.

Caterpillar green; feeds on Cruciferae, including cultivated spp, but not *Brassica*. T, ex Ic, far north. [5]

Orange-tip *Anthocharis cardamines* PIERIDAE ws 38–48 mm. ♂ white with outer third of forewings bright orange; ♀ lacks orange; hindwings of both sexes white, dappled green. 1 brood, May–Jun. Caterpillar bluish-green, inconspicuous; feeds on green seed-pods of various Cruciferae, including cultivated rock-cress and dame's-violet. T, ex far north. [♀ 6] [♂ 7]

Brimstone *Gonepteryx rhamni* PIERIDAE ws 52–60 mm. Pointed wing-tips; ♂ lemon-yellow, ♀ greenish-white. At rest, both sexes leaf-like. Adults hibernate in open among leaves remaining on bushes, reappearing early spring to late Jun. 1 brood Jul–Aug. Caterpillar green, powdered with black specks; feeds on buckthorn and alder buckthorn. Early name 'butter-coloured fly', contracted to 'butterfly'. T, ex Ic, far north. [♂ 8]

Wall Brown *Lasiommata megera* SATYRIDAE ws 38–50 mm. Bright orange-brown on upperside with dark brown veins, margins and transverse lines; white-centred 'eye-spot' near tips of forewings. Often rests on ground in sun. 2 broods, May–Jun, Jul–Aug. Caterpillar whitish-green, dotted with white; feeds esp on meadow-grasses and cock's-foot. T, but rare north of 60°N. [9]

Peacock *Inachis io* NYMPHALIDAE
WS 54–58 mm. 'Peacock eye' marks on
each wing; underside black. Visits garden
flowers, esp *Buddleja*. Adults hibernate in
hollow trees, buildings; reappear Mar–
Jun. 1 brood, Jul–Aug. Caterpillar spiny,
black; feeds in clusters on nettles. T. [1]

Red Admiral *Vanessa atalanta*
NYMPHALIDAE WS 55–62 mm. Forewings
black with scarlet band, subapical white
spots; hindwings with black-dotted
scarlet band. Migrant from south,
breeding in summer; commonest late
autumn. Often on *Buddleja*; at fallen
fruit in autumn. Caterpillar spiny,
greenish to blackish; feeds on nettles,
in loose 'tent'. T, but vagrant Ic, far
north. [2]

Painted Lady *Cynthia cardui* NYMPHA-
LIDAE WS 54–58 mm. Upperside orange,
flushed pink, many black markings; white
spots near tips of forewings. Migrant from
south, breeding in summer, unable to
survive winter. Often on *Buddleja*.
Caterpillar spiny, grey-green to blackish,
broken yellow line on sides; feeds on
thistles, nettles, many other plants, esp on
wasteland. T, but rare in north. [3]

Small Tortoiseshell *Aglais urticae*
NYMPHALIDAE WS 44–50 mm. Upperside
red-orange, with yellow and black patches,
dark borders with blue spots. Abundant
in gardens; visits flowers, esp *Buddleja*,
Sedum. Hibernates in buildings, reappears
early spring to June. 2 broods, Jun, Aug.
Caterpillar spiny, yellowish with black
speckles and lines; feeds in clusters on
nettles. T. [4]

Comma *Polygonia c-album* NYMPHALIDAE
WS 44–48 mm. Irregular wing-edge
distinctive; white comma on underside of
hindwings. Visits flowers, esp *Buddleja*,
also fallen fruit. Hibernates among tree
branches, reappears early spring–May.
2 broods, Jun–Jul, Aug. Caterpillar spiny,
grey-black, speckled reddish, large part of
back white; feeds on hops and nettles.
T, ex Ic, far north. [5]

Small Copper *Lycaena phlaeas*
LYCAENIDAE WS 24–30 mm. Forewings red
with black spots, dark border; hindwings
black with red lower border. Flies fast,
often rests on stones; visits garden flowers,
esp Compositae. Usually 3 broods,
Apr–Oct. Caterpillar slug-like, greenish;
feeds on docks on wasteland, roadside
verges. T, ex Ic. [6]

Holly Blue *Celastrina argiolus* LYCAENIDAE
WS 30 mm. ♂ lilac-blue, ♀ similar with
dark wing-tips; underside pale bluish-
white, dotted black. Usually flies high,
will settle on ground. Well-wooded parks,
gardens. 2 broods, Apr–May, Jul–Aug.
Caterpillar slug-like, variable in colour;
feeds on flowers, *eg* holly, ivy. T, ex Ic,
far north. [♀ 7] [♂ 8]

Common Blue *Polyommatus icarus*
LYCAENIDAE WS 28–36 mm. ♂ shining
blue; ♀ brown to bluish-brown, orange
spots at edges. Commoner on wasteland.
2 broods in south, May–Jun, Jul–Aug;
one in north, mid-summer. Caterpillar
slug-like, greenish; feeds usually on
common bird's-foot-trefoil. T, ex Ic.
[♀ 9] [♂ 10]

Small Skipper *Thymelicus sylvestris*
HESPERIIDAE WS 25–31 mm. Orange-
brown with dark veins, ♂ with black
streak on forewings; tips of antennae
orange below. Gardens, parks, where
grass uncut. 1 brood, Jun–Aug.
Caterpillar light green; feeds on grasses.
T, ex nBr, Ir, Ic, FS. [11] Essex Skipper
T. lineola, similar but tips of antennae
dark, also occurs in some towns; extends
into sFS.

Large Skipper *Ochlodes venata*
HESPERIIDAE WS 28–34 mm. Similar to
Thymelicus sylvestris, but wider, darker
outer wing margins, more spotted. Flight
rapid, best seen perched on flower. Flies
Jun–Jul, usually where tall grass; enters
gardens and parks from countryside.
Caterpillar feeds on grasses. T to 64°N,
ex Ir, much of nBr. [12]

Ghost Swift *Hepialus humuli* HEPIALIDAE
WS 44–64 mm, ♀ slightly larger than ♂.
Upperside of ♂ shining white, underside
dark; forewings of ♀ yellowish-orange
with orange marks, hindwings smoky-
yellow (♂ coloured like ♀ in north). Flies
Jun–Jul; common in wasteland, gardens.
Caterpillar feeds on roots of weeds,
garden plants. T, ex Ic. [♂ 1]

Orange Swift *Hepialus sylvina* HEPIALIDAE
WS 31–45 mm, ♀ larger than ♂. ♂ orange-
brown with greyish-edged, pale marks on
forewings; ♀ variable, orange-brown or
grey-brown. Flies early evenings, Jul–
Aug; common in gardens. Caterpillar
feeds on roots of weeds, garden plants. T,
ex Ic. [♀ 2]

Common Swift *Hepialus lupulina*
HEPIALIDAE WS 24–38 mm. Extremely
variable: usually dirty-brown with pale
marks on forewings; ♀ with less markings,
often none. Flies at night, Jun, sometimes
later; often abundant in gardens. Caterpillar glossy whitish with brown head;
feeds on roots of grass, often in lawns.
T, ex Ic, far north. [♂ 3] (Adults of all
these 3 *Hepialus* spp never feed, so not
associated with flower beds.)

Wood Leopard *Zeuzera pyrina* COSSIDAE
WS 40–65 mm, ♀ larger than ♂. Both sexes
shining white with many black spots;
abdomen of ♂ white, of ♀ black. Flies Jul;
common in some towns, ♂s attracted to
lights, otherwise not often seen. Caterpillar
dull white with black spots; feeds inside
branches of trees; mature in *c*3 years. T,
ex Ic. [♂ 4] [caterpillar 5]

Currant Clearwing *Synanthedon
salmachus* SESIIDAE WS 18–20 mm.
Transparent wings with black marks and
veins; bronze patch near tips of forewings;
body black with 3 yellow belts on ♀, 4 on
♂. Flies by day, easily mistaken for small
wasp; common where fruit bushes.
Caterpillar feeds inside stems of currants,
gooseberries. T, ex Ic. [♀ 6]

Mother-of-pearl *Pleuroptya ruralis*
PYRALIDAE WS 30–34 mm. Shining, pearly
white wings with brownish markings. Flies
Jun–Jul; common where nettles, often
disturbed by day from them; readily
attracted to lights at night. Caterpillar
green; feeds on nettles, remains concealed
in rolled-up leaf. T, ex Ic, far north.
[7]

Small Magpie *Eurrhypara hortulata*
PYRALIDAE WS 30 mm. White with black
markings. Flies Jun–Jul; habits similar to
Pleuroptya ruralis, usually found in same
patches of nettles. Caterpillar feeds on
nettles, Aug–Sep. T, ex Ic. [8]

Garden Pebble *Evergestis forficalis*
PYRALIDAE WS 25–29 mm. Pale brown
with darker brown markings. Nocturnal,
but often disturbed by day from vegetable
patch; common where crops grown. 2
generations, May–Jun, Aug–Sep.
Caterpillar feeds on cabbages, turnips,
other crops; can eat centre out of cabbage.
T, ex Ic, far north. [9]

Chinese Character *Cilix glaucata*
DREPANIDAE WS 20–25 mm. Silvery-white
with conspicuous black mark on forewings; resting on leaf, looks like bird
dropping. Common in gardens, parks, in
some areas. 2 generations, May–Jun, Jul–
Aug. Caterpillar red-brown, darker line
along back, paler stripe to pointed tail;
feeds on leaves of bushes, esp hawthorns.
T, ex Ic, Fi, No. [10]

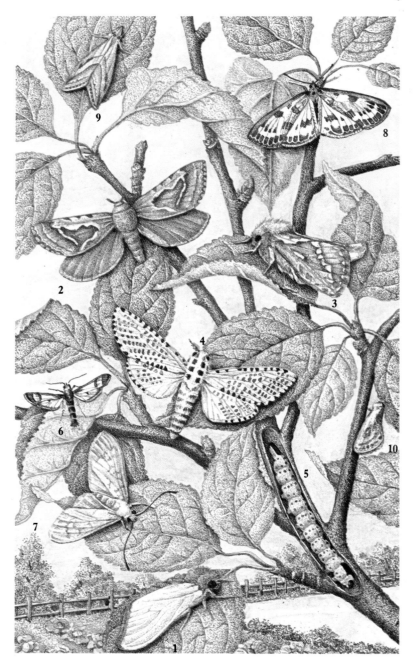

Buff-tip *Phalera bucephala* NOTODONTIDAE
WS 56–62 mm, ♀ slightly larger than ♂.
Forewings grey, tinged violet, with
conspicuous buff patch on outer third;
hindwings pale yellow. Nocturnal, Jun–
Jul; sits motionless by day, 'buff tip'
resembling end of broken twig. Caterpillar
more often seen, yellow with broken black
lines, black head; feeds in clusters on
leaves of trees, esp limes, elms. T, ex Ic.
[1] [caterpillar 2]

Puss Moth *Cerura vinula* NOTODONTIDAE
WS 58–72 mm, ♀ slightly larger than ♂.
Wings transparent white with many grey
markings and veins; body fluffy. Nocturnal,
May–Jun; common in parks. Caterpillar
green with red-brown saddle, 2 tails,
prominent face-like markings; when
threatened, elevates thorax and tails in
grotesque and menacing way, ejects
irritating fluid; feeds on willows, poplars;
more often found than moth in late
summer. T, ex Ic. [3] [caterpillar 4]

Sallow Kitten *Harpyia furcula*
NOTODONTIDAE WS 32–38 mm. Like
diminutive puss moth *Cerura vinula*, but
conspicuous band on forewings. Nocturnal
May–Jul, sometimes later; common in
gardens, but rarely seen except occasionally
at lights. Caterpillar similar to *C. vinula*,
but smaller; feeds on willows. T, ex Ic,
Fi. [5]

Garden Tiger *Arctia caja* ARCTIIDAE
WS 50–70 mm. ♀ slightly larger than ♂.
Unmistakable: wings and body boldly
patterned with white, chocolate-brown and
red. Nocturnal, often comes to lights;
common in gardens, wasteland. 'Woolly
bear' caterpillar conspicuous, hairy; feeds
on many garden plants, esp nettles.
Both moth and caterpillar distasteful,
avoided by predators. T, ex Ic. [6]
[caterpillar 7]

White Ermine *Spilosoma lubricipeda*
ARCTIIDAE WS 35–42 mm. Wings white,
abdomen yellow, both dotted black.
Nocturnal, Jun–Jul; often found by day
resting on fences; common in gardens,
wasteland. Caterpillar hairy, brown with
reddish stripe along back; feeds on weeds,
garden plants. T, ex Ic. [8]

Buff Ermine *Spilosoma luteum* ARCTIIDAE
WS 34–40 mm. Forewings deep yellow,
hindwings pale yellow, both with black
spots. Nocturnal, Jun–Jul; common in
gardens. Caterpillar hairy, grey-brown
with yellowish or whitish-grey stripe on
each side; feeds on most low-growing
plants. T, ex Ic. [9]

Ruby Tiger *Phragmatobia fuliginosa*
ARCTIIDAE WS 28–34 mm. Forewings
brown with black mark; hindwings black
and crimson. Time of appearance variable,
possibly 3 generations in some years;
occasionally comes to light. Caterpillar
more often seen, hairy, grey-brown with
reddish line along back and spots on sides,
becoming black; feeds on weeds, garden
plants, *eg* dandelions, plantains, golden-
rods. T, ex Ic, Fi. [10]

Turnip Moth *Agrotis segetum* NOCTUIDAE
WS 33–41 mm. Forewings variable, pale
brown to blackish, with darker markings;
hindwings white. Nocturnal, Jun, sometimes late autumn, feeding from flowers,
fallen fruit. Caterpillar grey-brown, tinged
yellow or pinkish; feeds on stems of
plants near ground, sometimes destructive
to turnips, related crops. T, ex Ic. [1]

Heart and Dart *Agrotis exclamationis*
NOCTUIDAE WS 34–40 mm. Extremely
variable: forewings usually pale brown
with conspicuous darker markings;
hindwings of ♂ white, of ♀ dirty pale
brown. Nocturnal, Jun–Jul, sometimes
later. In some years, immigrants swarm
from south, offspring make return
journey. Caterpillar brownish; feeds on
weeds, low plants. T, ex Ic. [2]

Shuttle-shaped Dart *Agrotis puta*
NOCTUIDAE WS 29–31 mm. Forewings of
♂ brownish with darker markings; ♀ much
darker, forewings almost black. Nocturnal,
Apr–May, Jul–Aug; often feeds from
fallen fruit in late summer. Caterpillar
feeds on low-growing plants, *eg* dandelions
Taraxacum. T, ex Ic, far north. [♂ 3]

Flame *Axylia putris* NOCTUIDAE WS 29–33
mm. Forewings pale brown with bold
dark leading edge; hindwings dirty white.
Nocturnal, Jun–Jul; not common, but in
most gardens. Caterpillar grey-brown
mottled with black, darker central line
with whitish line on each side; feeds on
weeds, *eg* docks, plantains, also garden
lettuce. T, ex Ic. [4]

Flame Shoulder *Ochropleura plecta*
NOCTUIDAE WS 27–29 mm. Pale 'shoulders'
of dark, pink-tinged forewings distinctive;
hindwings pure white. Nocturnal, May–
Jun, Aug–Sep; common in gardens,
wasteland. Caterpillar yellow-brown to
red-brown with paler stripe on sides,
dark-edged line on back; feeds on low-
growing plants, vegetables. T, ex Ic. [5]

Large Yellow Underwing *Noctua
pronuba* NOCTUIDAE WS 48–56 mm.
Forewings very variable, yellow to dark

brown or purplish, with darker markings;
hindwings yellow with black border.
Nocturnal, Jun–Oct, abundant Jul; often
disturbed from vegetation by day.
Caterpillar fat, ugly, brown, tinged yellow
or green, with yellowish lines, blackish
bars on back; feeds through winter on
roots of grasses, low plants. Shiny brown
pupa often dug up in gardens in early
summer. T. [6] [caterpillar 7]

Lesser Yellow Underwing *Noctua comes*
NOCTUIDAE WS 38–45 mm. Very like
N. pronuba, but smaller, with black spot
in middle of hindwings. Nocturnal, Jul–
Aug; common in gardens, but not often
seen except at lights. Caterpillar yellow-
brown with 3 yellowish, partly black-
edged lines on back; feeds on many
herbaceous plants. T, ex Ic, far north. [8]

Setaceous Hebrew Character *Xestia
c-nigrum* NOCTUIDAE WS 34–39 mm.
Forewings variable but usually shining
brown, tinged pink, with distinctive
wedge-shaped mark near leading edge;
hindwings whitish. Nocturnal, chiefly
autumn, but immigrants from south early
summer. Caterpillar pale brown to green-
grey with 2 series of black streaks and
dark-edged pale line on back; feeds on
docks, ragwort and other low-growing
plants. T, ex Ic. [9]

Square-spot Rustic *Xestia xanthographa*
NOCTUIDAE WS 34–38 mm. Forewings
brown or grey, often reddish tint, distinctive square spot near centre; hindwings
greyish. Nocturnal, Aug–Sep, attracted to
lights; common in gardens, wasteland;
feeds on fallen fruit. Caterpillar yellow-
brown with dark-edged yellowish lines,
black wedges along back; feeds on docks,
plantains, grasses. T, ex Ic. [10]

Gothic *Naenia typica* NOCTUIDAE WS 35–
45 mm. Brown, with delicate white marks
on forewings; hindwings dusky brown.
Nocturnal, Jun–Jul, attracted to lights.
Caterpillar grey-brown to yellow-brown
with dark and light marks; feeds on
plants in herbaceous borders, esp dead-
nettles, also fruit trees. T, ex Ic, No. [11]

Cabbage Moth *Mamestra brassicae*
NOCTUIDAE WS 33–43 mm. Grey-brown,
with irregular spot outlined in white on
forewings. Nocturnal, Jun–Jul, sometimes
autumn; common in gardens. Caterpillar
purplish-pink with black-edged, yellow-
brown line, broken by red-brown
triangles, along back; feeds mainly on
Brassica spp. T, ex Ic. [1]

Dot Moth *Melanchra persicariae*
NOCTUIDAE WS 37–41 mm. White spot on
blue-black forewings distinctive. Common
in gardens. Caterpillar green or brown
with darker markings; feeds on plants in
herbaceous borders. T, ex Ic. [2]
[caterpillar 3]

Bright-line Brown-eye *Lacanobia
oleracae* NOCTUIDAE WS 35–40 mm.
Forewings with distinctive brown spot,
white marginal line. Common in gardens.
Caterpillar, more often seen than moth,
varies from green to light brown, dotted
with black and white; feeds on herbaceous
plants, *Brassica*; can be greenhouse pest.
T, ex Ic. [4] [caterpillar 5]

Broom Moth *Ceramica pisi* NOCTUIDAE
WS 35–39 mm. Similar to *Lacanobia
oleracae*, but with straighter marginal line,
no brown 'eye'. Nocturnal, Jun–Jul.
Caterpillar green, brown or blackish with
yellow stripes; feeds on leaves of woody
plants, *eg* roses, brambles, willows. T,
ex Ic. [6]

Broad-barred White *Hecatera bicolorata*
NOCTUIDAE WS 29–33 mm. Forewings
white with broad, black band; hindwings
greyish-white. Nocturnal, Jun–Aug; often
found by day resting on tree trunks and
fences; common in some towns, esp parks.
Caterpillar yellow-brown blotched with
dark grey; feeds on flowers of hawk's-
beards. WE, CE, not Ic. [7]

Varied Coronet *Hadena compta*
NOCTUIDAE WS 29–31 mm. Forewings

blackish with irregular white bar, also
speckled white; hindwings grey. Flies at
dusk, Jun–Jul; common in gardens.
Caterpillar brown with broad, dark stripe
along back; feeds on sweet-william. T,
ex Ic, No, extending northwards. [8]

Clouded Drab *Orthosia incerta* NOCTUIDAE
WS 34–37 mm. Forewings very variable,
pale greyish to deep purplish-brown;
hindwings grey-brown. Flies early spring,
attracted to catkins of sallow; common in
towns, esp parks. Caterpillar green,
freckled whitish, with 3 white lines on
back, black and white stripes along sides;
feeds on oaks, willows, hawthorns.
T, ex Ic. [9]

Hebrew Character *Orthosia gothica*
NOCTUIDAE WS 31–35 mm. Forewings pale
purplish-grey, usually with conspicious
black markings. Flies early spring; visits
catkins of sallow. Caterpillar green above,
yellowish below, with 3 whitish lines on
back, yellowish stripe on sides; feeds on
docks, dandelions, leaves of trees and
bushes. T, ex Ic. [10]

Common Wainscot *Mythimna pallens*
NOCTUIDAE WS 31–35 mm. Forewings
more or less uniform pale yellow-brown;
hindwings white. Nocturnal, Jun–Jul,
sometimes Aug–Sep; common visitor to
flowers, fallen fruit. Caterpillar pale
whitish-brown with 3 black-edged whitish
lines on back, greyish and pink-brown
stripes along sides; feeds on grasses. T,
ex Ic. [11] Several similar spp in gardens.

Shark Moth *Cucullia umbratica* NOCTUIDAE
WS 40–52 mm. Grey with dark veins and
marks, esp on forewings; looks stream-
lined. Nocturnal, visiting flowers in
herbaceous borders; by day well
camouflaged on fences, palings; common
on wasteland, sometimes gardens.
Caterpillar grey-ochre with blacker
patterning; feeds on sow-thistles. T, ex
Ic. [12]

Early Grey *Xylocampa areola* NOCTUIDAE
WS 31–35 mm. Grey, marked with black.
Nocturnal, early spring, visiting catkins
of sallow, often attracted to lights; by day
resting on tree trunks; common in town
parks, gardens. Caterpillar rather large,
yellow-brown; feeds on honeysuckles.
T, ex Ic, Fi. [1]

Lunar Underwing *Omphaloscelis lunosa*
NOCTUIDAE WS 31-35 mm. Forewings pale
red-brown to dark blackish-grey;
hindwings grey with darker patches.
Nocturnal, Sep–Oct, visiting fallen fruit;
common in gardens. Caterpillar brownish
with 3 whitish lines along back, 1 along
each side, some blackish edging; feeds
esp on meadow-grasses. Br, Fr, Be, Ne.
[2]

Poplar Grey *Acronicta megacephala*
NOCTUIDAE WS 40–42 mm. Forewings
grey, intricately marked with black;
hindwings white with dark veins.
Nocturnal, May–Aug, resting on tree
trunks in town parks by day. Caterpillar
more often seen, yellow-brown to grey-
brown marked with blackish, hairs
whitish; feeds on poplars. T, ex Ic. [3]

Sycamore Moth *Acronicta aceris*
NOCTUIDAE WS 40–44 mm. Similar to
A. megacephala, but paler, less boldly
marked on forewings. Nocturnal, Jun–Jul,
resting on tree trunks by day; often in
town parks. Caterpillar has black-edged
white marks along back, yellow hairs;
feeds on sycamore. T, ex Ic. [4]

Grey Dagger *Acronicta psi*
NOCTUIDAE WS 35–41 mm. Grey forewings
with dagger-like markings; white
hindwings. Nocturnal, Jun–Jul, commonly
resting by day on tree trunks in town
parks. Caterpillar hairy, yellow-backed,
with conspicuous hump; feeds on leaves
of trees, roses. T, ex Ic. [5]

Marbled Beauty *Cryphia domestica*
NOCTUIDAE WS 22–27 mm. Small,

whitish-grey, marked darker grey.
Nocturnal, Jul–Aug, attracted to lights,
resting on walls by day; common in older
suburbs. Caterpillar grey with black-
spotted, yellowish stripe on back; feeds on
lichens on walls. T, ex Ic, Fi. [6]

Mouse *Amphipyra tragopoginis* NOCTUIDAE
WS 30–38 mm. Forewings uniform shining
brown, with 3 black specks; hindwings
pale brown. Nocturnal, Jul–Aug, visiting
fallen fruit in gardens; sometimes
disturbed by day among vegetation,
scuttling away like mouse. Caterpillar
green with white lines along back and
sides; feeds on leaves of willows,
hawthorns, woody plants. T, ex Ic. [7]

Old Lady *Mormo maura* NOCTUIDAE
WS 60–70 mm. Large, brown with paler
brown markings. Nocturnal, Jul–Aug;
common in towns, esp London, often
comes into houses, hides behind curtains.
Caterpillar yellow-brown with darker
diamond pattern on back; feeds on low
plants in autumn, on birches, willows,
hawthorns in spring after hibernation.
Br, Ir, Fr, Be, Lu, Ne, Ge, Cz. [8]

Straw Underwing *Thalpophila matura*
NOCTUIDAE WS 37–44 mm. Forewings dark
brown with pale lines, white-edged spots;
hindwings pale straw, edged brownish.
Nocturnal, Jul–Aug, attracted to lights,
fallen fruit; common in gardens.
Caterpillar yellowish or red-brown with
grey-brown marks along back, brown-
edged line on sides; feeds on grasses. T,
ex Ic. [9]

Small Angle Shades *Euplexia lucipara*
NOCTUIDAE WS 29–35 mm. Pinkish-
purplish-brown with black-banded
forewings, each with obvious pale spot.
Nocturnal, Jun–Jul; common in gardens.
Caterpillar green or pink-brown, with 3
faint lines and dusky V-marks on back,
white line along sides; feeds on plants in
herbaceous borders, also woody shrubs,
eg birches. T, ex Ic. [10]

Angle Shades *Phlogophora meticulosa*
NOCTUIDAE WS 44–50 mm. Pale brown
patterned with dark greenish, tinged pink
when fresh; at rest, like crumpled leaf.
Almost all year, esp May–Jun, Sep–Oct.
Caterpillar green or brown, with pale
central line, dusky V-marks; feeds on
garden plants, weeds, even in winter. T.
[1]

Dark Arches *Apamea monoglypha*
NOCTUIDAE WS 44–50 mm. Forewings
normally pale brown intricately marked
with darker brown, but melanic individuals
often in towns; hindwings pale whitish-
brown. Nocturnal, Jun–Aug or later;
common in gardens, rarely seen. Caterpillar greyish, tinged red or brown; feeds
on garden plants, weeds. T, ex Ic.
[melanic 2]

Rustic Shoulder-knot *Apamea sordens*
NOCTUIDAE WS 33–38 mm. Variable brown
forewings with distinct black 'shoulder-
knot' near base. Nocturnal, May–Jun,
attracted to lights; common in gardens.
Caterpillar pale grey-brown, greyish line
along back edged with black marks; feeds
on grasses through winter. T, ex Ic. [3]

Common Rustic *Mesapamea secalis*
NOCTUIDAE WS 27–33 mm. Forewings
usually brown or black with white-edged
spot in middle; hindwings greyish. Nocturnal, Jul–Aug, at fallen fruit, flowers;
common in gardens. Caterpillar green
with yellow head, 2 reddish lines along
back; feeds in grass stems. T, ex Ic. [4]

Rosy Rustic *Hydraecia micacea*
NOCTUIDAE WS 31–39 mm. Brown, with
pink tint; dark line through hindwings
distinctive. Nocturnal, autumn; frequent
in gardens, esp near coast. Caterpillar
pinkish with yellow head, darker stripe on
back; feeds in stems of docks, other
plants, crops. T, ex Ic. [5]

Mottled Rustic *Caradrina morpheus*
NOCTUIDAE WS 28–33 mm. Dull grey-
brown, with darker bands on forewings,
paler hindwings. Nocturnal, Jun–Aug or
later; visits fallen fruit, garden flowers.
Caterpillar grey-brown to yellow-brown,

whitish central line edged with blackish
arrow marks; feeds on weeds. T, ex Ic. [6]

Burnished Brass *Diachrysia chrysitis*
NOCTUIDAE WS 33–37 mm. Forewings
with striking metallic-green patches;
hindwings brownish. Nocturnal, Jun–Aug;
visits garden flowers. Caterpillar pale
green, white-streaked; feeds on nettles,
dead-nettles, burdock. T, ex Ic. [7]

Golden Plusia *Polychrisia moneta*
NOCTUIDAE WS 36–38 mm. Forewings
pointed, brown with dark line through
centre and dark-edged spot; hindwings
pale brown. Jun–Jul, Aug–Sep; esp at
flowerbeds. Caterpillar green, dotted with
white; feeds on *Delphinium*. T, ex Ic. [8]

Silver-Y *Autographa gamma* NOCTUIDAE
WS 37–41 mm. Y-mark on forewings
distinctive; hindwings grey with broad,
dark border. Immigrants produce 1 or 2
late summer generations; flies by day and
night, feeds at garden flowers. Caterpillar
green; on garden plants, as is black pupa in
silk cocoon. T, ex Ic. [9] [caterpillar 10]

Spectacle *Abrostola triplasia* NOCTUIDAE
WS 30–37 mm. Forewings dark, paler
at edges and base; hindwings dark brown.
Nocturnal, May–Aug, often at garden
flowers. Caterpillar pale green with white-
edged, dark green V-marks on back, 3
whitish lines on sides; feeds on nettles,
dead-nettles, hops. T, ex Ic. [11]

Herald *Scoliopteryx libatrix* NOCTUIDAE
WS 40–46 mm. Forewings angular, marked
with brick-red and white lines; hindwings
brownish. Appears late autumn, hibernates
in buildings, flies again early spring–June;
visits fallen fruit, flowers of ivy, willows.
Caterpillar long, thin, green; feeds on
willows. T, ex Ic. [12]

Snout *Hypena proboscidalis* NOCTUIDAE
WS 33–37 mm. Body thin, forewings
pointed at tips, brown with darker bands.
Active at night, Jun–Jul, resting by day
on plants; common on wasteland,
occasional in gardens. Caterpillar green
with darker green line along back, 2 along
sides; feeds on nettles. T, ex Ic. [13]

Vapourer *Orgyia antiqua* LYMANTRIIDAE
WS ♂ 25–35 mm. ♂ red-brown with white
spot on forewings; fat ♀ has only stumps
of wings, cannot fly. ♂ flies by day in
summer; often in city streets. ♀ lays
cluster of eggs on cocoon from which she
has emerged. Caterpillar violet or grey
with black-edged, creamy line along back,
dotted and fringed with red spots,
broken yellowish line on sides, 4 brushes
of yellow hair on back; feeds on leaves of
most deciduous trees, bushes. T. [♂ 1]

Pale Tussock *Dasychira pudibunda*
LYMANTRIIDAE WS 42–58 mm, ♀ larger
than ♂. Greyish-white; forewings marked
darker grey. Nocturnal, May–Jun, resting
by day on herbage; common in gardens,
town parks. Caterpillar usually green or
yellow, mottled whitish or greenish,
marked with black spots, 4 brushes of
yellow hair, 1 of reddish; feeds on birches,
oaks. T, ex Ic, No. [2]

Lime Hawk *Mimas tiliae* SPHINGIDAE
WS 66–75 mm, ♀ slightly larger than ♂.
Forewings pale pinkish-grey or red-
brown marked with green, whitish patch
towards tip; hindwings pale brown,
bordered black, edged orange. Nocturnal,
May–Jun; rests by day on tree trunks,
resembling leaf; common in towns where
limes, elms. Caterpillar rough-skinned,
green with 7 yellow and reddish-purple
oblique stripes on sides, blue horn at rear
with yellowish tip; feeds on elms, limes,
Jul–Aug. T, ex Ic. [3]

Eyed Hawk *Smerinthus ocellata*
SPHINGIDAE WS 70–80 mm, ♀ larger than
♂. Forewings marbled with shades of
brown, often tinged rosy; hindwings
pinkish with black and blue-grey 'eyes'.
Nocturnal, Jun; rests by day on tree
trunks, where difficult to see, opening
forewings to reveal eye-spots if disturbed;
common in well-wooded suburbs, parks.
Caterpillar large, rough-skinned, yellowish-
green, with 7 white oblique stripes on
sides, conspicuous blue-green horn at rear;
feeds on willows, poplars. T, ex Ic. [4]

Poplar Hawk *Laothoe populi* SPHINGIDAE
WS 66–78 mm, ♀ larger than ♂. Large,
grey (♀ sometimes pinkish) with dull red
patch at base of hindwings. Nocturnal,
May–Aug; rests by day on tree trunks;
common in well-wooded suburbs, gardens.
Caterpillar rough-skinned, green, with 7
yellow oblique stripes on sides, reddish-
tipped horn at rear; feeds on poplars,
willows, Jul–Oct. T, ex Ic. [5]

Humming-bird Hawk *Macroglossum
stellatarum* SPHINGIDAE WS 45–51 mm.
Forewings dark; hindwings orange. Flies
in bright sunshine, hovers in front of
flowers, like large bee. Migrant from south,
numbers fluctuate from year to year.
Caterpillar feeds on bedstraws. T. [6]

Elephant Hawk *Deilephila elpenor*
SPHINGIDAE WS 58–66 mm. Pink and
green, with pink and black hindwings.
Flies at dusk, Jun; common in towns
where willowherbs *Epilobium*, but seldom
seen. Large caterpillar (L <8 cm) more
often found, blackish, grey-brown or
green dotted with black, horn at rear;
feeds on willowherbs, esp rosebay, on
wasteland. T, ex Ic. [7] [caterpillar 8]

Blood-vein *Timandra griseata*
GEOMETRIDAE WS 27–31 mm. Wings pale
buff with pinkish-red fringes, pinkish-red
diagonal from apex of forewings to middle
of inner margin of hindwings. Nocturnal,
summer; rests by day on leaves, easily
disturbed; common in wasteland, also
gardens. Caterpillar brown-grey, with 4
darker lozenges and 3 whitish lines on
back; feeds on docks. WE, CE. [1]

Riband Wave *Idaea aversata* GEOMETRIDAE
WS 27–30 mm. Wings variably grey-white
or grey-buff with dark lines or dark band,
distinct spot in middle of each. Nocturnal,
Jun–Jul; common in wasteland, gardens.
Caterpillar brownish, yellower at rear and
in line along sides, with whitish line in
darker strip broken by V-marks on back;
feeds on dandelions, docks, primroses,
bedstraws. T, ex Ic. [2]

Dark-barred Twin-spot Carpet
Xanthorhoe ferrugata GEOMETRIDAE WS 22–
24 mm. Forewings pale yellow with broad,
dark central band, usually dark base;
hindwings greyish-white, finely lined with
darker scales. Nocturnal, May–Jun, Aug;
common in wasteland, gardens. Caterpillar yellow-brown, mottled greyish, with
pale diamonds and black spots in middle
of back; feeds on many weeds. T, ex Ic.
[3] Several similar spp in gardens.

Garden Carpet *Xanthorhoe fluctuata*
GEOMETRIDAE WS 22–24 mm. Forewings
white with dark area at base and variable
dark markings in centre; hindwings white
or grey. Nocturnal, Apr–Oct; often rests
indoors by day on curtain or wall;
common in gardens, wasteland. Caterpillar
dark grey to dull green, with pale blotches
and black spots on back; feeds on Cruciferae, including cabbage. T, ex Ic. [4]

Common Carpet *Epirrhoe alternata*
GEOMETRIDAE WS 23–25 mm. Similar to
Xanthorhoe fluctuata, but usually with
dark central band, more obvious markings
on hindwings. Nocturnal, Jun–Jul; esp
gardens. Caterpillar pale yellow-brown to
green, 3 darker lines along back, yellow
stripe on sides; feeds on bedstraws. T. [5]

Yellow Shell *Camptogramma bilineata*
GEOMETRIDAE WS 23–28 mm. Wings
usually yellow, sometimes brownish,
intricately marked and lined with darker
pattern. Nocturnal, through summer;
often found on vegetation by day, easily
disturbed; esp on wasteland, common in
many areas. Caterpillar yellow-green,
with dark green and 2 yellowish lines
along back, pale line on sides; feeds on
grasses. WE, CE. [6]

Mallow *Larentia clavaria* GEOMETRIDAE
WS 30–40 mm. Forewings brown with
broad, dark central band; hindwings paler
with dark lines. Nocturnal, autumn; rests
by day on undersides of leaves; common
on wasteland, in gardens where hollyhocks.
Caterpillar long, green, with slightly
darker lines on back and sides; feeds
on mallows, hollyhocks. T, ex Ic, far
north. [7]

Spinach *Eulithis mellinata* GEOMETRIDAE
WS 29–34 mm. Forewings pale yellow-
brown, clouded darker brown, with 3
dark cross-lines; hindwings pale yellow.
Nocturnal, Jul–Aug, attracted to light;
common where there are currants.
Caterpillar long, green, with dark green
and 2 whitish lines along back, whitish
line on sides; feeds on currant leaves.
T, ex Ic. [8]

Magpie Moth *Abraxas grossulariata*
GEOMETRIDAE WS 36–43 mm. Wings white
and yellow with black spots. Nocturnal,
Jul–Aug; common in gardens. Caterpillar
white with rows of black blotches and dots;
feeds on leaves of currants, gooseberry, in
towns esp spindle tree. Pupa black and
yellow, also on these plants. T, ex Ic. [9]
[caterpillar 10]

Brimstone Moth *Opisthograptis luteolata*
GEOMETRIDAE WS 29–38 mm. Wings and
body bright yellow; front margin of
forewings marked with red. Flies at dusk,
spring, summer; common in suburbs, esp
where flowering cherries. Caterpillar twig-
like, brownish, tinged with green or
purple; feeds on hawthorns, cultivated
Prunus. T, ex Ic. [11]

Canary-shouldered Thorn *Ennomos alniaria* GEOMETRIDAE WS 34–37 mm, ♀ slightly larger than ♂. Forewings yellow-brown with 2 brown lines; hindwings yellowish; thorax canary-yellow. Nocturnal, autumn; common in well-wooded suburbs, parks. Caterpillar brownish, mottled purplish; feeds on birches. T, ex Ic. [1]

Dusky Thorn *Ennomos fuscantaria* GEOMETRIDAE WS 33–38 mm. Similar to *E. alniaria*, but outer half of wings dusky, thorax brownish-yellow. Nocturnal, Aug–Sep; common wherever ash. Caterpillar green, sometimes pale brown or red-brown; feeds on ash lvs. T, ex Ic. [2]

Early Thorn *Selenia dentaria* GEOMETRIDAE WS 34–41 mm. Forewings grey-brown with 3 transverse lines, dark patch near tip; hindwings grey-brown, sometimes slightly spotted. Flies early spring, 2nd brood Jul–Aug (latter smaller, browner); common in wooded parks. Caterpillar twig-like, orange or red-brown; feeds on birches, willows, hawthorns. T, ex Ic. [3]

Scalloped Hazel *Odontopera bidentata* GEOMETRIDAE WS 40–48 mm. Forewings grey-brown with 2 dark lines, dark-edged central spot; hindwings similar, but with 1 line; in some areas, black individuals common. Nocturnal, May–Jun. Caterpillar pale blue-green and black, resembling lichen, or purplish mottled yellow and brown; feeds on privet, also other trees, bushes. T, ex Ic. [4]

Scalloped Oak *Crocallis elinguaria* GEOMETRIDAE WS 34–37 mm. Forewings pale buff, with dark-edged, pale brown central band containing dark spot; hindwings pale buff, with dark central spot; outer margins of both dotted brown. Nocturnal, Jul–Aug; common in well-wooded suburbs, parks. Caterpillar yellow-grey to dark grey tinged purple, diamond marks on back; feeds on most

deciduous trees, bushes. T, ex Ic. [5]

Swallow-tailed Moth *Ourapteryx sambucaria* GEOMETRIDAE WS 42–56 mm. Large, pale yellow, with 2 dark lines on forewings, 1 on hindwings; projection at point of hindwings, marked with 2 brown spots, forms 'swallow tail'. Flies at dusk, Jul; often in suburbs. Caterpillar long, thin, brownish marked with red-purple, mimicking twig; feeds on ivy, elder. T, ex Ic, Fi, No. [6] [caterpillar 7]

Brindled Beauty *Lycia hirtaria* GEOMETRIDAE WS 38–50 mm. Forewings grey, tinged green, with lines and speckles; hindwings paler. Nocturnal, Mar–Apr; resting by day on tree trunks; urban moth, often in city streets, parks. Caterpillar purplish-grey or red-brown, freckled darker, marked yellow; feeds on limes, elms. T, ex Ic. [8]

Peppered Moth *Biston betularia* GEOMETRIDAE WS 42–52 mm, ♀ larger than ♂. Wings white, peppered black; in many towns, entirely black; intermediates occur. Nocturnal, May–Jul, ♂s attracted to lights; common wherever trees. Caterpillar green, brownish-green or purplish-brown; feeds on birches, willows, beech. T, ex Ic. [9]

Waved Umber *Menophra abruptaria* GEOMETRIDAE WS 29–35 mm. Dark-banded, pale brown hindwings distinctive; at rest on fence or tree trunk, resembles dead leaf. Nocturnal, Apr–May; common in some towns. Caterpillar grey-brown, sometimes tinged green, with pink-brown blotches along back; feeds on privet, lilac. T, ex Ic, Fi, Sw. [10]

Light Emerald *Campaea margaritata* GEOMETRIDAE WS 36–48 mm. Wings pale whitish-green with white lines. Nocturnal, Jun–Jul, resting by day among herbage; common in towns wherever trees. Caterpillar green-brown to purple-brown; feeds on oaks, birches, beech. T, ex Ic, Fi. [11]

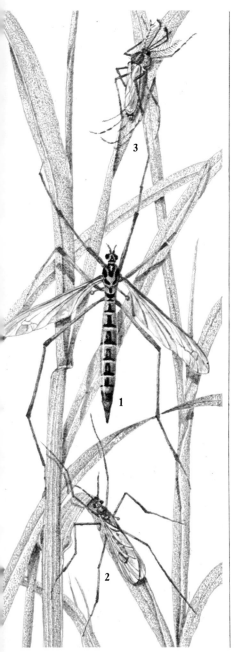

True flies (Diptera) are immensely varied, tiny to medium-sized. Adults distinguished by single pair of wings; hindwings reduced to short balancing organs (halteres). Membraneous wings may be patterned, but are usually partly transparent. A few spp, mainly parasitic, are wingless. Sucking or piercing mouthparts. Distinct larval and pupal stages, but much variation in form associated with different life histories. Perhaps the most abundant order of insects in towns, with many spp in an average garden.

crane-fly, daddy-long-legs *Nephrotoma appendiculata* TIPULIDAE BL 15–20 mm. Body conspicuously banded with yellow and black; very long legs; transparent wings. Nocturnal, May–Sep; often disturbed by day from vegetation. Larva or 'leather-jacket' greyish, thick-skinned; feeds on plant roots, often damages garden crops. T, ex Ic. [1] Many similar spp, some more gnat-like.

winter gnat *Trichocera relegationis* TRICHOCERIDAE BL 6–7 mm. Like small crane-fly; distinguished by short, curved lower vein in wings. Does not bite. Seen dancing in air in winter swarms; occurs throughout year. Larva feeds on decaying vegetation, fungi. T, ex Ic. [2]

Common Gnat, Northern House Mosquito *Culex pipiens* CULICIDAE BL 4·5–6 mm. Slender, leggy; wings with 10 veins or vein branches reaching margin. ♂ with plumed antennae; does not bite.

♀ with piercing mouthparts; sometimes bites man. Hibernates in buildings. Abundant where standing water; larva commonly in puddles, ponds, water tanks. T, ex Ic. [3]

mosquito *Culiseta annulata* CULICIDAE BL 8–10 mm. Dark spots on wings; white rings on legs. ♀ hibernates indoors; often bites and extracts blood, even in winter if warm weather breaks hibernation. T, ex Ic. [4]

fever-fly *Dilophus febrilis* BIBIONIDAE BL 4–6 mm. Black, hairy-looking; wings transparent in ♂, slightly smoky in ♀. Diurnal, Mar–Oct; often visits flowers. ♂ dances in air above ♀ on vegetation. Breeds in manure, leaflitter; may damage plant roots. 'Fever-fly' has no connection with fevers. T. [5]

biting midge *Culicoides pulicaris* CERATOPOGONIDAE BL 1·5–2·5 mm. Wings with dark spots; ♂ with plumed antennae. ♀ with piercing mouthparts, more often felt than seen: bites especially at dusk on warm summer evenings (hence 'no-see-ums' in USA). Larva in mud. WE, CE, ex Ic. [6] Related spp suck blood of caterpillars.

owl midge, moth-fly *Psychoda alternata* PSYCHODIDAE BL 1·5–2·5 mm. Wings and body covered with small hairs. Often on windows or clustered on tree trunks. Runs jerkily. Larva in mud, abundant in sewage filters. T, ex Ic. [7] Related spp also in towns.

Hoverflies (Syrphidae), separated from other flies by the presence of veins running parallel to the hind margin of the wings, are by far the most obvious group of Diptera in towns and gardens. Usually brightly coloured, they may be recognized by their hovering flight in sunshine, feeding from flowers, fallen fruit, honeydew.

hoverfly *Platychirus peltatus* SYRPHIDAE BL 8–10 mm. Small; ♂ with conspicuous thickening at tips of legs (as in all *Platychirus*); abdomen black with 6 yellow spots, yellow tip. Larva feeds on decaying vegetation, fungi, in damp places. T. [1] Several related spp common in gardens.

hoverfly *Melanostoma scalare* SYRPHIDAE BL 7–8 mm. Small, slender; abdomen with pairs of dark yellow spots on upperside. Abundant in gardens; feeds on flowers. Larva slug-like; feeds on aphids on garden plants, vegetables. T, ex Ic. [2] Several related spp in gardens, with *M. ambiguum*, BL 7–8 mm, sometimes commonest of genus.

hoverfly *Scaeva pyrastri* SYRPHIDAE BL 13–15 mm. Rather large; body black, with 3 pairs of white half-moon marks on upperside of abdomen. Usually singly on flowers, sometimes common; will visit and feed from drinks, *eg* beer, left outdoors. Migrant, appearing in swarms in coastal towns. Larva feeds on aphids. T, ex Ic. [3]

hoverfly *Syrphus ribesii* SYRPHIDAE BL 11–14 mm. Rather large; body dark brown, with 4 yellow bands, 1st broken in middle, on upperside of abdomen. Common in gardens at flowers, at honeydew on trees. Swarms during dry weather, sometimes in immense numbers on coast. Larva slug-like; feeds on aphids on garden plants. T. [4] Several related and equally common spp differ in arrangement and shape of yellow abdominal bands, *eg S. corollae*.

hoverfly *Syrphus balteatus* SYRPHIDAE BL 10 mm. Body dull orange; upperside of abdomen with black belts. Migrant; common in gardens. Larva feeds on aphids. T, ex Ic. [5] [larva 6]

Large Narcissus-fly *Merodon equestris* SYRPHIDAE BL 10–12 mm. Large, robust, hairy; several distinct colour forms, each mimicking sp of bumblebee. On leaves, flowers, May–Jun. Larva feeds on bulbs; can become pest. WE, CE. [7]

hoverfly *Syritta pipiens* SYRPHIDAE BL 8–9 mm. Small; hindlegs noticeably large, thickened; upperside of abdomen dark with pale markings. Very common at flowers in gardens. Larva feeds on decaying matter. WE, CE, ex Ic. [8]

Drone-fly *Eristalis tenax* SYRPHIDAE BL 12–14 mm. Large; body brown with variable paler markings; remarkably similar to drone of honey bee. Feeds on nectar and pollen. Migrant; extremely common in some years, esp autumn. Eggs laid in decomposing plant, animal remains. Larva moves to water, extends tube which acts as snorkel for air breathing. WE, CE, ex Ic. [9].

hoverfly *Eristalis arbustorum* SYRPHIDAE B6 11 mm. Smaller and less like honey bee than *E. tenax*; body brown, with pair of pale orange-brown patches on front segments of upperside of abdomen. Very common in gardens, Apr–Sep, esp where *Aster* flowers. Larva feeds on decomposing matter. WE, CE, ex Ic. Several related spp in gardens.

Lesser Bulb-fly *Eumerus strigatus*
SYRPHIDAE BL 5–7 mm. Small, squat,
black. Not often noticed, but, together
with very similar *E. tuberculatus*, extremely
common in gardens. Larva feeds on bulbs;
can become pest. WE, CE, ex Ic. [1]

hoverfly *Rhingia campestris* SYRPHIDAE
BL 8–9 mm. Rather large, orange, with
conspicuous proboscis. Often seen at
flowers, esp *Buddleja*. Comes into gardens
from farmland where larva feeds in cow-
dung. Widespread; rarely common. WE,
CE, ex Ic. [2]

hoverfly *Sphearophoria scripta* SYRPHIDEA
BL 10 mm. Long body; upperside of
abdomen with black and yellow bands;
yellow stripes on side of thorax. Common
at flowers. Larva feeds on aphids. T. [3]

hoverfly *Baccha elongata* SYRPHIDAE
BL 9–10 mm. Small, narrow-waisted,
resembles ichneumon fly. Usually seen
flying slowly in sheltered corners of
garden; rarely at flowers. Larva feeds on
aphids. CE, WE, ex Ic. [4]

thickhead fly *Conops quadrifasciata*
CONOPIDAE BL 8·5–12 mm. Wasp-like;
abdomen banded; antennae clubbed.

Active in bright sunshine, usually at flowers. ♀ lays eggs while in flight, on bumblebees. Larva internal parasite, eventually kills bee. T, ex Ic. [5] Several similar spp, none esp common.

Celery-fly *Philophylla heraclei* TRYPETIDAE BL 5 mm. Small; dark patterns on wings; iridescent green eyes. ♀ lays eggs on Umbelliferae, *eg* celery. Larva mines into leaf tissue; often lives in small groups. Common where food-plants. WE, CE, ex Ic. [6]

Carrot-fly *Psila rosae* PSILIDAE BL 4–6 mm. Wings with distinctive cross-fold, but fly small and inconspicuous. Larva yellowish, attacks carrots, related crops; often seen with rear end sticking out of root. Usually 2 generations per year. Common in gardens where larval food-plant grown. T. [7]

Holly Leaf-miner *Phytomyza ilicis* AGROMYZIDAE BL 3–4 mm. Small, rarely noticed, like tiny house-fly. Can be disturbed from holly *Ilex aquifolium*, May. Larva causes conspicuous blotches on holly leaves, best seen in winter, early spring. Truly urban, common wherever holly. WE, CE, ex Ic, Fi. [8]

Small Cluster-fly *Thaumatomyia notata* CHLOROPIDAE BL *c*3 mm. Tiny; eyes brightly coloured. Most often seen in autumn: enters buildings in large numbers before hibernation. WE, CE, ex Ic. [1] Many related spp; most have plant-feeding larvae.

Common Dung-fly *Scatophaga stercoraria* SCATOPHAGIDAE BL 9·5–10·5 mm. Medium-sized, greenish-yellow, furry. More often seen at cow-dung in country; comes into gardens throughout summer. Feeds on smaller flies. Larva feeds on dung. W, not Sw. [2]

tachinid fly *Gonia sicula* TACHINIDAE BL 10–12 mm. Looks like large house-fly; head swollen between eyes; wing venation characteristic; abdomen black, hairy, with white bands on anterior part. Mar–Apr. Eggs scattered in flight by ♀. Larva internal parasite in caterpillars of noctuid moths, also other insects. WE, CE, Fi, Sw. [3]

bluebottle *Calliphora vicina* CALLI-PHORIDAE BL 8·5–11 mm. Large, blue-bodied, hairy, with black checks. ♀ enters houses in search of meat on which to lay eggs; ♂ feeds from flowers. Common everywhere. T, ex Ic. [4] Several related spp collectively known as blue-bottles.

greenbottle *Lucilia caesar* CALLIPHORIDAE BL 9–10 mm. Similar to *Calliphora*, but body metallic-green. ♀ lays eggs on dead animals: larvae important decomposers. ♂ feeds from flowers. Common every-where but rarely enters houses. T, ex Ic. [5] Several *Lucilia* spp in gardens.

blow-fly *Protocalliphora azurea* CALLI-PHORIDAE BL 9·5–10·5 mm. Resembles *Calliphora*, but smaller. Feeds at flowers.

Larva dirty-white, 8 mm long when full-grown; sucks blood of, and may kill, nestling birds. Pupates in the bird's nest. T, ex Ic. [6]

Grey Flesh-fly *Sarcophaga carnaria* CALLIPHORIDAE BL 14·5–15·5 mm. Large, grey, speckled, with conspicuously big feet. ♀ viviparous: deposits tiny larvae on to meat, dead animals. These pupate in ground. Common in towns. T, ex Ic. [7]

House-fly *Musca domestica* MUSCIDAE BL 8–9 mm. Grey; buff-tinted abdomen. Closely associated with human habitation: most flies entering houses try to escape through windows, *M. domestica* does not. Larva feeds on refuse, esp excrement. Transmits diseases. T. [8]

Lesser House-fly *Fannia canicularis* MUSCIDAE BL 6–8 mm. Similar to *Musca domestica*: ♀ dull-coloured, thorax grey, abdomen yellowish; ♂ thorax grey, abdomen buff with greyer tip and light patch at base. Common round houses, summer. In rooms and under trees, flies in steady, angled course; occa-sionally darts off-course before resuming circling, but rarely settles (contrast *M. domestica*). Larva has protuberances with small hairs along body which help movement in liquid; feeds in decaying, semi-liquid matter or excrement. T. [♀ 9]

Common Bee-fly *Bombylius major* BOMBYLIIDAE BL 8–12 mm. Resembles bumblebee but only 1 pair of wings; furry, brown body; obvious long proboscis (tongue); anterior margin of wings darker, posterior transparent. Agile, hovers actively above flowers, often touching with feet, Mar–May. Larva parasitic in nest of solitary bee. Pupates in bee cell: 2 pupal stages, 2nd has strong circle of spines to cut way out. T. [10]

Woodwasps, sawflies (Hymenoptera: Symphyta) have no waist. Larvae mostly free-living, resembling Lepidoptera caterpillars but with 6 or more pairs of abdominal legs; plant-boring spp legless. Larvae more often noticed than adults.

Rose Sawfly *Arge ochropus* ARGIDAE BL 7-10 mm. Orange-yellow, with black mark on thorax, dark head. Eggs laid near growing point of rose. Larva caterpillar-like, green, spotted; feeds in groups on leaves of garden roses. Common where food-plant. WE, CE, ex Ic. [1] [larva 2]

Large Hawthorn Sawfly *Trichiosoma tibiale* CIMBICIDAE BL 13-24 mm. Large, black. Larva more often seen, pale green; feeds singly on leaves of hawthorn. Hard cocoon attached to twigs in winter contains pupa. Common where hawthorns. T, ex Ic. [3] [larva 4] [cocoon 5]

sawfly *Allantus cinctus* TENTHREDINIDAE BL 7-9 mm. Black; upperside of abdomen with conspicuous yellow band. Larva green, dark-headed; feeds in companies at edges of rose leaves. Fairly common where food-plant. T, ex Ic. [6] [larva 7]

Poplar Sawfly *Trichiocampus viminalis* TENTHREDINIDAE BL 7-9 mm. Abdomen yellow-orange, thorax black, legs orange. Larva yellow, black-spotted, spiny; feeds in groups on leaves of poplar. Abundant where poplars. T, ex Ic. [8] [larva 9]

sawfly *Pontania proxima* TENTHREDINIDAE BL 3-4 mm. Dark black-brown, inconspicuous. Larva causes bright red gall on upperside of leaf of willow. WE, CE, NE, ex Ic. [galls 10]

Gooseberry Sawfly *Nematus ribesii* TENTHREDINIDAE BL 6-11 mm. ♂ black, ♀ yellow. On currants, gooseberry, also at

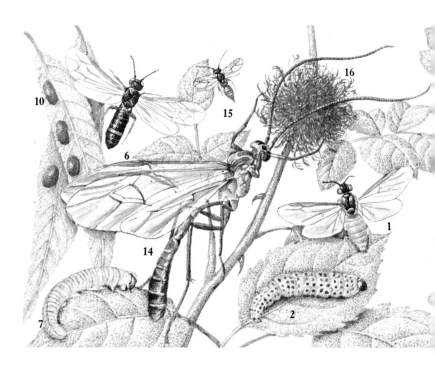

flowers. Larva pale green, dark-spotted; common on currants, gooseberry; feeds on leaves, sometimes defoliates. Can become pest. T, ex Ic. [♀ 11] [larva 12]

Wasps, ants, bees, ichneumons and other parasitic wasps (Hymenoptera: Apocrita) are narrow-waisted. Many have stings, *eg* digger wasps, bumblebees, some ants; most ants bite, or secret an irritant. ♀s of large ichneumon flies can pierce human skin with ovipositor.

parasitic wasp *Apanteles glomeratus* BRACONIDAE BL 2–5 mm. Small, black. Parasitizes caterpillars of large white butterfly; <100 larvae live in, eventually kill, single host; leave host when fully fed. Pupae in yellowish cocoons around host. T, ex Ic. [cocoons 13]

parasitic wasp *Ophion luteus* ICHNEUMONIDAE BL 15–18 mm, WS 30 mm. Large, brown. Flies at night, is attracted to lights in houses. Parasitizes caterpillars of wide variety of large moths. T. [14]

parasitic wasp *Pteromalus puparum* CHALCIDAE BL 3 mm. Small, black. Eggs laid on pupae of white butterflies: <100 larvae produced from division of single egg. T, ex Ic.

Robin's Pin-cushion Gall Wasp
Diplolepis rosae CYNIPIDAE BL 3–4 mm. Tiny adults rarely noticed. Larva causes gall on roses. Often on ramblers in gardens; rarely on ornamental varieties. T, ex Ic. [15] [gall 16] Related spp cause 'oak apples' and other galls on oaks.

ruby-tailed wasp *Chrysis ignita* CHRYSIDIDAE BL 7–10 mm. Small, brilliant metallic-green and bronze. Active flier in bright sunshine. Parasitic in nests of solitary bees, wasps. T, ex Ic. [17]

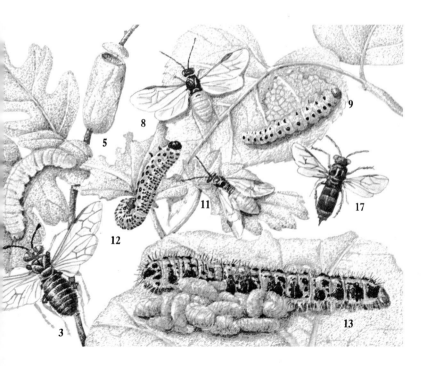

Pharaoh's Ant *Monomorium pharaonis*
FORMICIDAE BL 3–5 mm, ♀ larger than ♂.
Small, yellow with dark tip to abdomen;
♂ and ♀ winged, ☿ wingless. Nests
indoors, behind ovens, in cellars; pest in
warehouses, factories. T, ex Ic. [1]

Garden Black Ant *Lasius niger*
FORMICIDAE BL 3·5–9 mm, ♀ larger than
♂. Dark brown. Nests under paving
stones, often in or near buildings; common
in gardens, enters houses for food. Mating
flights in summer produce great swarms.
T, ex Ic. [2] [queen 3]

Argentine Ant *Iridomyrmex humilis*
FORMICIDAE BL 3–5 mm, ♀ larger than
♂. Dark-bodied, legs paler. In heated
buildings; not outdoors in Europe. T,
ex Ic. [4]

Wall-mason Wasp *Ancistrocerus
parietum* VESPIDAE BL 4–6 mm. Dark with
dull yellow bands. Commonly seen

inspecting fences, walls for suitable nest
sites. Caterpillars are stung and carried
paralysed to cell of fine soil mixed with
saliva; then single egg is laid and nest
sealed. T, ex Ic, uncommon Fi, No.
[5]

Common Wasp *Vespula vulgaris*
VESPIDAE BL 14–18 mm. Very similar to
V. germanica and *Dolichovespula sylvestris*:
distinguished by facial and abdominal
patterns. Black anchor-mark on face;
black triangle, bands and spots on yellow
abdomen. Social with large queens, ☿s,
drones (♂s). Builds large paper nest in
hole in ground. Commonest of the 3 spp
in towns. T, ex Ic. [6]

German Wasp *Vespula germanica*
VESPIDAE BL 13–20 mm. 3 black dots on
face; diamond and more distinct black
central marks on abdomen. Often almost
as common as *V. vulgaris*. Similar habits.
T. [7]

Tree Wasp *Dolichovespula sylvestris*
VESPIDAE BL 15–19 mm. Black dot on face;
more simply banded abdomen without
lateral spots. Constructs large paper nest
in hollow tree, roof. Much less common in
towns, gardens. T, ex Ic. [8]

Mournful Wasp *Pemphredon lugubris*
SPHECIDAE BL 10–12 mm. All black.
Solitary; nests in holes in fences. Stocks
cells with aphids to feed larvae. T, ex Ic.
[9]

Two-girdled Digger *Argogorytes
mystaceus* SPHECIDAE BL 11–13 mm. Black
with narrow yellow bands, yellow legs.
Solitary. Stocks nest in ground with
nymphs of spittlebug *Philaenus spumarius*.
T. [10]

solitary bee *Lasioglossum* (*Halictus*)
malachurus APOIDEA BL 9–11 mm. Black
with buff bands, buff legs; ♀ (like all
Halictus ♀s) with groove at tip of
abdomen. Most *Halictus* spp are solitary,
but *L. malachurus* semi-social: a few
workers in 1st brood. Nests in burrow
provisioned with pollen for larvae: several
cells with 1 egg in each. T, ex Ic.
[11]

Lawn Bee *Andrena armata* APOIDEA
BL 5–7 mm. ♀ hairy, red; ♂ browner, less
hairy. No sting. Common in spring,
early summer, flying over lawns. Small
piles of earth on lawns are burrows for
nests. Feeds on nectar, pollen. T, ex Ic.
[♀ 12]

Flower Bee *Anthophora retusa* APOIDEA
BL 13–16 mm. Large, blackish, hairy,
resembles bumblebee; ♂ with strikingly
hairy legs, ♀ with orange hairs on pollen
baskets of hindlegs. Nests in ground:
each earthen cell provisioned with pollen
nectar, before eggs laid; cell sealed.
Common in gardens in spring. WE, CE,
NE, ex Ic. [♀ 13]

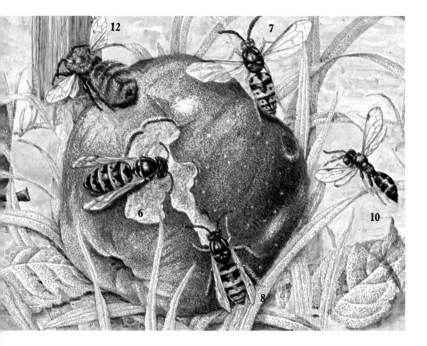

Common Garden Bumblebee *Bombus pascuorum* APOIDEA BL 14–18 mm. *Bombus* spp are social, with large queens (♀s), smaller ♀s and ♂s. Queen makes nest in early spring: produces workers throughout summer. Potential queens and ♂s both appear later and mate; ♂s die, queens overwinter. Queens and ♀s with pollen baskets on hindlegs. *B. pascuorum* all brown. Makes mossy nest above ground. T, ex Ic. [queen **1**]

Large Red-tailed Bumblebee *Bombus lapidarius* APOIDEA BL 15–22 mm. Black with red tail; wings clear. Nests in holes in banks. Attracted esp to Labiatae, *eg* white dead-nettle, bugle. T, ex Ic. [queen **2**] [♂**3**] [♀ **4**]

Buff-tailed Bumblebee *Bombus terrestris* APOIDEA BL 18–25 mm. Queen very large; white tail (yellow in British form); otherwise black with yellow bands on front of thorax, abdomen. Nests in holes in ground. Queen often covered with mites on emergence in spring; usually first *Bombus* sp to appear. T, ex Ic, Fi. [queen **5**]

Small Earth Bumblebee *Bombus lucorum* APOIDEA BL 14–23 mm. Black with white tail, broad yellow bands on front of thorax, abdomen. Known to build nests in bird nest-boxes. T, ex Ic. [queen **6**]

Early Bumblebee *Bombus pratorum* APOIDEA BL 13–18 mm. Resembles *B. lucorum* but tail bright brown; ♂ fluffy with yellow-green hairs on body. Will nest in old bird's nests. ♂ appears earlier than other *Bombus* ♂s. T, ex Ic. [queen **7**]

Vestal Cuckoo-bee *Psithyrus vestalis* APOIDEA BL 16–20 mm. Resembles *Bombus terrestris*, but lacks yellow band on less hairy abdomen. Nest parasite, usually of *B. terrestris*. Infrequent in gardens. T, ex Ic, Fi. [queen **8**]

Hill Cuckoo-bee *Psithyrus rupestris* APOIDEA BL 20–25 mm. Black with red tail; resembles *Bombus lapidarius* but wings dark smoky-brown. T. [queen **9**] [♂ **10**]

Honey or Common Hive Bee *Apis mellifera* APOIDEA BL 13–18 mm. Social; kept in hives for honey; many nest in hollow trees. Frequently swarms. ♀s leave sting in the flesh and die soon afterwards. (T.) [♀ **11**]

Beetles (Coleoptera) are distinguished by hardened forewings (wingcases or elytra) and membraneous hindwings; a few groups have reduced wingcases. All have biting mouthparts. Most larvae have well-developed legs on thorax; those which burrow into plant tissue are legless.

Violet Ground Beetle *Carabus violaceus* CARABIDAE BL 25 mm. Shiny, black; wingcases, thorax with violet borders. Active, nocturnal predator of insects, earthworms; lurks under stones by day. T, ex Ic. [1] Several other *Carabus* spp, some flightless.

ground beetle *Nebria brevicollis* CARABIDAE BL 9–12 mm. Black, small, flattened; legs reddish. Active, nocturnal predator of insects; under stones by day. Common in gardens. T, ex Ic, but uncommon Fi, No. [2]

ground beetle *Harpalus affinis* CARABIDAE BL 8·5–12 mm. Black with striking bronze or green sheen; legs, antennae reddish. Active, nocturnal predator of insects; under stones by day. T, ex Ic. [3]

ground beetle *Amara aenea* CARABIDAE BL 6–8 mm. Black with metallic-green or yellowish sheen; bases of antennae red. Hides under stones, also active by day, esp early spring. Feeds on insects, seeds. T, ex Ic. [4]

Black Burying Beetle *Necrophorus humator* SILPHIDAE BL 18–28 mm. Black, angular; rear abdominal segments project beyond wingcases; red-tipped antennae clubbed. Buries corpses of small mammals, *eg* mice. ♀ lays eggs in excavated chamber near buried corpse, feeds newly-hatched larvae with regurgitated carrion; older larvae eat corpse. T, ex Ic. [5]

sexton beetle *Necrophorus vespillo* SILPHIDAE BL 15–20 mm. Resembles *N. humator*, but smaller, wingcases with conspicuous orange bands. Habits also similar; attracted to lights. T, ex Ic. [6]

Devil's Coach-horse *Staphylinus olens* STAPHYLINIDAE BL 20–28 mm. Rove beetles (Staphylinidae) are mostly small, elongate; short, stumpy elytra expose much of abdomen; usually dull black or black and orange, often downy. All-black *S. olens* among largest. Nocturnal; under cover by day. Widespread, common. Opens large jaws, curves abdomen, if alarmed. WE, CE, not Ic, Fi. [7]

Stag Beetle *Lucanus cervus* LUCANIDAE BL 20–50 mm, ♂ larger than ♀. Black with red-brown wingcases; ♂ only has huge, antler-like (but weak) jaws. Flies at night; in daytime on tree trunks. Larva feeds on rotten wood, esp roots. WE, CE, not Fi, No. [♂ 8]

Common Dor Beetle, Lousy Watchman *Geotrupes stercorarius* GEOTRUPIDAE BL 16–23 mm. Shiny black with metallic sheen; hairy legs and underside. Flies early evening, often attracted to lights; hums in flight, falls to ground if strikes solid object. Eggs laid in dung. Usually infested with mites, hence 'lousy watchman'. T. [9]

Garden Chafer, Bracken-clock *Phyllopertha horticola* SCARABAEIDAE BL 8–11 mm. Wingcases orange-brown; head, thorax and underside dark green; conspicuous claws on feet. Day flier, Jun; sometimes large swarms. Feeds on flowers, leaves; may damage fruit trees. Larva feeds on roots; can be serious pest. T, ex Ic. [10]

Cockchafer, Maybug *Melolontha melolontha* SCARABAEIDAE BL 20–25 mm. Wingcases orange, powdered; thorax, abdomen black; ♂ antennae red, fan-like. Flies at dusk, May–Jun; often crashes into windows. Larva feeds on roots. WE, CE, not Ic, Fi, No. [11]

Rose-chafer *Cetonia aurata* SCARABAEIDAE BL 14–20 mm. Brilliant metallic-green; underside bright orange-red to copper. Feeds on flowers, esp roses. Larva eats roots. T, ex Ic. [12]

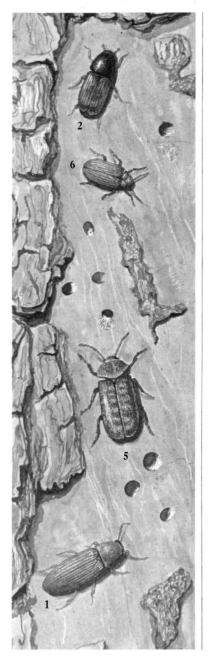

wireworm, click beetle *Agriotes obscurus* ELATERIDAE BL 7–9 mm. Brown, elongate; projections on thorax. Falls to ground if disturbed: if on back, springs into air with click to right itself; repeats click-jump if handled. Nocturnal; hides on ground by day. Adult feeds on pollen, nectar. Larva is tough leathery 'wireworm'; eats roots, *eg* potatoes, tubers. T, ex Ic. [1]

Large Elm-bark Beetle *Scolytus scolytus* SCOLYTIDAE BL 3–6 mm. Dark brown with redder wingcases, legs. Apr–May, Jul–Aug. Radiating galleries beneath bark of elms made by adults and then larvae. Damages trees, transmits fungus causing Dutch elm disease. T, ex Ic, Fi, rare No. [2] Other spp in this family bore under bark of various trees.

Bacon or **Larder Beetle** *Dermestes lardarius* DERMESTIDAE BL 7–9 mm. Black with broad, pale band across front half of elytra, usually marked with 3 dots on each side. Mainly indoors, in houses, warehouses. Larva hairy; feeds on furs, skins, wool; bores into wood to pupate. Often common; can be serious pest. T, ex Ic. [3]

Leather or **Hide Beetle** *Dermestes maculatus* DERMESTIDAE BL 5·5–10 mm. Resembles *D. lardarius*, but greyer-black and without pale band across elytra; underside covered with white down. Common indoor pest; outdoors on carrion. Larva feeds on dry animal remains, also clothing; sometimes used to clean museum skeletons. T. [4]

Death-watch Beetle *Xestobium rufovillosum* ANOBIIDAE BL 5–7 mm. Dull brown, stout; not often noticed. Sexes communicate by tapping heads against wood: heard at night when people sat up with the dead (hence name). Larva bores into dead wood, beams, rafters, furniture; can cause considerable damage in old buildings. T, ex Ic. [5]

Furniture Beetle, Woodworm *Anobium punctatum* ANOBIIDAE BL 3–4·5 mm. Small, red-brown with short, yellowish down; rarely noticed. Flies at night, Jun–Jul. Common in houses: numerous tiny holes in woodwork and little piles of wood-dust indicate presence. Larva bores into and feeds on wood. T. [6]

White-marked Spider Beetle *Ptinus fur* PTINIDAE BL 2·5–4 mm. Small, ♀ round-bodied, ♂ narrower; long legs, antennae. Common in houses. Larva scavenges stored food. T. [♀ 7]

Mealworm *Tenebrio molitor* TENEBRIONIDAE BL 12–16 mm. Blackish, elongate; lines on elytra. Larva pale brownish; feeds on flour, bran. Produced commercially as pet bird food, fish bait; pest of stored food. T. [8] Several other spp, *eg* much smaller *T. confusum* BL 3·5–4·5 mm: common pest of stored cereals. T. [9]

Pea-weevil *Bruchus pisorum* BRUCHIDAE BL 4–4·5 mm. Small, dark; short elytra expose white markings at tip of abdomen. Larva feeds on stored peas, beans. Not true weevil. T. [10]

Grain Weevil *Sitophilus granarius* CURCULIONIDAE BL 2–3·5 mm. Like most weevils, head has prominent 'snout'; body brown or red-brown. In stored cereals. Larva lives in single grain. T, ex Ic, rare Fi. [11] Many other weevils in urban gardens attack plants.

Turnip Flea-beetle *Phyllotreta nemorum*
CHRYSOMELIDAE BL 2·5–3 mm. Small;
black with 2 bold yellow stripes on elytra;
hindlegs well-developed for jumping
(hence 'flea' in name). Fly Jul;
important in aerial plankton. Adult and
larva feed on leaves, esp Cruciferae. T,
ex Ic. [1] Many related spp; all plant-
feeders.

Colorado Beetle *Leptinotarsa decemlineata*
CHRYSOMELIDAE BL 12 mm. Unmistakable:
yellow with black lines on elytra. Larva
red with black spots; feeds on potato, can
become pest. Appears periodically; usually
rare or absent. Special efforts made to
control numbers: sightings in Br should
be reported. (WE, CE, sSw, rare Fi,
from N America.) [2]

Ten-spot Ladybird *Adalia 10-punctata*
COCCINELLIDAE BL 3–4 mm. Distinguished
from *A. bipunctata* by yellow (not black)
legs, not by number of spots. Variable:
often red with black spots; unspotted
forms black, yellow and black, pale brown
and yellow. Common in gardens. Larva
feeds on Homoptera, *eg* aphids. T, ex Ic.
[3] [4]

Two-spot Ladybird *Adalia bipunctata*
COCCINELLIDAE BL 3–5 mm. Variable: red
with 2 black spots [5]; black with 2 or
more red spots; or red with black pattern
[6]. Common in gardens. Hibernates in
buildings, outhouses. Larva feeds on
aphids. T.

Seven-spot Ladybird *Coccinella
7-punctata* COCCINELLIDAE BL 5·5–7·5 mm.
Largest common ladybird; usually with 7
black spots. Invades gardens in vast
numbers in some years; rare or absent in
others. Feeds on aphids, nectar, honeydew, juices of fallen fruit. Hibernates
outdoors, often in groups, among
vegetation. Larva feeds on aphids. T. [7]
[larva 8]

11-spot Ladybird *Coccinella 11-punctata*
COCCINELLIDAE BL 3–4 mm. Red with 11
black spots, not variable; looks like small
C. 7-punctata. Invades gardens in large
numbers in some years; rare or absent in
others. Hibernates outdoors in vegetation.
Larva feeds on aphids. T. [9]

14-spot Ladybird *Propylea 14-punctata*
COCCINELLIDAE BL 3–4 mm. Yellow and
black, boldly marked; elytra with clear,
black crescent. Associated with woody
vegetation; sometimes common in gardens.
Larva feeds on aphids. T, ex Ic. [10]

22-spot Ladybird *Thea 22-punctata*
COCCINELLIDAE BL 2–3 mm. Small; yellow
with black spots; pale legs. Fairly
common, conspicuous on garden plants.
Larva feeds on mildew. T, ex Ic. [11]

Eyed Ladybird *Anaitis ocellata*
COCCINELLIDAE BL 7·5–9 mm. Large; red
with pale-edged, black spots. Occasionally
in gardens, esp on conifers. Larva feeds
on aphids. T, ex Ic. [12]

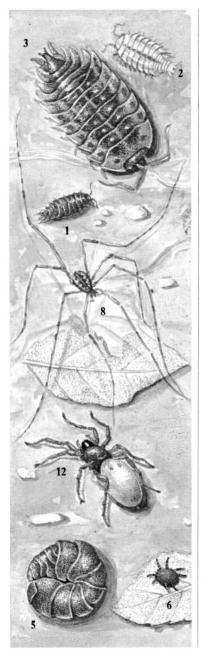

woodlouse *Trichoniscus pusillus*
TRICHONISCIDAE BL 3–5·5 mm. Small,
smooth, shiny red-brown, mottled white.
In damp places, under stones, bark;
moves into soil during frosty or dry
weather. Feeds on decaying vegetation.
Abundant, but less often noticed than
next 4 spp. T. [1]

woodlouse *Androniscus dentiger*
TRICHONISCIDAE BL 6–8 mm. White, pink
or even red with median white stripe;
transparent; body minutely tuberculate.
Locally common, esp in gardens, greenhouses, waste ground, basements of
houses; also in caves. WE, in greenhouses
eastwards to De, Po, FS. [2]

woodlouse *Oniscus asellus* ONISCIDAE
BL 15–18 mm. Grey with paler patches;
sometimes orange or yellowish. The
common sp avoiding desiccation under
stones in gardens. ♀ carries young in
brood-pouch on underside. As with all
woodlice, young are miniatures of adults:
aggregation under stones may contain
variety of sizes. T, ex Ic. [3]

woodlouse *Porcellio scaber* PORCELLIONIDAE
BL 11–18 mm. Body tuberculate; usually
grey, sometimes (esp ♀) yellow or orange
dotted with black; bases of antennae
orange. Commoner in dry places than other
spp, eg old walls; often indoors. T. [4]

Pill-bug *Armadillidium vulgare*
ARMADILLIDIIDAE BL 15–21 mm. Large,
grey woodlouse, with well-defined body
segments. Rolls into ball when alarmed.
Among stones, bricks; common in old
walls. T. [5]

red spider mites TETRANYCHIDAE BL < 1
mm. Plant-feeding mites, sometimes
destructive. Extract fluid from plant cells,
causing cell collapse: leaf appears crisp.
Adults of most spp red; spin webs over
foliage. *eg Panonychus ulmi*, BL 0·45 mm,
outdoor pest of fruit trees. [6] *Tetranychus
urticae*, pest outside and in greenhouses.
T. cinnabarinus, BL 0·6 mm, pest only in
greenhouses; outside in S Europe. Family
T, ex nBr, Ic, nFS.

false-scorpion *Chelifer cancroides*
CHELIFERIDAE BL 2·6–4·5 mm. Large
anterior pincers recall true scorpion, but
lacks tail; harmless to man. 4 pairs of
legs. Active predator. In gardens, running
on fences, walls. T. [7]

harvestman *Phalangium opilio*
PHALANGIIDAE BL 4–9 mm. All harvestmen,
unlike spiders, have no waist: cephalothorax and abdomen united. Legs, 4 pairs,
very long. Many spp nocturnal. Feed on
insects, spiders, other harvestmen; also
scavenge dead insects, even bird droppings. *P. opilio* partly diurnal, in gardens,
occasionally on walls, fences. T. [8]

Spiders (Araneae) have 4 pairs of legs; 2
divisions to the body, cephalothorax and
abdomen, joined by a narrow waist; silk
glands opening from spinnerets on
abdomen. Prey on small invertebrates.
About 50% of spp use silk for building
traps: from simple webs of crisscrossed
threads to circular orb–webs. Other spp, *eg*
Lycosidae and Salticidae, have good vision
and hunt prey.

spider *Amaurobius similis* AMAUROBIIDAE
BL ♀ 6–12 mm, ♂ smaller. Dark brown
with light abdominal markings. Spins
bluish, meshed web to entangle insects,
on tree trunks, walls. T, ex Ic, Fi, Sw. [9]

spider *Oonops domesticus* OONOPIDAE
BL 1·5–2 mm. Tiny, pinkish. In houses,
usually seen at night on walls; builds silk
cell in corner, crevice. Feeds on small
insects. Br, Fr, De, Cz. [10]

spider *Segestria senoculata* DYSDERIDAE
BL 7–10 mm. Slender; yellow, patterned
abdomen. Builds silk tube in crevice under
bark, in wall. Threads radiate from
opening of tube: when insect alights,
threads vibrate and spider rushes out to
seize prey. T, ex Ic. [11]

spider *Dysdera crocata* DYSDERIDAE BL 9–
15 mm. Carapace and legs red, abdomen
pale grey to yellowish. Common in
gardens, under stones; spins silk cell.
Hunts woodlice at night. T, ex Ic, Po,
Fi, Sw. [12]

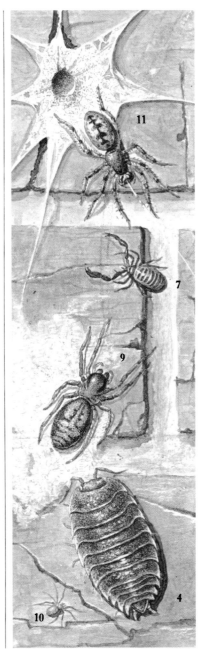

Spitting Spider *Scytodes thoracica* SCYTODIDAE BL 5–6 mm. Pale yellow with many black spots; characteristic domed carapace. In houses. Hunts at night by squirting gum which immobilizes small insects. Once considered rare. Br, Fr, Be, Ge, Cz. [1]

Long-bodied Cellar Spider *Pholcus phalangioides* PHOLCIDAE BL 8–10 mm. Long-legged, resembling harvestman; body long, pale yellow with grey abdomen. Hangs upside down in corner of room; makes cobweb. ♀ carries cluster of eggs in her jaw. T, ex Ic, Fi, Sw. [♀ 2]

spider *Drassodes lapidosus* GNAPHOSIDAE BL 6–24 mm. Carapace light yellowish to red-brown; abdomen greyer, downy. Abundant, under stones, in grass clumps; often in silk cell. Hunts insects at night. T, ex Ic. [3]

Zebra Spider *Salticus scenicus* SALTICIDAE BL 5–7 mm. Black and white abdominal markings distinctive. Commonly found on walls, fences, esp in gardens, houses. Active in bright sunshine; locates prey visually, creeps and pounces like cat. ♂ performs courtship dance. At rest, hides in crevice in sac-like retreat. T. [4]

crab spider *Xysticus eanio* THOMISIDAE BL 5–7 mm. Body and sideways movement crab-like; red-brown fairly distinctive. No web; lurks in low trees, bushes, seizes insects. T, ex Ic. [5]

wolf spider *Pardosa amentata* LYCOSIDAE BL 5·5–8 mm. Dark brown. Active in bright sunshine, running over bare ground; hunts insects. ♀ carries cluster of

eggs around in silk cocoon attached to
spinnerets. Young spend first days on ♀'s
back. T, ex Ic. [♀ 6]

Common House Spider *Tegenaria
gigantea* AGELENIDAE BL 11–14 mm.
Brown, hairy. Usually in sheds or dark
places outdoors; makes extensive web in
corner. Br, Fr, Ge, [7] *T. domestica*
similar, but smaller: T. ♂s of *Tegenaria*
spp leave webs in autumn to search for
♀s; often fall into baths, sinks, occasionally enter via overflows.

spider *Steatodea bipunctata* THERIDIIDAE
BL 4–7 mm. Chocolate-brown abdomen
with lighter striping; waxy appearance;
shiny eyes. Spins web to catch crawling
insects, in houses, garages. T. [8]

spider *Meta segmentata* TETRAGNATHIDAE
BL 5–8 mm. Very variable pattern, but
with central black band. Builds orb-
web fastened to vegetation, entangles
flying insects. Common in gardens. T,
ex Ic. [9]

Garden Spider *Araneus diadematus*
ARANEIDAE BL ♀ 10–12 mm, ♂ 4·5–8 mm.
Hairy; variable colour, but usually
yellowish to black with distinct white
cross-pattern on abdomen. Characteristic,
sticky orb-web common in gardens, esp late
summer; hides behind leaves, rushes into
web to secure trapped insects. T. [♀ 10]

money spider *Erigone atra* LINYPHIIDAE
BL 2–2·5 mm. Tiny. Ascends into air,
pulled up by its silk thread; often caught
by swifts. T. [11] This and related spp all
very small; live in litter on ground;
make sheet-like webs in vegetation.

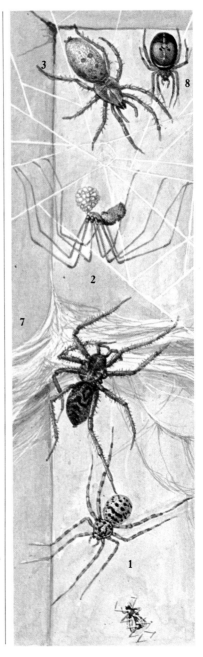

Mallard *Anas platyrhynchos* ANATIDAE
L 55–64 cm. ♂ yellow bill, green head,
white collar, purplish breast, grey
underparts, curled central tail-feathers. ♀
mottled brown; bill greenish, often dull
orange at sides. Only ♀ quacks. Any fresh
or salt water; common on urban rivers,
reservoirs, park ponds; in some areas
partly domesticated. Nests among under-
growth, often on islands in ponds, but
also far from water. Feeds on aquatic
vegetation, small invertebrates; accepts
bread in town parks. T, but only summer
nFS. [♀ 1] [♂ 2]

Tufted Duck *Aythya fuligula* ANATIDAE
L 41–46 cm. ♂ black with drooping crest,
white sides; ♀ browner, often with light
patch at base of bill. Common on open
fresh water: reservoirs, large rivers, large
ponds in town parks. Nests, often
sociably, among rushes or bushes on lake
islands. Feeds on small aquatic animals,
vegetation; becomes quite tame, takes
bread. Dives repeatedly. T, but only
summer Cz, ePo, Fi, nSC. [♀ 3] [♂ 4]

Moorhen *Gallinula chloropus* RALLIDAE
L 31–34 cm. Blackish, distinguished from
Coot *Fulica atra* by smaller size, bold
white streak along flanks, white under-
tail-coverts, red frontal shield, red bill
with yellow tip. Loud croaking calls,
mainly disyllabic. Streams, rivers, ponds,
lakes; common in parks in Br, Ir, but
more secretive on Continent. Nest of dead
reeds, sedges, over or near water, on
ground or in low bush; tiny young black
with pink bill and shield, blue skin above
eyes. Feeds on seeds, grasses, insects,
worms, slugs. Swims jerkily; dives
occasionally. T, ex Ic, nFS, but only
summer Cz, Po, Fi. [5]

Coot *Fulica atra* RALLIDAE L 36–40 cm.
Black, with white frontal shield and bill.
Short, explosive calls, mainly monosyllabic.
Prefers large areas of open water; also
coasts, harbours in winter. Nest of reeds,
sedges, over water or hidden in similar
vegetation; tiny young black with much
red on head. Feeds mainly on aquatic
plants, some small animals, *eg* molluscs,

tadpoles, insects. Swims rather jerkily; dives constantly. T, ex Ic, nFS, but only summer Cz, ePo, Fi. [6]

Black-headed Gull *Larus ridibundus* LARIDAE L 36–39 cm. Rather small gull with red bill, legs; head brown in summer, white with blackish marks near eyes in winter; juv has yellow-pink bill, legs, brown on upperparts, black-tipped tail. In flight, always white leading edge to wings. Harsh calls, esp 'kraar'. Common inland, coasts; often by water, also refuse tips, parks, farmland, even gardens in cold weather. Feeds on insects, worms, crustaceans, molluscs, fish; scavenges scraps. Swims buoyantly, perches in trees, hawks insect swarms, *eg* ants. T, ex nFS, but only summer Fi. [winter 7]

Common Gull *Larus canus* LARIDAE L 39–42 cm. White with grey back and wings, black and white wing-tips, but head streaked grey in winter; green-yellow bill, legs; juv marked brown above, black tip to tail. Calls high, shrill.

Moorland in summer; coasts, estuaries, lakes, farmland, parks in winter. Feeds on insects, earthworms, seeds, marine animals, refuse. Seldom hawks insects. T, but only winter/passage Fr, Lu, Be, Cz, only summer Fi, much of SC. [winter 8] Herring gull *L. argentatus*, also seen in towns, bigger with red-spotted yellow bill, usually pink legs, juv mainly brown tail.

White/Pied Wagtail *Motacilla alba* MOTACILLIDAE L 17–18 cm. ♂ conspicuously black, white and grey, with long tail; ♀ greyer, less black on head and breast. [♂ summer 9]. Pied wagtail *M. a. yarrellii* (ssp breeding in Br, Ir, adjacent coasts of Continent) has black rump, not grey; ♂ black back also. [♂ summer 10]. Flight-note characteristic 'tchizzik'. Towns, gardens, farms, open country, often by water. Nests in holes in walls, banks, cliffs, also in ivy. Feeds chiefly on insects, esp flies. Runs short distances, wags tail constantly. Large social roosts in some towns. T, but only summer Ic, Ne, De, Ge, Cz, Po, FS.

Kestrel *Falco tinnunculus* FALCONIDAE
L 33–36 cm. ♂ upperparts black-spotted
chestnut, head and black-tipped tail blue-
grey; ♀ rufous-brown above, barred
blackish, including tail. Shrill 'kee-kee-
kee' in breeding season. Lowlands,
mountains, moors, coasts, locally in
towns. Nests in old nests of other birds,
tree-hollows, cliffs, buildings. Feeds
on mice, voles, small birds, large insects,
even earthworms; hunts by habitual
hovering, often near motorways, railways,
then dropping to ground. T, ex Ic, but
only summer ePo, Fi, nSC. [♀ 1] [♂ 2]

Feral Pigeon *Columba livia* COLUMBIDAE
L 31–34 cm. Obvious, often abundant
town pigeon. Colour and pattern
extremely variable, *eg* whites, red-browns,
blacks, but often blue-grey with white
rump and 2 black bars across wings, like
rock dove ancestor. Voice 'oo-roo-coo'.
Towns, parks, granaries; also sea cliffs,
open country. Nests on buildings, cliffs.
Feeds on scraps, grain, some weed seeds.
T, ex far north. [3]

Collared Dove *Streptopelia decaocto*
COLUMBIDAE L 27–29 cm. Pale brown
upperparts; white-edged, black half-collar
on back of neck; pink-grey head and
breast; white-ended, black-based
underside to rather long tail. Flight call
nasal 'kwurr'; song monotonous 'coo-
cooo-cu' (accent on mid syllable). Mainly
suburban; also villages, farms, granaries.
Nests in trees, sometimes on buildings.
Feeds on grain, also scavenges. T, ex Ic
(has bred), Fi, nSC, but still spreading.
[4]

Tawny Owl *Strix aluco* STRIGIDAE L 37–
39 cm. Large, round head, no ear tufts;
black eyes, grey-brown facial discs;
variably red-brown to grey, mottled and
streaked lighter and darker brown. Call
sharp 'ke-wick'; familiar hooting song
'hoo-hoo-hoo' ends with long-drawn,
tremulous 'hoooooooooo'. Suburban areas,
parks, old woods. Nocturnal; more often

heard than seen; sometimes disturbed
from tree by day, seen at night on roof-
top. Nests in holes in trees, takes to
special nest-boxes. Feeds on small
mammals, birds, large insects, earthworms, even fish. T, ex Ic, Ir, nFS. [5]

Swift *Apus apus* APODIDAE L 16–17 cm.
Distinguished from swallows (Hirundinidae) by long, scythe-shaped wings;
short, forked tail; all sooty-black except
pale throat. Distinctive flight, with rapid
beats of stiff wings. Noisy when breeding,
screaming parties chasing round buildings.
Exclusively aerial, over towns, villages,
water; also open country, cliffs. Nests
socially in holes under eaves, also in tree
holes (FS). Feeds on insects and spiders
caught in air. Summer T, ex Ic, nSC. [6]

House Martin *Delichon urbica*
HIRUNDINIDAE L 12–13 cm. Blue-black,
with white rump and underparts;
distinguished from swallow *Hirundo
rustica* by short-forked tail, white rump.
Twittering song; chirruping calls in flight
and at nest. Almost entirely aerial, over
towns, villages, water; also open country
near dwellings, locally on cliffs. Cup-
like mud nest under eaves, often in
colonies. Feeds on insects caught in air.
Summer T, ex Ic. [7]

Starling *Sturnus vulgaris* STURNIDAE
L 21–22 cm. Blackish, glossed metallic-
green and purple; much speckled in
winter; short tail, pointed wings; sharp
bill, brown turning yellow in early spring;
juv mouse-brown with whitish throat.
Rambling song of warbles, whistles, clicks,
rattles, also mimicking other birds and
noises; call harsh 'tcheerr'. Towns, parks,
woods, open country. Nests in holes in
masonry, trees. Feeds on insects, earthworms, other invertebrates; seeds, berries,
fruit; kitchen scraps, esp in winter.
Social: roosts in great numbers on city
buildings, also in conifer woods, reedbeds.
T, but only summer Cz, ePo, Fi, nSC.
[summer 8] [winter 9]

Black Redstart *Phoenicurus ochruros*
TURDIDAE L 13–14 cm. Rufous tail,
constantly flickering; otherwise, breeding
♂ sooty-black except for white wing-
patch, winter ♂ much greyer, ♀ and juv
grey-brown. Short, warbling song ends
with gravelly rattle; calls 'tsip' and ticking
note. Large buildings in towns, power
stations, ruins; also cliffs, rocky ground.
Nests in holes in buildings, walls, rocks.
Feeds mainly on insects; some berries and
small crustaceans in autumn/winter. All
year sBr, Fr; summer Lu, Be, Ne, De,
Ge, Cz, Po, sSw, winter sIr. [♀ 1] [♂ 2]

Blackbird *Turdus merula* TURDIDAE L 24–
26 cm. ♂ all-black with orange-yellow
bill and eye-ring; ♀ dark brown above,
paler and more rufous below, with brown
or yellowish bill, whitish throat; juv paler,
more rufous, more mottled on breast;
imm ♂ black-brown with black bill. Song
rich and warbling; chattering alarm.
Gardens, town parks, hedges; also woods.
Nests in bushes, hedges, trees, sheds,
walls, buildings. Feeds on earthworms,
insects, seeds, berries, fruit, also scraps.
T, ex nFS, but only winter Ic. [♀ 3]
[♂ 4]

Blue Tit *Parus caeruleus* PARIDAE L 11–12
cm. Bright blue crown, wings and tail;
white cheeks with black line through eyes,
black chin; yellow underparts; juv green-
brown above, with yellow cheeks.
Commonest calls variations of 'tsee-tsee';
similar notes begin characteristic trilling
song. Gardens, hedges, parks; also mixed
woods. Nests in holes in trees and walls,
commonly in garden nest-boxes. Feeds on
insects, esp caterpillars, aphids, also
spiders, various seeds; in winter, takes
nuts, fat, scraps from bird tables. T, ex
Ic, nFS. [5]

Great Tit *Parus major* PARIDAE L 13–14
cm. Head glossy blue-black with white
cheeks; yellow underparts with black band
down middle; greenish to blue-grey
upperparts; juv has browner crown,
yellowish cheeks. Very varied vocabulary;
song distinctive, ringing 'teechew-
teechew'. Gardens, hedgerows; also mixed
woods. Nests in holes in trees and walls,

often in nest-boxes. Feeds on insects,
spiders, slugs, snails, earthworms, various
seeds and buds; so often searches on
ground. T, ex Ic. [6]

Greenfinch *Carduelis chloris* FRINGILLIDAE
L 14–15 cm. ♂ olive-green with yellowish
rump, obvious yellow on wings and tail;
♀ greyer, with less yellow; juv browner,
streaked. Song warbling twitter, often
accompanying bat-like display flight; calls
include characteristic, prolonged, nasal
'tsweee' of ♂ in breeding season. Gardens
with trees, parks; also wood edges,
farmlands. Nests in bushes and small
trees, esp evergreens, often socially. Feeds
on seeds, of both crops and many weeds,
also berries and fruit buds; young fed
partly on insects. T, ex Ic, nFS. [7]

House Sparrow *Passer domesticus*
PASSERIDAE L 14–15 cm. ♂ dark grey
crown and nape, chestnut at sides, grey-
white cheeks and underparts; black throat
and upper breast, ♀ and juv much duller,
dark-streaked brown above, grey-brown
below, without distinctive features. Very
noisy: variety of chirping and twittering
calls. Familiar town bird; also common
round farms and cultivation. Untidy nest
of straw and feathers in hole or under
eaves, in tall hedge or dense tree. Feeds
mainly on scraps in towns, but opportunist, even taking aphids and butterflies in
air; elsewhere much corn, some seeds and
buds, various insects. T, ex Ic (has bred).
[♀ 8] [♂ 9]

Tree Sparrow *Passer montanus* PASSERIDAE
L 13–14 cm. Sexes alike, smaller and
neater than house sparrow *P. domesticus*,
with chocolate crown, neat black bib,
black spot on purer white cheeks; juv
similar, but duller crown, greyer-black
bib and spot. Metallic 'chip' and hard
flight-call 'tek, tek' distinctive. In west,
locally in suburbs, but more in old
hedgerows, trees, open woods, orchards,
also in riverain willows, even on exposed
islands; in east, commonly in towns, also
extending to tundra in FS. Nests in holes
in trees or buildings. Feeds on seeds,
insects, spiders; also takes scraps. T, ex
Ic, much of Fi, nSC. [10]

Hedgehog *Erinaceus europaeus* ERINACEIDAE
BL 225–274 mm. Sharp spines on
upperside; pointed snout; truncated head
and neck; short legs. Grunts quietly;
often detected by rustling among dead
leaves. Gardens, hedgerows, woods, esp
where damp grassland nearby; needs
cover for nest. Feeds on insects, slugs,
snails, also mice, frogs, berries; garden
visitors accept milk. Nocturnal; by day
after rain. Rolls into ball if frightened.
Hibernates in moss- or leaf-lined hole
among shrubs. T, ex Ic, nFS. [1]

Long-eared Bat *Plecotus auritus*
VESPERTILIONIDAE BL 37–48 mm, FA 34–42
mm. Small; long, conspicuous ears; broad
wings. Voice sharp, shrill. Aerial over
trees, bushes in suburbs. Feeds on flying
insects. Largely nocturnal; spends day
in hollow trees, lofts, steeples. Hibernates
singly in cellars, stables, hanging from
wall or roof. Some migrate long distances.
T, ex Ic, nFS. [2]

Pipistrelle *Pipistrellus pipistrellus*
VESPERTILIONIDAE BL 33–45 mm, FA 28–35
mm. Small; short ears; rather narrow
wings. Flies with fast, jerky movements.
Squeaks in flight. Aerial over open
country, towns. Feeds on flying insects.
Crepuscular, nocturnal, occasionally by
day; usually spends day in buildings (often
large colonies), hollow trees among ivy.
Hibernates in groups in buildings. T, ex
Ic, Fi, nSC. [3]

Serotine *Eptesicus serotinus* VESPERTILI-
ONIDAE BL 58–75 mm, FA 48–55 mm.
Large, robust; broad wings; tail projects
beyond tip of wing membrane. Flight
fluttering, hesitant, rather like large moth.
Aerial over towns, parks, wood edges.
Feeds on flying insects. Crepuscular,
nocturnal; spends day in small groups in
buildings, fissures in walls. Hibernates in
hollow trees, cellars, barns, churches. T,
ex nBr, Ir, Ic, nDe, FS. [4]

Red Fox *Vulpes vulpes* CANIDAE BL 55–75
cm, TL 30–50 cm. Upperside red-brown,
underside whitish; sharp muzzle; pointed
ears; long, bushy tail. Barking call, also
high-pitched wailing. Scrub, tall
vegetation, woods, parks, railway
embankments. Underground den, often
enlarged rabbit hole. Eats rats, rabbits,
birds, frogs, earthworms, beetles;
scavenges from dustbins, refuse tips.
Nocturnal, usually solitary. T, ex Ic. [5]

Red Squirrel *Sciurus vulgaris* SCIURIDAE
BL 195–280 mm, TL 140–240 mm.
Upperside red-brown (occasionally black),
underside white; ears conspicuously
tufted in winter; long, bushy tail. Voice
chattering, scolding. Mainly lowlands,
but also mountains; prefers conifers, but
also in broadleaved trees, esp beech
Fagus sylvatica; urban parks and gardens,
on the Continent. Nest a ball of twigs,
moss, bark, high in tree. Eats conifer
seeds, nuts (often stored in ground),
also birds' eggs, fungi, bark, berries.
T, ex Ic (but now replaced by grey
squirrel *S. carolinensis* in much of
Br, Ir, where not town animal).
[1]

Grey Squirrel *Sciurus carolinensis*
SCIURIDAE BL 245–300 mm, TL 195–250
mm. Upperside grey, underside paler; in
summer, rather reddish; long, bushy tail;
looks larger than red squirrel *S. vulgaris*,
ears never tufted. Voice chattering,
rasping. Mainly broadleaved trees, esp
beech, oaks, hazel; urban parks, gardens.
Nest ball of twigs, leaves, usually high in
tree. Eats nuts, bark, buds, fungi; in
countryside, much persecuted for damage
to trees; in towns, becomes very tame,
even taking bread, scraps from the hand.
(Br, Ir, from N America). [2]

House Mouse *Mus musculus* MURIDAE
BL 75–100 mm. Grey or grey-brown;

small and slender. Repeated squeaking. Particularly associated with houses and buildings of all kinds, but also fields, hedges, bushes. Mainly nocturnal, but also active by day. Digs tunnels, climbs. Nests in holes. T. [3] Wood mouse *Apodemus sylvaticus* is red-brown above, silvery beneath, with bigger eyes and ears, shorter tail.

Ship or **Black Rat** *Rattus rattus* MURIDAE BL 160–235 mm. Brown or blackish with grey or white underside; pointed muzzle; conspicuous ears; tail longer than head and body. Closely associated with buildings, including warehouses, barns, stables; often in ships. Scavenges on human refuse. Nocturnal. Seldom burrows, but climbs, jumps, swims. T, ex Ic, but local Br, De, FS, where usually confined to large towns, esp on coast. [4]

Common or **Brown Rat** *Rattus norvegicus* MURIDAE BL 215–270 mm. Mostly brown with grey underside; large, robust; rather blunt muzzle; short ears; tail slightly shorter than head and body; fur stiff, sleek. In winter mainly in buildings, but in summer moves into fields, gardens, sewers, river banks, harbours. Largely dependent on man, commonly scavenges on human refuse; also eats green plants. Swims well, when easily confused with water vole *Arvicola terrestris* (very blunt muzzle, shorter ears and tail, fur soft, shaggy). T, ex nFi. [5]

FURTHER READING

Much of the information on the flora and fauna of towns and gardens is buried away in scientific periodicals which are not always readily accessible. Two of these periodicals, *Environmental Conservation* and *Biological Conservation* have in the past few years published articles on wildlife in towns. The following list gives at least one book per topic in the order of the field guide.

London's Natural History, R. S. R. Fitter (Collins, 1945, London)
A Natural History of New York City, J. Kieran (Houghton Mifflin, 1959, Boston)
The Natural History of the Garden, M. Chinery (Collins, 1977, London)
What is Ecology, D. F. Owen (Oxford University Press, 1974, London)
Pesticides and Pollution, K. Mellanby (Collins, 1970, London)
The Thames Transformed, J. Harrison, P. Grant (André Deutsch, 1976, London) The Jarrold Nature Series: *eg Wild Animals in the Garden*, H. Angel (Jarrold Colour Publications, 1976, Norwich)
The Wild Flowers of Britain and Northern Europe, R. Fitter, A. Fitter and M. Blamey (Collins, 1974, London)
The Concise British Flora, W. Keble Martin (Ebury Press and Michael Joseph, 1969, London)
The Dictionary of Garden Plants, R. Hay and P. Synge (Ebury Press and Michael Joseph, 1969, London)
The Oxford Book of Garden Flowers, E. B. Anderson (Oxford University Press, 1963, Oxford)
Flora Europaea, 4 vols, T. G. Tutin (ed) (Cambridge University Press, 1964–72, Cambridge)
A Field Guide to the Trees of Britain and

Northern Europe, A. Mitchell (Collins, 1974, London)
Trees and Bushes of Europe, O. Polunin and B. Everard (Oxford University Press, 1976, Oxford)
Flowers of Europe, O. Polunin (Oxford University Press, 1969, Oxford)
Grasses, C. E. Hubbard (Penguin, 1968, London)
The Oxford Book of Invertebrates, D. Nichols, J. Cooke and D. Whiteley (Oxford University Press, 1976, Oxford)
The Young Specialist looks at Molluscs, H. Jancs (Burke, 1965, London)
A Field Guide to the Insects of Britain and Northern Europe, M. Chinery (Collins, 1973, London)
Grasshoppers, Crickets and Cockroaches of the British Isles, D. R. Ragge (Warne, 1965, London)
A Field Guide to the Butterflies of Britain and Europe, L. G. Higgins and N. Riley (Collins, 1970, London)
The Moths of the British Isles, Series One and Two, R. South (Warne, 1961, London)
Flies of the British Isles, C. W. Colyer and C. O. Hammond (Warne, 1968, London)
The World of Spiders, W. S. Bristowe (Collins, 1971, London)
A Field Guide to the Birds of Britain and Europe, R. Peterson, G. Mountfort and P. A. D. Hollom (Collins, 1954, London)
Birds of Town and Suburbs, E. Simms (Collins, 1975, London)
Man and Birds, R. K. Murton (Collins, 1971, London)
A Field Guide to the Mammals of Britain and Europe, F. H. van den Brink (Collins, 1967, London)
The Handbook of British Mammals, G. B. Corbet and H. N. Southern (Eds.) (Blackwell, 1977, Oxford)

ACKNOWLEDGEMENTS

page
6   Adam Woolfitt/Susan Griggs Agency
11 John Markham/Bruce Coleman Ltd
14 A–Z Botanical Collection
18 Eric Hosking
18 Gordon Langsbury/Bruce Coleman Ltd
22 Heather Angel
22 Heather Angel
23 Stephen Dalton/NHPA
25 Kelvin Brodie/Thomson Organization Picture Service
27 Denis Owen
27 Stephen Dalton/Bruce Coleman Ltd
30 Jane Burton/Bruce Coleman Ltd
35 S. C. Bisserot/Bruce Coleman Ltd
38 Robert Harding Associates
42 John Markham/Bruce Coleman Ltd
47 Adam Woolfitt/Susan Griggs Agency
49 Popperfoto
50 I. Beames/Ardea London
54 Pamela Harrison
55 John Markham/Bruce Coleman Ltd
59 Jane Burton/Bruce Coleman Ltd
64 Eric Hosking
68 S. Roberts/Ardea London
71 Denis Owen
73 Walter J. C. Murray/NHPA
74 Karen Goldie-Morrison
75 L. Hugh Newman/NHPA
81 I. and L. Beames/Ardea London
83 Denis Owen

INDEX